# POLLING
# MATTERS

★★★★★★★★★★★★★★★★★

# POLLING MATTERS

★★★★★★★★★★★★★★★★★

## Why Leaders Must Listen
## to the Wisdom of the People

# FRANK
# NEWPORT

**WARNER BOOKS**

NEW YORK   BOSTON

Warner Books

Time Warner Book Group
1271 Avenue of the Americas, New York, NY 10020
Visit our Web site at www.twbookmark.com.

Printed in the United States of America
First Printing: July 2004
10  9  8  7  6  5  4  3  2  1


Library of Congress Cataloging-in-Publication Data

Newport, Frank.
    Polling Matters : why leaders must listen to the wisdom of the people / Frank
  Newport.—1st Warner Books Printing
        p. cm.
    Includes bibliographical references and index.
    ISBN 0-446-53064-6
    1.  Public opinion polls. 2.  Public opinion—United States. 3.  Elections—
  United States.   I. Title: Why leaders must listen to the wisdom of the people. II.
  Gallup Organization. III. Title.
    HM1236.N48 2004
    303.3'8'0973—dc22                                              2004000831

*Book design by Giorgetta Bell McRee*

To Kim

# CONTENTS

# INTRODUCTION

This book is about polls—what they are, where they come from, why they are important, and how they can and should be a more integral part of the functioning of our democratic society.

Polling is a wonderful application of scientific principles to the challenge of understanding and extracting the insights, emotions, and attitudes of the millions of people aggregated into a common society. There is great wisdom bound up in these collective views. Polling is by far our best, most efficient, and most productive way of extracting this wisdom. Rather than fearing the influence of polls or denigrating their value, we should be spending more time and devoting more energy to a focused effort to use them wisely.

We don't see a lot of movies and television shows devoted to pollsters (in fact, we sadly don't see any at all, although *The West Wing* has the recurring character of a pollster), but we should. Polling is complex, fascinating, and important. Pollsters give themselves the task of figuring out what millions of people are thinking about a given topic and report the results in a matter of days or even hours. These results provide pooled wisdom and insights built out of the experiences of millions of people across numerous generations.

This process isn't new. Polling has been around in one form

or another for well over one hundred years. Some historians recognize the first poll as having been conducted as far back as 1824. (That poll supposedly focused on the presidential election between Andrew Jackson and John Quincy Adams.) By the end of the 1800s, straw polls were very common across the United States. Newspapers and magazines began to publish polls of one sort or another—focusing on elections—in ever-increasing numbers as the twentieth century dawned. Pollster David Moore has a fascinating chapter on the history of polls in his book *The Superpollsters*,[1] pointing out that by the 1924 and 1928 elections, the Hearst newspaper chain was running presidential preelection polls involving almost all states of the Union. Then came 1936, which along with 1948 (although for different reasons) is perhaps polling's most famous year. In 1936, a young man named George Gallup proved the value of a scientific approach to polling when he made the daring prediction, contrary to much conventional wisdom, that President Franklin Roosevelt would win reelection. Of course, FDR did win, and George Gallup went on to be a polling hero.

Polling's influence has grown exponentially since. Most presidents from Roosevelt on have relied on polls to gain insights into the mood of the electorate. Every major news outlet in the United States today not only reports on polls but commissions them directly. Polling is also common in other countries around the world.

Polls provide routine and frequent assessment of the public's views on almost any topic one can name. Polling measures public reaction to major news events, often within hours or days of their occurrence. Polling provides the public's views on important policy issues facing the country, ratings of leaders, and assessments of actions taken by elected representatives. Polling provides an appraisal of the public's mood, reaction to sports and entertainment events, and insights into the ways in which people are thinking, feeling, and living. Polls, in short, function as a form of scientific gossip, telling us not just what the neighbor across the backyard fence is thinking but what *all* of our neighbors across all of our fences are doing and feeling.

A friend once gave me a T-shirt that had the words "Famous Polls" at the top, with pictures of all sorts of different uses of that word: the pope (who is from Poland), the North Pole, a Maypole, a polar bear, polo poles, the pole vault, and so forth. Of course, none of these are the polls we're talking about here. This book deals with polls that ask questions and as a result help us understand people by gathering, organizing, and summarizing their answers. In this book, I'll be using the word "polling" to describe any process by which the views of a group of people are systematically tabulated and released back to the public.

But there's more to it than that. The polls on which I'll be focusing use the results of interviews with relatively small numbers of people to estimate what would have been found if it had been possible to interview every person in enormously large groups. Pollsters, in other words, aren't interested only in the opinions of the people actually interviewed. We're interested in using these sample data to estimate the opinions of much, much larger numbers of people.

The results of polls reflect the combined experience and backgrounds of the amazingly disparate group of citizens that makes up our nation's population. Americans in a randomly selected poll sample come from all areas and walks of life, are of both genders and all ages and ethnicities, and from all levels of socioeconomic status. By the luck of the draw, a poll might contain a billionaire, a janitor, a chemistry professor, a seventy-year-old with a lifetime's experience as a plumber, a PTA homeroom mother, or a single mother working two jobs in an attempt to get by. Americans in such a random sample vary widely in terms of their background and experiences, having seen live plays, having flown on an airplane, having been in a big city, having milked a cow, having worked with their hands for a living, having been in court, having had a major medical operation, and having served in the military.

And, of course, polls include respondents who have widely varying combinations of education, knowledge, and intelligence. It's impossible to know exactly what types of knowledge are most valuable at any point in the nation's history, or in any specific situation. But the blend of the experience and background that is accessed by polling provides an extraordinarily valuable resource to use in directing and guiding the society's progress. The purpose of this book is to examine this tremendous resource and how we can make better use of it.

Not everyone agrees that polling is valuable. Indeed, the history of polling is also the history of antipolling sentiment. Dr. George Gallup, who founded the Gallup Organization in 1935, ran into disbelief about the polling process almost from the first day he released public polls in the 1930s. He spent a good deal of time attempting to explain his processes in articles, books, and speeches—as have many other survey researchers and pollsters in the years since.

Gallup put it best a few years after his polls started to become famous when he said, "We are now witnessing a paradoxical but unavoidable phenomenon—the polls of public opinion are themselves becoming an issue of public opinion. There are those who see more vice than virtue in this new instrument."[2] Indeed, a Columbia University professor named Lindsay Rogers was so upset by the growing influence of polls that he wrote a whole book about it in 1949. Rogers titled his book *The Pollsters*, and its cover carried claims that the book was "A forceful *Warning* to those who rashly assume that the only *Shortcoming* of the Polls is their *lack of Accuracy*. An acute *Analysis* of the *Polls* as a *Threat* to Representative Government and the Democratic Process. An *Indictment* of the destructive *Influence* of the Polls on Newspapers, Legislators and the Public itself."[3]

Variants of these views are still with us. We receive messages every day from good Americans across the country who are asking, in the immortal words of one such correspondent, "Just what the hell are polls?"

Here is a sample of what we heard around the beginning of the 2003 war in Iraq, when polls were showing that 70 percent of Americans supported President George W. Bush's determination to go to war with that country:

- Dear Gallup Poll—I have never been polled by you, and I have only known one person in my entire life of 52 years who has ever been polled by you. Therefore I am deeply skeptical of your recent polling of American opinion on the war in Iraq. If you polled me, and all my friends and relatives, you might see that there is much less support for this war than you think. Thank you.
- I do not believe the findings of your recent poll.
- I would like to know how to get to vote on the polls you take. And just how many people you poll on your questions. Because my polls on the war and such don't add up to your polls. Wondering if you are polling in a widely populated Republican state or whatever?
- I keep wondering who and how you are polling the country? I meet many people in my work and there is severe opposition to this war, which I have not seen reflected in your polls. Please help me understand why the opposition to the war is not being heard.
- Your statistic of a 70% support rate does not reflect my opinion.
- Your poll does not represent the majority.
- I don't know where your [sic] finding all of the people who you claim support the war.

These complaints, questions, and plaintive pleas reflect a number of different reasons why people take issue with polls.

*People resent specific poll results that differ from their own personal positions.* The fact that polling results are publicly disseminated means that the average citizen is directly confronted with them. The news media talk about polls and announce their results. Americans can't avoid polls, and ultimately those who don't agree with certain poll results can be resentful that these polls are taken seriously.

*People don't like the fact that policy makers and politicians pay attention to the results of polls.* Some people who agree that polling accurately represents the views of the general population don't think it matters. They argue that representatives and lawmakers shouldn't be paying all that much attention to what the average Joe or Jane thinks in between elections. Too much slavish devotion to what the whimsical masses might be thinking, it is argued, reduces the type of individual and courageous leadership that made this country great.

*People believe that the average American is too ill informed to have opinions worth paying attention to.* There's a strain of elitism on the part of some Americans that produces disdainful views of the ability of common people to offer opinions that have significant value. Polls, of course, measure what those common people are thinking and feeling.

*People don't understand the process.* Most profoundly, many people simply don't understand how polling works. The fact that polling uses incredibly small samples (on a relative basis) to generalize to huge populations of millions is simply unbelievable to many. I must have been asked a thousand times, "How can polls be accurate? I've never been called."

*People think questions can be manipulated.* Some people take issue with the way poll questions are asked. Even if they understand the rudiments of how random sampling works, they argue that pollsters miss the mark totally because they ask either the wrong or biased questions. The "truth" is out there in the American population, but poll-sters aren't getting at it because they're asking biased questions or questions that are too simplistic to gauge sophisticated opinions and emotions.

These arguments about the value of polls aren't just trivial dinner table abstractions. Some people became so agitated by the proliferation of polling results during the initial stages of the war in Iraq in 2003 that they accused Gallup of "helping to kill American soldiers" because our results showed a majority in favor of war. Others were upset by polls showing that the majority of Americans wanted Bill Clinton to remain in office during the impeachment crisis of 1998 and 1999, and argued that polls were leading to the ruination of the "rule of law" and helping push America further down the road to a pernicious hell of moral decay.

Syndicated columnist Arianna Huffington became so exercised by polls that she started a "Partnership for a Poll-Free America" organization, saying, "Polls are polluting our political environment, and there is an urgent need to clean it up."[4] George W. Bush claimed to be so dead set against the sneakily negative input of polls that he proclaimed in his 2000 presidential campaign not only that he would not pay attention to polls but that he would go so far as to "not pay attention to public opinion" at all should he be elected.

But, as I've noted, none of this criticism of polls is new. Indeed, here I sit confronting exactly the same issues George Gallup faced in his pioneering efforts to establish polling as a legitimate aspect of democratic societies some sixty years ago. Thus, in a way I'm revisiting Dr. Gallup's 1940 *The Pulse of Democracy*, a book he coauthored with Saul Rae in an attempt to head off criticism of polls and their increasingly frequent use in America, and to explain exactly what the Gallup poll was doing and why it was so valuable.[5]

Polling is in many ways a rather miraculous process, as is

the sampling theory upon which it is built. It's not that conducting the interviews themselves is so astounding, although getting that done is not as simple as it sounds. The amazing part is our ability to assume that these interviews accurately represent the opinions and feelings of millions of people spread out all over the country.

The whole polling process is perhaps a little too amazing for many people. Disbelief about the way in which a small sample of people can represent millions seems to be a major problem for a good proportion of the general public. That's why explaining just how polling is done is going to occupy a good deal of this book. As I've noted, it is both a fascinating process and one that—when understood—goes a long way toward alleviating some of the concerns people have about polls and their influence today. I'm convinced that once people go behind the scenes and learn how polling really works, they will be much more likely to appreciate the valuable role polling can play in a democratic society.

But before we get to that, I think it's good to begin with the most important question of all: why do we have polls? We may agree that polls provide us with the ability to figure out what a large—very large—group of people is thinking and doing, while avoiding the costs and effort to talk to all of them. But what good does this do us? In other words, who cares?

1. David W. Moore, *The Superpollsters* (New York: Four Walls Eight Windows, 1995).

2. George Gallup and Saul Forbes Rae, *The Pulse of Democracy* (New York: Simon & Schuster, 1940).

3. Lindsay Rogers, *The Pollsters* (New York: Alfred A. Knopf, 1949).

4. Arianna Huffington, "A Modest Proposal," filed October 3, 1996, http://www.ariannaonline.com/columns/files/100396.html.

5. George Gallup and Saul Forbes Rae, *The Pulse of Democracy* (New York: Simon & Schuster, 1940).

# POLLING MATTERS

★★★★★★★★★★★★★★★

# CHAPTER 1

# The Lure of Knowing What Other People Think

At some personal level, it is pretty obvious that an awful lot of people care what other people around them are thinking. Almost every one of us does informal polling. We ask friends, neighbors, even people next to us on the bus what they think or feel about an issue or problem. We share opinions, listen to gossip, and get a general feel for the lay of the land—opinionwise—of those around us. Everybody likes to talk about their opinions, and we listen back as others give us their thoughts. In fact, gossip, discussion, and verbal interaction have been the mainstays of the human species since speech first evolved. There's a lot of speculation about why this should be the case, but it is probably correct to say that we as a species benefit from our drive to hear and understand what other people are doing and thinking. It keeps us in tune with our environment and helps us stay alert to developments that may affect us. People may deride gossip as negative, nasty, and counterproductive, but scholars tell us that gossip is a very important element of human social interaction.

The bottom line is that knowing what other people feel or think appears to be of basic importance to the species. Humans live with and around other people. Acquiring a knowledge of these people is an important way in which humans manage to survive, get along, and come together to accomplish common goals. Thus, I think one of the most important rationales for polling is the *fundamental interest that humans have in the opinions of those around them.*

Indeed, a social psychologist named Leon Festinger—one of the great minds in the development of social psychology in the 1950s and 1960s—developed a "theory of social comparison" which attempted to explain the interest humans have in the opinions of others. He argued that humans have an *innate* drive to compare themselves to others. Festinger said that we constantly seek a reference standard against which to analyze our own thinking. "Festinger postulated that there is a basic drive in human beings to evaluate their opinions and abilities; he stated once again that when physical reality checks are not available in making these evaluations the person will use others as a point of reference . . ."[1] In other words, when it is not possible to check our attitudes, opinions, and feelings against a concrete reality (as is the case most of the time when it comes to attitudes and opinions), we are interested in comparing them to the attitudes, opinions, and feelings of others. As Festinger said, "An opinion, a belief, an attitude is 'correct,' 'valid' and 'proper' to the extent that it is anchored in a group of people with similar beliefs, opinions and attitudes."[2] We are driven to want to know what other people think in order to put our own opinions in context.

At previous times in history, most residents of small villages or towns had little trouble following through on this drive. They essentially knew what everyone in their restricted social world was thinking. There was enough gossiping and sharing of opinions that most people were fairly knowledgeable about where those around them stood on the key issues of the day.

But there have been changes over the years in the ability of humans to compare themselves to people in the social systems around them. Human societies have gotten bigger. It is impossible, for the most part, to know what everyone in our social sphere is thinking. We don't have the social networks and highly frequent face-to-face interaction that we once did. Instead, there's been movement toward surrogate interaction brought about by technology—mainly radio, television, and the Internet.

Harvard political scientist Robert Putnam documents this transition in his fascinating 2000 book, *Bowling Alone*. He makes the case that Americans are increasingly less likely to engage in activities that bring them into contact with their fellow humans (exemplified by the decline in group participation in bowling leagues that forms the rationale for the title). Putnam amasses evidence to show that

> across a very wide range of activities, the last several decades have witnessed a striking diminution of regular contacts with our friends and neighbors. We spend less time in conversation over meals, we exchange visits less often, we engage less often in leisure activities that encourage casual social interaction, we spend more time watching (admittedly, some of it in the presence of others) and less time doing. We know our neighbors less well, and we see old friends less often.[3]

In other words, we don't spend as much personal, experiential time to find out what others are thinking as we may have had in the past, for a variety of reasons.

However, I don't think these facts of life suggest that there's less interest in being with and finding out about friends and neighbors than there has been in the past. On the contrary, the drive is still there. But in many ways, the structure of our society today encourages people to seek to fulfill their social comparison drive in different (and perhaps less satisfying) ways than the old face-to-face patterns that dominated in the past.

Mass media are a big factor here. Much of television, a lot of talk radio, and a good deal of the Internet, in one way or another, are an expanded version of old-style face-to-face talk and discussion. Indeed, as we move into the electronic digital age, maybe it is not surprising that aspects of the media that appear to fascinate us most are those that give us the chance to hear from or about other people. Much television programming today, from sitcoms to cable news, is a window into the lives and thoughts of others. Television (and movies) provide surrogate neighbors, friends, and families. In recent years, television has turned increasingly to talk programming and "reality" shows that allow us to observe and hear from and about other "real" humans. Radio talk shows have become important mechanisms by which Americans get their news and information about the world around them (particularly the political world). Some of the most popular features of the Internet are e-mail, chat rooms, and instant messaging that allow us to talk back and forth with others. People apparently still thrive on getting to know other people and like to tune in to find out just what other people are doing, how they are doing it, and what they're thinking about. They're just doing it in a different way.

I'm fascinated with local television newscasts—which in today's American society can be a prominent way in which we figure out what our friends and neighbors are doing and thinking. Television consultants point out that the on-air crew of the typical evening newscast in many ways represents a family setting to viewers: the father figure (typical male anchor), the mother figure (female anchor), the bratty brother or sister (weathercaster), and the visiting uncle (sportscaster). We tune in to the 6 and 11 p.m. news as much to spend time with these surrogate family members as we do to find out about the latest murder, fire, or car wreck.

In other words, the electronic mass media have helped meet the need for learning about others in a world in which there are millions of people and in which many individuals no longer live in the intense, highly networked, smaller social environments of the past.

Polling performs a parallel function in a different way. It compiles and compresses the opinions of millions of people. Polling gives us the ability to understand—fairly precisely—what the people around us think and feel about the key issues of the day. It provides the same types of insights into our neighbors that we might have obtained in days gone by from gossip at the village pub, but on an expanded basis that involves literally all of our neighbors.

When we polled people about polls (which pollsters do) in June 2001, for example, we found significant support for the idea that people like the *content* of polls:

- 76 percent of Americans were interested in polls about political campaigns and elections, including the presidential election (34 percent said they were very interested, and 42 percent said they were somewhat interested). Only 23 percent said they were not too interested or not at all interested.
- There was an even higher interest in hearing about the results of polls "which measure how Americans feel about the major political issues of the day, including those on which Congress is debating and voting": 77 percent of those polled said they were interested in these types of polls, with only 22 percent not too interested or not at all interested.
- 64 percent of Americans were interested in polls about Americans' religious attitudes and behaviors, 85 percent were interested in polls measuring Americans' feelings about the economy and business and industry, and 66

percent were interested in polls measuring Americans' attitudes about the entertainment industry.

- The highest interest level of all was in polls measuring Americans' attitudes about enduring social issues such as gun control, abortion, and affirmative action. A whopping 88 percent were interested in these types of polls, including 57 percent who said they were very interested. Only 12 percent were not interested.

This human drive to want to know about the opinions and feelings of others is certainly the reason why newspaper editors and broadcast producers use polls as a significant part of their daily news coverage. Most media gatekeepers are fairly cold-blooded when they make decisions on the content of their publications and broadcasts. They want material that will interest their readers and viewers and increase circulation and ratings. Thus, it's significant that these gatekeepers seem to be committed to the idea of getting the views of the common people into their news coverage. In the old days this was done with "man in the street" interviews, by which reporters provided flavor and texture to news coverage.

Polling today simply provides information from all of the "men in the street." The fact that polls have moved to a prominent position in the media firmament is confirmation of their interest to the average consumer. In a big, mass world, polling provides a shorthand way to figure out what our fellow humans are thinking and feeling.

As we will discuss later in this book, this interest on the part of humans to know about others has its perverse side. We often don't like it if we find that other people do not share our personal opinions and views. It is, I think, a love-hate relationship. We want to know what others are thinking, but we may not like what we find. Fundamentally, however, the fact remains that much of the reason we have polling today is that humans find it interesting and fascinating to understand the people around them.

## THE SCIENTIFIC RATIONALE

Understanding things is the role of science. Scientists study their subject matter—insects, trees, molecules, asteroids, rock formations—because it exists. Mathematicians study the properties of numbers because they are there to be studied. By studying "things" (that is, matter, nature, natural processes, etc.), scientists add to the fund of human knowledge about the world. Scientists assume that this is a true and noble goal. The scientific desire to understand what goes on around us has been at the forefront of progress of the human species as far back as we have written and oral records.

The motivation of the social scientists, psychologists, and pollsters who study human beings for a living most certainly reflects this same sentiment. The human species forms a fascinating subject of study. For many, in fact, humans are the single most fascinating topic in the world.

My own initial interest in sociology and polling came about when I was in high school in Texas and became more and more interested in the ways the people around me were behaving. I found the status hierarchies and social patterns at school to be weirdly compelling. I wasn't interested in bugs or the planets or chemical reactions, but in people. What interested me most was the extraordinarily powerful impact that social categorization had on the daily lives of all of us in high school. There was no printed list or official rules that designated students as members of the jocks, nerds, cool kids, rejects, cowboys, and so forth, yet these informal social categories (and who belonged in each one) were well known and well understood by everyone at the school. One's positioning on the subjective ladder of popularity was so important that it could be a make-or-break factor in one's enjoyment of the entire high school experience (as we learn when school shootings give tragic witness to the power of rejection and feelings of isolation on the part of student loners).

Thus, for me—and most social scientists and survey researchers—the drive to study and understand human beings is part and parcel of the same motivation to acquire knowledge and understanding that has propelled science forward over the ages.

There are a wide variety of ways to study individual humans on a one-by-one basis. But there are very few ways to study large numbers of humans without developing some system for systematically collecting information about them. That's particularly true in modern societies, when we're talking about the analysis of tens and hundreds of millions of people. Polling is thus of particular interest to scientists who study people: it provides an effective, quick, and cost-efficient way to analyze very large groups of humans without having to extract measures from each one of them individually. It would take an army of anthropologists to find and interview all of the residents of a state or country (something the U.S. government attempts only once every ten years). Polling short-circuits that process, and thus provides great practical value to social scientists.

Polling also takes advantage of another very powerful fact of life. Humans have the unique ability to talk about themselves. (After all, language is one of the key things that separate us from our close cousins the apes.) Humans can self-report their own behavior and save the scientist/observer the time and trouble of having to constantly observe human actions him- or herself. This includes reports of actual behavior ("I went to church last Sunday") and the emotional orientations to objects which we usually call attitudes (one's reaction to the question "How do you react when I say the word 'abortion'?"). Humans can report on their own history and—with varying degrees of precision—predict their behavior in the future. Humans can also introspect and report on what they perceive to be the reasons behind their behavior.

Polling thus provides the scientist interested in studying large groups of humans a decided advantage in the scientific process of measurement and discovery. Rocks, asteroids, ants, and neutrons cannot cooperate directly with an investigator and talk about their own history, why they are doing or feeling certain things, or inform others on what they intend to do in the future. Humans can. Humans reflect, examine, remember, and project. Humans study themselves and—of course—know themselves better than anyone else. This opens up enormous possibilities. A subject that cooperates and can summarize and analyze itself—on demand—provides amazingly fertile possibilities for investigators.

Polling, which for the most part consists of asking people questions about their feelings, opinions, past behavior, and future behavior, takes advantage of this uniquely human ability. And because of the miracle of sampling, polling allows these measures to be obtained in ways that generalize to literally millions of people. Polling is in many ways uniquely situated as a major component of any scientific effort to study and understand the human species.

Polling thus has two primary benefits: it allows us to generalize—with a good deal of precision—to very large groups of people without having to study each of them individually, and it takes advantage of the ability of humans to self-report.

A tour through the journals of most branches of social science, particularly sociology and political science, reveals the degree to which polling forms the methodological basis for a great deal of what these sciences are about. The study of the fundamentals of politics and governance, race relations, gender differences, power, status, inequality, sexual behavior, child rearing, health, and so forth is greatly enhanced by polls that provide insights from large groups of people. Historians can only drool at the valuable information we would have if there had been accurate polls throughout history. What did the people of the Roman Empire really feel about condemning and crucifying Jesus Christ? How did the French populace feel about Napoleon? Did the people of France and England wholeheartedly support the idea of opposing the Germans in the trenches of World War I? Did the people of Japan support the expansionist dreams of their government in the 1930s and early 1940s? Did the Chinese people support Mao Tse-tung or Chiang Kai-shek? Even in recent years, scholars wonder what the people who live in countries with totalitarian regimes think about their leaders and the structure of their societies.

In the most general sense, the basis for science is measurement and description. That's exactly what polling does: it measures and describes the feelings, opinions, and projected behavior of the people living in specific social groups. Polling provides us a way of summarizing or typifying human societies based on what the people who live in those societies think and feel. Polling is thus an invaluable tool for those interested in studying humans and the ways in which they organize themselves and live their lives.

1. Edward E. Jones and Harold B. Gerard, *Foundations of Social Psychology* (New York: John Wiley & Sons, 1967), 312.

2. Leon Festinger, "Informal Social Communication," in *Classic Contributions to Social Psychology*, ed. Edwin P. Hollander and Raymond G. Hunt (New York: Oxford University Press, 1972), 340.

3. Robert D. Putnam, *Bowling Alone* (New York: Simon & Schuster, 2000), 115.

# CHAPTER 2

# The Bottom-Up Approach

We can turn now to what I believe is the single most important reason why polls are so valuable. Polling provides us with a way of collecting and collating a distilled, summarized wisdom based on the input of the members of a society. This wisdom can be used as the basis for altering and improving the direction of the societies in which we live.

This is based on the key proposition that *groups of people often have more wisdom among them than does any one person alone.* The collected opinions, observations, and attitudes of all of the individuals in a population provide a distillation of knowledge and insights that is more likely to be sensible and useful than the insights and knowledge of single individuals or small groups of people independently. There is a great deal that can be done with that wisdom—more than just measuring it, studying it, and talking about it. It can be used to help guide a society forward.

In a mass society, polling is the only practical way to bring this knowledge together. The power of polling lies in its ability to harness wisdom and apply it to the problems of governing societies and making decisions about what those societies should do.

This is a pretty radical thesis. It implies that insight, wisdom, and knowledge levels increase with larger and larger numbers of people. This flies in the face of the feelings of many who hold just the opposite thesis: that wisdom and knowledge *decrease* as groups become larger and larger. There is in fact a long history of distrust of the mob or group, with a concomitant reverence accorded the contributions made by individuals and brilliant, single-minded leaders. Here I'm arguing that the views of the mob, as it were, have the potential to be extremely valuable to all concerned, and that the views of individuals or small elites often leave much to be desired.

One of the ways to approach this issue, I think, is to look around us. There is something very natural about the derivation of great value from many discrete actions collected together. It appears as if nature itself operates such that the combined actions of millions of entities in a social system can ultimately work to produce the most adaptive and useful structural patterns and actions for that system. Similarly, while the attitudes of single individuals in human social systems may seem insignificant in and of themselves, one attitude coupled with another and another and another ultimately brings together a totality of thought that is much more than the sum of its parts. Every person in a human social system is distinct in many ways and has a different genetic inheritance. In addition, by adulthood, humans have lived through and experienced life in distinctly different ways, reflecting the results of their *cultural* exposure. When the results of all of these differences in background and exposure are brought together, it constitutes the basis for an extraordinarily powerful body of knowledge. And that knowledge is gathered and processed by polls.

The core principle here is straightforward. The bringing together of *all* of the experiences and knowledge of a group of individuals allows for a distillation of truth that is more profound than an alternative that involves only the experience and knowledge of a few. It is my conviction that in many situations *no individual or small group knows as much about the real world in which problems originate (and in which they must be solved) as larger groups and populations*. No one physician knows as much about a disease or treatment as do all physicians combined, and no one rocket scientist knows as much about the space shuttle as do all rocket scientists put together.

No single football coach or sportswriter can decide on the best college football team in the nation as fairly as a group of many coaches or sportswriters. No single corporate purchasing agent's views on the progress of the economy are as likely to be accurate as are the views of hundreds of purchasing agents amalgamated together. No central economic authority can determine the value of companies as efficiently as the actions of millions of stock buyers and sellers acting individually on the major stock exchanges. No juror is as likely to produce a fair decision in a court case as are twelve jurors with their collectively combined views. And, in the most general sense, no individual can make as effective and efficient a decision on the broad direction a society should take as the collected views of all that society's citizens.

It is this last point that seems to generate the most resistance from observers. Many well-meaning citizens feel that powerful or smart people—rather than the public and its collected insights—are in the best position to provide the information and understanding that a society needs to rely on for direction.

Of course, nothing is absolute. There are certainly situations in which individual guidance is exactly what is needed. No one argues that the opinions of a broad cross section of society can provide the same insights into the treatment of cancer as can the judgment of trained specialists. No one argues that the views of all of the people in a society are as valuable in making a decision on the course of a hurricane as are the insights of meteorological specialists, or that random samples of average citizens can provide meaningful insights into decisions on the selection of the proper flu vaccine at the beginning of the influenza season.

But the broad principle here is that the thoughts, opinions, and insights of larger groups of people *in many cases* have the potential to be more valuable than the thoughts, opinions, insights, or wisdom of just one person or a small number of people. Or at the least, they add significant value to the decision making of whoever is in power. And as I will discuss later, even in the realm of specialists, it is increasingly evident that the knowledge of larger groups of individuals in a given area (for example, all diabetes specialists across the world) can be more powerfully wise than the opinions of just one or two brilliant people by themselves (one or two diabetes specialists).

There is no shortage of examples. One of the most contentious issues facing the United States today is health care. Certainly, Harvard professors and legislative committee staffers who focus on health care can have encyclopedic knowledge of health care statistics and the intricacies of how health payment systems work. But these experts may never have set foot in a charity hospital, have probably never had to sit in an emergency waiting room for hours seeking diagnosis and treatment, and have never gone without medical help as a result of not knowing where to go or how to pay for it. Average Americans, on the other hand, have collectively seen it all: hospitals, bad doctors, bureaucracy, HMOs, Medicaid, and ridiculously expensive drugs. Their combined experiences could provide the basis for a textbook of health care wisdom far exceeding that of the experts.

It is thus no surprise that the health care plan proposed by the Clinton administration in the 1990s, guided by experts meeting behind closed doors, failed miserably. What was missing? At least in part, a strong reliance on the wisdom of the people. Hillary Clinton and her task force gave short shrift to the tremendous expertise lodged in the "collected together" insights of the people, and proposed a system that the people were unwilling to accept. Imagine how much better the proposed health care reform system might have been if every aspect of it incorporated comprehensive polling of the people who were expected to live with it, examining how individuals dealt with health care issues in the real world and what they thought might most effectively be changed to make the system work to the greater benefit of all involved.

Another example was suggested to me by the fascinating book *Ghost Soldiers*, by journalist Hampton Sides.[1] The book deals with the daring World War II commando raid that rescued Allied prisoners being held by the Japanese in the Philippines. Some of the most intriguing parts of the book were Sides's descriptions of the ways in which the prisoners over their three- or four-year captivity created their own small-scale social structures and interactive patterns that maximized chances of survival. Small, closely bonded social groups of no more than three men gradually evolved. These small groups seemed to provide the most effective way of dealing with the exigencies of getting food and shelter and surviving interactions with the Japanese authorities and guards.

The prisoners, in other words, essentially evolved their own social structures that were crucial in maximizing their chances of survival. There was no autocratic control from the Japanese—in fact, there were few leadership directives at all. The prisoners were free to arrange their daily lives and social structures any way they wanted in all of the camps in which they were held.

Moving beyond what actually occurred in the Philippines, I speculated on what might have happened if all of the prisoners had been transferred to one big camp and all social arrangements had been started from scratch. What would have been the best way of determining how to arrange the social structure in this new camp? Would it have been better to let one Allied officer or a handful of Allied officers make that decision? I think not. Even if the highest-ranking Allied officer had the right to make the final decision on how the new camp was to be arranged, he would have done well to take advantage of the pooled wisdom and insights of the prisoners themselves—gathered from their experiences in different camps across the Philippines. The Allied leader would ideally have interviewed the prisoners about their views on what worked and what didn't. He would have collected their opinions, analyzed them, and looked for the common threads that seemed to reflect a consensus. The men would have seen and witnessed a variety of prison situations and as a group would have the best possible insights on how to structure the new camp. Put together, their suggestions would lead to patterns that would have the greatest ability to enhance survival in the camps—far greater than the views or opinions of any one officer or small group of officers alone.

As I've noted, the use of collective opinions may not apply in all circumstances and is certainly not appropriate as the basis for decision in every situation. The collected wisdom of all of the people in a society isn't of as much value when those in positions of power are making informed decisions about the best way to send astronauts into space, arguing arcane principles of law, deciding on which submarine systems to fund, or revising complex elements and loopholes in the tax code. But many of the major decisions made by those in power don't deal with highly specialized issues. They're concerned with matters quite close to the daily experience of the average person in a society. These include social policies relating to such matters as race relations, welfare and poverty, deciding on the best way to define certain activities as deviant (sexual

behavior, alcohol, smoking, drugs, abortion) and impos-
ing sanctions when they occur, the impact of specific economic policies on daily life, and such issues as taxes,
health care, and education. The citizens of a society can
and do have a great deal of knowledge about these areas
of concern. It is my conviction that the average people of
a society are able to provide wisdom that has great value
when these types of issues and problems are on the policy-
making agenda.

In an ideal world, the systemwide opinions and views
of the people should be collected, analyzed, and synthe-
sized, with a focus on plurality and majority agreement
patterns. If there appears to be a convergence of opinion
about a course of action in the collective opinions of the
members of a society, then we can assume that this direction encapsulates genetics, experience, and observations
across literally millions of collection points (humans).
The combination of all this provides a coherent whole
that is often more powerfully useful than what could be
provided by smaller entities—elites, kings, congresses—
by themselves.

## DOCTORS, JURIES, AND BUSINESS

Doctors are increasingly figuring out that they simply
can't make the best possible and most informed decisions
about the diagnosis and treatment for their patients all by
themselves—no matter how smart the doctors may be.
There is simply too much to take into account. Physicians
are thus relying more and more on the collective wisdom
of their colleagues to help guide their decision making.
What's called the evidence-based medicine (EBM) movement assumes that any one physician, no matter how well
trained, cannot have all of the knowledge at his or her fin-
gertips that is needed to properly diagnose and prescribe

treatment for every condition that presents itself. The EBM approach argues that the individual physician should rely on the collective insights of many different experts (and the existing database of research findings) in deciding how to handle any given patient diagnosis and treatment plan. It may be damaging to the doctor's ego to admit that help is needed, but it's ultimately more beneficial to the patient.

Indeed, patients are figuring out the same thing for themselves. While the collective opinions of the masses wouldn't be much help in advising doctors how to perform surgery, the collected opinions of those who have had the surgery can be important in helping prospective patients figure out whether or not they should have the surgery to begin with and/or what consequences to be aware of. That's exactly the function that medical Web sites and chat rooms are playing today, and their popularity is testimony to their perceived value. Patients diagnosed with a disease or condition about which they know little are less and less likely to simply accept the advice of one or two medical experts. They're increasingly likely to use the Internet to access the collective wisdom of hundreds or thousands of people who have been confronted by the same medical challenge. The people, in other words, find themselves looking for the aggregated opinions of other people in their search for wisdom and guidance.

There are many other examples of this principle in our culture. The American jury system assumes that a group of individuals with various backgrounds and experiences will reach a verdict that has a higher probability of being just and fair than would occur if any one person—including even a learned and highly experienced judge—made the decision. Each juror brings a different perspective to bear on a case. Each has different levels of background knowledge. All of these varied skills and differing perspectives help make sure, so the theory goes, that the jury renders a just decision.

The stock market is a method of pooling thousands of individual perceptions of the value of a business and arriving at an assessment of what that value is. The pricing of a stock through this mechanism is often called a perfect process that takes into account a vast amount of knowledge and input that extends far beyond what would be possible if only a selected subset of stock analysts were called upon to value the stock.

Other mechanisms for pooling knowledge have acquired significant importance in the business world. Purchasing agents across the country are asked to estimate what they are going to buy over a specified period of time in the future, under the assumption that their pooled insights provide valuable guidance on the direction of the commercial economy. A number of other systems are in place in the financial world in which large groups of analysts or others are asked their opinion about an economic issue (for example, where consumer confidence is headed), under the assumption that the averaged-out set of opinions embodies more wisdom than would be available by asking just one or two experts to deliver their views. As the 2004 election primary season got under way, Web sites collected the predictions of a group of varied political insiders, assuming that their combined opinions would distill down into valuable insights much more valuable than the opinions of just one or two pundits or observers.

In one of the most intriguing developments in recent years, new search engines on the World Wide Web operate by analyzing which sites are most frequently used by the individuals who begin a search on a given topic. The assumption behind the algorithms that drive these sites is that the record of the collective actions of a large group of people looking for information on a topic can be the most valuable guide for future individuals seeking information about that same topic. And preference marketing, which is gaining prominence in business circles, attempts to follow the purchase decisions of individuals in order to build a trail that suggests the products or services they might like in the future—based on the collective actions of others with similar interests. If an individual buys two or three books on Amazon.com, a preference-marketing process pools the data of every other purchaser who bought those same books and provides the initial purchaser with suggestions for future purchases based on the additional books these other individuals bought. The aggregated behavior of large groups of customers is often a better guide for purchase decisions than the recommendations of individual book critics or the old-fashioned idea of asking clerks in bookstores.

Sellers of products and services on the Internet are now evaluated by thousands of individual users, not by one expert or single evaluator. One's decision on buying something from a seller on eBay, for example, may hinge critically on how hundreds or thousands of other individuals have rated that seller, based on past experience. The sellers who generate a portfolio of positive customers begin to prosper, while those who don't, wither away.

This type of evaluation by the masses is immensely powerful. The coalesced, communal rankings that develop out of individual experiences take on a life of their own and far outstrip what it might be possible to do with the more old-fashioned, top-down approach to such evaluations provided by individual critics. Who needs an expert's evaluation of online sellers when a constantly updated, continuous, collective evaluation from all of the buyers is available based on thousands of actual, real-world experiences?

When I'm looking for a book to read these days, I spend less time reading one or two reviews in *The New York Times Book Review* or similar sources and more time going online and plowing through the dozens and dozens of reviews submitted by average readers on sites like Amazon.com. One or two of these reviews aren't of great value by themselves. By the time I go through a good number of them, however, I begin to recognize certain themes and insights. And I benefit from offbeat observations that come out of left field from individual reviewers who have unusual backgrounds or perspectives. This type of evaluation of a book based on the opinions of many, many individual readers often ends up being much more valuable than the learned opinion of one man or woman who reviews books for a living. In similar fashion, the J.D. Powers and Associates ratings of initial automobile quality provided by random samples of thousands of car buyers or the car repair experiences of thousands of *Consumer Reports* readers are now recognized as signficant factors in the success or failure of specific automobile lines.

In a broader sense, the wisdom of the people, pooled together, is the fundamental basis of the marketplace in a capitalist society. The ultimate test of a new product or service is how it plays out among large groups of individuals to whom it is exposed. There is general agreement that these pooled actions of the marketplace represent an effective and efficient way to distribute products and services. A new car, or a new Web site, or a new technology, or a new approach to a problem is successful to the degree that it begins to gain acceptance from large numbers of people who approach it from many different perspectives, and who thus provide wide-ranging reactions in ways that any small group of product testers could not. In all of these cases, it is assumed that great insights arise from many different opinions or actions. It's that simple.

One of the other reasons collective opinions of a broad group are valuable is the fact that they produce effective decisions. Experts focusing on social issues and policies often come up with programs or laws doomed for failure when they ignore the views of the people potentially affected by such measures. When experts and bureaucrats spin out programs and impose them on a people who don't understand them and don't want them, they simply don't work in the long run. When decision makers and bureaucrats view the opinion of the people upon whom programs must be imposed as irrelevant, the programs have a lower probability of success.

All of these examples underscore the premise that there is great wisdom in the pooled opinions and behavior of large numbers of people. As Benjamin I. Page and Robert Y. Shapiro summarize near the end of their book *The Rational Public*:

> . . . our work indicates that *collective* public opinion reflects a considerably higher level of information and sophistication than is apparent at the individual level . . . In substantial part, collective wisdom results from collective deliberation based on a division of labor. For all these reasons, collective public opinion far outshines the opinion of the average individual. It is both an aggregation of many individual opinions and the result of a process in which many individuals interact.[2]

Survey research in its simplest form provides a mechanism for bringing this wisdom together in a way that accurately represents what would happen if it were possible to pool the opinions and attitudes of all of the individuals in a population.

None of these thoughts are new, or in fact specific to the human species. Polling—a systematic way of assembling estimates of what all of the people in a group or society think and feel—is part of a more general set of processes that revolve around the power of many different individual actions of living entities. The advantages of polling as I've described them are part of one of the most profound and fascinating principles in nature: the fact that an approach that aggregates, combines, and coalesces creates a final result that is more valuable than the sum of its parts.

## BOTTOMS UP

Polling exemplifies the process by which a new reality—in this case summary measures of opinions and attitudes—comes into existence based on the collected actions or thoughts of a widely diverse group of elements. I like to call this a bottom-up approach because it involves the process of building up from a variety of building blocks, as opposed to a "top-down" approach, which involves decisions or plans that individuals or very small groups make from above.

I mentioned the relationship between this central component of polling and a process that seems to be prevalent and fundamental in the natural world. The complex and powerful ways in which plant and animal systems have developed and operate are not the result of a plan "imposed from above." Instead, they are the result of the actions and behaviors of millions of individual entities over a lengthy span of time. These actions and behaviors—shaped, selected, or extinguished by the relentless power of evolutionary forces—result in systemwide patterns that allow natural systems to adapt to the environment and thus to have the highest probability of surviving.

There's an extension of the evolutionary approach, popularly known as emergence theory, that caught my attention. This approach focuses on the idea that thousands or millions of actions by a group of individual plants, animals, or humans coalesce into something powerful and functional despite the fact that each of the individual entities involved is doing nothing but operating out of self-interest or according to some other simple, individually based rule of action. I'm not sure if there is a direct parallel between these processes and the aggregation of opinions through polling, but I'm intrigued by the ways scientists who work in this field talk about what is going on:

- "The whole is smarter than the sum of its parts."[3]
- ". . . novel outcomes that are not sufficiently understood as a sum of their parts."[4]
- ". . . they solve problems by drawing on masses of relatively stupid elements, rather than a single, intelligent executive branch."[5]

In other words, successful solutions to problems emerge from the combining of the simple actions of relatively simple individual elements.

The upshot is that powerfully adaptive systems develop from the decisions and actions of millions of individuals. I think a word like "coalesce" works well in this context. It implies the coming together of streams of input from many different individual entities, leading to patterns or structures that benefit the group, yet—and this is the key—are not imposed from one master thinker or authority, but rather built off a bottom-up combination of individual actions.

The idea is that individual elements in a social system, left essentially to their own devices, will by virtue of their individual actions develop broad approaches that are adaptive to their environment. These approaches will have the highest probability of accomplishing that which systems are supposed to do: continue existing.

This book certainly isn't the place to review the diverse and voluminous literature on evolution and emergence theory, nor am I an expert in this fascinating approach to natural life. But the essence of these approaches seems to underscore a general conclusion that pertains to polling, even if indirectly: the simple fact that there is power in numbers. To say it another way: *from individual actions emerge powerful collective results.*

In polling terms, of course, we are talking about the insights and wisdom that come from combining the opinions and attitudes of the individual humans that make up a society. There is not only precedent but also excellent justification for the idea that bringing together the insights of the people in a society is a process that makes a great deal of sense.

## DESIGNING A SOCIETY FROM SCRATCH

Now I'd like to shift gears and approach this a little differently. I want to look a little more directly at the reasons it is important to pay attention to the aggregated opinions of the masses. One approach focuses on power, and the formal role that the collective views of the people in a society can or should play in the process of making decisions that affect them. There are strong parallels here to the thought that went into the development of democratic approaches to governance, and I'll turn to a consideration of the implications of polling for democratic societies in the next chapter of this book. But there's a somewhat different way of looking at this, and that's a focus on finding the best source of *wisdom* to use in making decisions about key issues facing societies, regardless of who has the actual power to implement those decisions. Even if a monarch or dictator is formally ruling a society, what input should he or she use as the basis for their decisions?

In other words, what if we were designing a society from scratch and had to decide exactly what sources of wisdom, insight, and guidance we wanted to use to make the decisions that affect the members of that society? What would we do? Let's assume we're not interested in who has the power to implement the decisions. That's a different question. The person or persons in charge could be a king, a dictator, a parliament, a congress, a tribal chief, or any other entity we might think of. Our concern in this scenario is determining the best *input* so that people in charge can use it to make decisions that positively affect the entire society. Looked at differently, I'm asking: what sources of insight, wisdom, and guidance can a society most effectively use as the basis for making the important decisions it faces?

We could look first for this wisdom by studying what already exists in a society, under an assumption that patterns that develop over generations have done so for a reason. I'm going to spend some time here talking about this approach because I think it illuminates some important points. Many observers have noted over the years that clues to how a society should be arranged can be derived from studying the patterns that seem to have developed or evolved naturally. This view is echoed by what sociologists have called functionalist theories of society, popular at various points in the twentieth century. Functionalists argue, like evolutionary theorists, that certain social patterns and social systems are more functional than others for the well-being and future of societies, and that these patterns and systems develop naturally over time *for good reason*. Therefore, the theorists argue, one should study societies and look for recurring patterns of social organization under the assumption that such patterns must exist because they help societies to continue to adapt and exist. Sociologists and anthropologists in the functionalist tradition thus study many different types of societies and have attempted to distill from them an understanding of basic principles, social forms, and social structures that seem to be universals.

One famous functionalist theorist was a Harvard sociologist named Talcott Parsons. Parsons, who died in 1979, was at one time the most famous sociologist in the world. A symbolic figure for this broad functionalist approach to society, Parsons argued (in a dense, Germanic prose style that was famous for its impenetrability) that every social system develops a set of specific social patterns and structures designed to meet basic societal needs. Parsons presented these in voluminous detail in his writings, and they became highly influential.

But for my purposes, it is important to note that the functionalist approach to society espoused by Parsons and many others has come under intense criticism over the years by scholars who argue that humans have become, in a way, smarter than the functionalist theories assume. Functionalism implies that basic social patterns existing across many different societies must be useful and appropriate by definition simply because they seem to have emerged so frequently. Critics, on the other hand, argue that many of the social patterns that exist in more advanced societies have been imposed by groups of humans who have intervened into the "natural" flow of things and who have arranged society to suit their personal benefit. Even if social systems and structures did arise initially out of natural and functional processes, the critics contend that humans have developed to the point where they *should* intervene and change things for the better even if that means disrupting natural processes. This latter point is important. It implies that humans have reached a developmental state in which they consciously decide what is adaptive and good and what isn't—essentially eschewing the slow forces of nature as arbiter.

For example, almost all societies develop stratification systems by which certain people end up with more of what is good in life than do others. Functionalists theorize that there must be a good reason that these systems exist if they are so commonly found in societies. Two sociologists, Kingsley Davis and Wilbert E. Moore, argued in a famous article ("Some Principles of Stratification"[6]) that some occupations and roles in society have more prestige and greater financial rewards attached to them than others because the occupants of those roles contribute more to society. In other words, inequality exists because it performs a functional benefit for society as a whole and increases the chances that society will be maximally adaptive. Doctors have larger salaries than garbage collectors because the prestige and financial rewards attached to the doctor role are necessary to attract and motivate talented people to fill it. This, in a way, is very similar to the analysis by animal ethnologists that describe dominance systems in lion and wolf societies. Some lions and wolves have more power in their social groups than others because the inequality of power allows all of the animal group to increase its chances of survival in a tough environment.

The Davis-Moore approach (and others like it) can be used as the basis for deciding that levels of unequal income and prestige associated with different jobs makes perfect sense. But this approach has been roundly criticized because it seemingly implies a justification for a vastly unfair status quo. (This is very similar to the criticisms that have been lodged against sociobiologists and other evolutionary theorists by those who argue that these approaches, when applied to human societies, seemingly sanction or provide a rationale for racism, oppression, and oligarchies.) Critics say that the functionalist approach is based on faulty assumptions, because humans now intervene and disrupt and change the "natural" ways in which systems developed in more primitive days. Humans may be guided by genetic influences that hail back to the days of the hunters and gatherers, and societies may all develop certain characteristics that emerge out of centuries of individual actions. But at some point there are disruptions. Essentially, these critics say, it is wrong to assume the positive functions that stratification plays in society because stratification systems no longer represent just the results of a slow, natural, evolutionary process. Indeed, sociologists advanced so-called conflict theories, arguing that it's illusory to believe that what exists is necessarily there for a good reason. Strong leaders or strong groups of individuals, conflict theorists argued, grasp power and change the society around them quickly in order to benefit themselves and exploit everybody else.

Doctors may make lots of money and have great prestige not because it's functional for everyone involved, but because doctors have managed to manipulate the system to create and maintain their rewards at the expense of others in their societies. Conflict theorists argue that men have more freedom, status, and power than women in many societies not because it is functional for the society as a whole, but because men have created systems and advanced cultural norms that support an oppressive system that benefits them at the expense of women. In other words, the progress of a society naturally or traditionally based on the collective actions of thousands or millions of people over time is unnaturally interrupted when an elite or a small group of individuals with common and selfish interests is allowed to take over and impose its version of what is wise and what should be done within the society. What's natural is no longer natural.

One famous example of this conflict approach is embedded in the writings of Karl Marx. Marx, of course, decided that capitalist societies were dysfunctional. Certain groups of people with specific relationships to the means of production had grasped power, Marx argued, and were benefiting from their position, while others were cheated and exploited and had much of the value of their labor power stolen as they slugged their unfortunate way through life.

Marx was convinced that capitalist societies had moved to the point where the individuals in positions of power and control over the means of production arranged *all* societal institutions and culture so that they perpetuated their dominant positions—exploiting all others in the process. Marx in some ways argued that the development of a system that allowed exploitation of the proletariat by the bourgeois capitalist class was itself a natural evolution, just as functionalists argued that what they found (*i.e.*, stratification systems) were natural. But one thing is certain. Marx argued that there needed to be, in essence, more intervention to correct the situation. This was in short a situation that demanded interruption—in Marx's case, a revolution by the proletariat. Society had become irretrievably corrupt, Marx argued, and humans needed to make it better. So Marx countenanced the active revolt of the proletariat (and their vanguard) to further disrupt the way human societies worked until the social structure attained a final state of development and organization that fit Marx's criteria of what a society should look like.

Marx the political theorist wasn't very good at figuring out what should come next, but as a social theorist, Marx's basic point was clear. Humans frequently and actively intervene and control the direction in which society moves. This may be because it is a natural part of the progression of evolutionary forces. Or it may be that the natural progression of evolution has been disrupted and that culture and social organization move in a way that is different. But in some ways, it really doesn't matter. Whatever the reason, intervention is happening.

In other words, humans have developed complex systems for intervening in the natural process of evolution and making decisions on the fly about altering and changing the way they are structured. Humans change and disrupt. And when they intervene in the natural flow of things, there is the abiding need for some type of criterion to use as the basis for deciding on systems and structures. Given the fact that humans can and do intervene and change the way their societies are structured, there needs to be a way of deciding exactly what the results should optimally look like.

Karl Marx certainly didn't hesitate in this regard. He had his own criteria and his own theory about the way in which human societies should move until they reached what he thought was the correct and appropriate end state. (Marx thought that societies should ultimately organize themselves in a way in which people collectively owned the means of production, in which people contributed according to their abilities and were rewarded according to their needs, and so on and so forth.) And Marx was just one among many who have dreamed up ideas about organizing societies, although it has appeared over the years to be much easier to criticize the status quo than it is to develop ideas for structuring societies that actually seem to work well. Indeed, Marx's viewpoints on the best way to organize society have for the most part been total failures when applied in the real world.

All of this is part of one of the most thoroughly examined and discussed areas of human thought: how can humans arrange things so that their social systems and societies move forward in the best possible way to maximize the well-being of everyone involved.

There's no shortage of answers to that question, in addition to those promulgated by Marx and other conflict theorists. Societies can use theology or tradition as the basis for their structure. Most important, the decision makers in charge of a society can adopt the theories or arguments of single individuals or small groups of elites (including themselves). In fact, all of these procedures have been used in some way for centuries. Rulers of societies through the ages, up to and including the current time (consider Fidel Castro or Saddam Hussein), believe that they have the insights and wisdom to make the decisions that are maximally beneficial for their societies (although of course these systems often end up being maximally beneficial to themselves).

But what other methods are there? Aren't there some other, more effective mechanisms or ways to acquire wisdom and guidance that would allow us to bring the powers of reason and scholarship to bear on problems facing society? Isn't it possible to use the methods of science or at least a systematic procedure to address these perpetually problematic and arguably important questions of guiding society? We can call this the search for "optimal wisdom" for the guidance of societies.

I think such attempts should involve two assumptions. First, what is optimal may vary from society to society and from time to time. We are not looking for *one* optimal decision or principle (for example, that there should always be communal ownership of the means of production or that everyone must believe in a single God of such and such characteristics). We are looking for *procedures* applicable to any particular social system or culture in which we are interested. Second, and more important, we are assuming that it is possible for a rational, systematic, and even scientific procedure to yield results that can help to answer this type of question. There is no compelling reason not to use the contributions of science in conjunction with attempts to answer society's tough questions.

I first became interested in this issue of finding optimal sources of wisdom for societies when I was writing my doctoral dissertation. My topic was equity theory, which has to do with investigating the ways humans look at the distribution of resources in their societies. Sociologists have long been interested in stratification, social class, and inequality—the fascinating ways in which societies allocate power, money, and prestige. I was interested in what the people themselves think about these types of distribution. This isn't a trivial area of concern. Many if not most of the revolutions in human history have revolved around the fact that certain groups in societies have felt that the resources were not being distributed appropriately—that there was too much going to the few at the top and not enough going to the many at the bottom. But in other situations (such as the contemporary United States), people view inequality as more legitimate and appropriate, and—at least so far—there has been no revolution.

Social scientists have argued that there may be some universal rules that apply to the ways in which people look at their situations—norms of equity that people in most societies agree on (for example, that one's reward should be proportionate to one's contribution). In a broader sense, in my research I was analyzing the process of determining the optimal or just process for distributing resources in society, based on measuring and determining the views of the people in that society.

This highlighted the important contrast between a "top-down" system and a "bottom-up" system. The former is most probably the more common in history. By top down, I mean a system that uses broad philosophic principles or some entity or some person (at the top of a societal pyramid) to generate decisions about how the society is organized, decisions that ultimately trickle down to the multitudes. As I have noted, the top-down approach has been dominant in human societies for centuries. Kings, dictators, religious leaders, tribal chiefs, philosophers—all of these embody the idea that great wisdom comes from on high and devolves down to the waiting members of a society below. This is nice in some ways if it works—for example, as in the benefits of the benevolent dictator who watches out for the best interests of his people. Untold thousands of philosophers, writers, pundits, and deep thinkers—from all ends of the ideological and political spectrums—toil away even today at developing theories and rationales to use as the basis for making crucial policy decisions.

But I studied the bottom-up approach because it seemed, ultimately, to be more important. No social system of stratification can continue to exist, generation after generation, if it doesn't have the acceptance of the people it affects. The people may accept a monarchy that hoards all of the society's riches, or the people may demand an equal society in which no one has more than anybody else. But whatever the outcome, it is the wishes and opinions of the people, I reasoned, that form the best and most useful criteria for deciding what societies and systems should look like. This bottom-up approach takes advantage of the power of aggregation and coalescing. A bottom-up approach generates decisions by aggregating input from a large number of entities or persons at the bottom—decisions that are eventually implemented by whoever is in power. It uses the power of the insights of a large aggregated group of people to provide the input into society's key decisions. This is exactly what seems to be such an important part of the way that nature is organized and that is the focus of my discussions in the previous chapter.

It is obvious why the bottom-up approach interests me. Not only is it in my opinion the most viable way that society can figure out how best to arrange itself, but by extension it leads directly to a significant reason why polling is so important.

If we believe in this approach, we need to take seriously the justification for polling I outlined above: that the collective views of the people of a society provide a fundamentally sound source of wisdom. In this chapter I have been calling attention to the assumption that the actions of large groupings of individuals/people/entities coalesce (in what seems like a mysterious process) to produce broad results that are adaptive for the social unit under consideration. Looked at differently, we can say that wisdom and ways of proceeding within a society can develop—and develop well—when the resources of many different entities within that society are involved. This is the "mass aggregation" process for which I have so much reverence. The assumption is that taking into account the views of many different members of a society produces a coherent whole that is efficient and effective in moving that society forward.

1. Hampton Sides, *Ghost Soldiers: The Epic Account of WW II's Greatest Rescue Mission* (New York: Anchor, 2002).

2. Benjamin I. Page and Robert Y. Shapiro, *The Rational Public* (Chicago: University of Chicago Press, 1992), 388.

3. Steven Johnson, "Emergence," from an interview by David Sims and Rael Dornfest, O'Reilly Emerging Technology Conference, May 13–16, 2002.

4. Jeffrey Goldstein, "Emergence as a Construct: History and Issues," *Emergence*, Vol. 1, Issue 1: 53.

5. Harold J. Morowitz, *The Emergence of Everything: How the World Became Complex* (New York: Oxford University Press, 2002), 14.

6. Kingsley Davis and Wilbert E. Moore, "Some Principles of Stratification," *American Sociological Review* 10 (1945): 242–49.

# CHAPTER 3

# The Pulse of Democracy

Those who agree in broad principle that the collective wisdom of the people is a powerful tool of which that society should take advantage probably think immediately of democracy—the system for societal governance that has at its core the concept that the will of the people should prevail. Democracy is built on the basic type of bottom-up assumptions I've discussed in the previous chapter, and many reactions to the use of polling are bound up with discussions of its relationship to democratic systems in place in U.S. society today. Indeed, George Gallup titled one of his important early books on polling *The Pulse of Democracy*, which I've used as the title for this chapter. But as I begin to discuss in more detail the way in which polling fits democracy, I first want to reiterate the important distinction between a *formal* power system that embodies democratic principles and the *informal* way in which the voices of the people are heard and used on a regular basis, particularly between elections.

I think many people believe that the principle of the value of the collective wisdom of the people is nice, but should be applied only so far. Democracy as practiced in the United States today seems to fit this "only so far" qualification nicely. The collective opinions of the public are used in a formal way to select representatives and the president, but from that point on, the views of the people are often viewed as too ill informed, whimsical, and unstable to be seriously considered on a regular basis. I believe this is a mistake. If the society is to prosper and move forward in an optimally adaptive fashion, it is vital that those charged with decision making take the people's views into account on as systematic and frequent a basis as possible.

In many ways, this discussion boils down to a focus on how democracy should work in the real world. Our democratic heritage recognizes the right of the people in a society to be the core element in its governance. But, as is often the case, nothing is as simple as it seems, and democracy is no exception. There are as many ways to institutionalize a democracy as there are societies that attempt it. And many democratic systems today take less than full advantage of the collective wisdom of their citizens.

Democracy can be viewed as the *formal* way decisions are made in society: the way in which the people legally and officially have their voice heard in governmental decisions. This should be differentiated from the *informal* way those who are entrusted with making decisions use the wisdom and insights of the people, regardless of the formal or official structure of the society. This informal process can range from a situation in which public opinion is less routinely taken into account (as is the case in most monarchies and dictatorships) to one involving an almost continuous reliance on public opinion. The process doesn't necessarily have to relate to the nature of the formal system of governing. Nothing prevents even the most hereditary of monarchs or the most controlling of dictators from constantly polling and assessing the views of the people. The core principle of relying on public opinion for societal wisdom and guidance can be applied in any situation, even one in which there is no formal role for the public's involvement.

Certainly, the formal and informal ways in which public opinion can be taken into account most often go together in rough parallel. Most dictatorial regimes don't waste a lot of time assessing public opinion. And almost any society in which there is a great deal of reliance on the wisdom of the people has at least some formal mechanism (for example, the vote) by which the public's voice can be officially manifested.

But here's the rub. Democracy as practiced in the United States today rests on the formal principle of the sovereignty of the people, but informally, the people's wisdom is often ignored and its value wasted. In other words, the views of the people are often lost on an ongoing basis as our democratic system plays itself out. Representatives are elected and sent to state capitals and to Washington, D.C., but their decisions can veer sharply from what their constituents back home want them to do. The people are often regarded as "ballot cattle"— to be dealt with only when election time comes around. Some elected representatives pay lip service to the effort to understand constituent feelings and attitudes, while others quite frankly take the position that they (the representatives) have no business trying to determine the will of the people, but rather should be spending their time figuring out, on their own, what is the "right" thing to do. These efforts to find the right thing to do often include paying attention to special interests, party leaders, and lobbyists.

All of this is a long-standing debate that harkens back to the Federalist Papers and the development of the U.S. Constitution. Is it important or necessary, it has been asked since the beginning of U.S. history, to pay attention to the collective voices of the people on a regular basis above and beyond the vote? In other words, although the United States has in place a formal system that recognizes the ultimate power of the people as exercised through periodic elections, there is no consensus within the country today on how powerful the people's voice should be on a continuing *informal* basis—between elections.

Representatives today have the ability to assess the attitudes and opinions of the people they represent in dramatically effective ways—if they choose to take advantage of them. Polling is a scientific tool that can assess collective public opinion on an essentially continuous basis, and if executed and analyzed properly, estimates the thoughts, attitudes, and perceptions of the entire country's population. The issue becomes one of just how important it is to assess and use this wisdom as a key input into societal decision making within our representative democratic framework. I think the answer is that it's *very* important. But there is far from unanimous agreement on this issue.

Here's how this argument is often framed. Some claim, on the one hand, that the input of the people should be limited to the periodic vote (with an underlying assumption, perhaps, that elected representatives know the opinions of the people they represent). On the other hand, others argue that elected representatives should widen their perspective and take advantage of the collective wisdom of the people as fervently and as frequently as possible between elections. Ultimately, it's a question of the *advisability* of taking into account the views and wisdom of the public. *There has never been agreement on the degree to which elected representatives should consider public opinion on a day-to-day basis.* (One extreme argument is that even the role of the representative is outdated and that the United States should move toward a direct democracy in which the people's vote is used to make all governmental decisions. I won't get into the pros and cons of this direct-democracy model, but it's unlikely that the role of the representative will be abolished in the United States in the near future; there are a number of reasons why it makes sense to have representatives in place to execute the will of the people.)

## Delegate Versus Trustee

There are labels for the two broad positions taken in the debate over the appropriate role for elected representatives. Political scientists have distinguished between a "delegate" model and a "trustee" model of representative democracy, and this broad distinction can help us get a grasp on what we're talking about here.

The *delegate* model assumes that elected representatives are sent off to serve at the pleasure of the people they represent. Representatives are to do their best to figure out what the people they represent are thinking and how those people would want them to vote. This viewpoint assumes that the ideal way for a democracy to function is to have each citizen participate as much as possible in each decision that faces the society and that representative democracy is a second-best solution *imposed primarily because of practical limitations*. In other words, the more frequently representatives can take the views of the people they represent into account, the better. This view leads to the immediate acceptance of mechanisms that allow for a more direct expression of the people's will if and when these mechanisms become available—that is, mechanical or electronic means by which the public's views can be assessed and taken into account on an ongoing basis. Polling is such a mechanism.

The *trustee* model is quite different. It argues that a representative democracy is the best way for democracy to function in all cases, *even if* mechanisms become available that allow for a more direct expression of the people's will. This orientation assumes that representatives are a good thing because they allow individuals who have experience and expertise (and who are not as subject to whims and passions as are the masses) to do most of the thinking and decision making on things that matter, subject to the occasional ratification of the public through the mechanism of the vote. Representatives, in this model, make decisions based on a variety of inputs (most notably their own judgment), only one of which is what those back in the districts and states might be thinking. As in a blind trust in which the trustees make their own judgments about investment decisions without consulting the client, the trustee model of representative democracy assumes that the representatives, elected periodically, should make their own judgments about legislative decisions without consulting the people.

In this trustee model, representatives are ultimately responsible to their constituents, but not on a regular or ongoing basis. The trustee representative model puts the elected official in charge, not liable to feedback from his or her constituency until the next election, at which point the official is either reelected or told not to return.

These two models represent two quite different perspectives. Both models assume that the people ultimately have the power in the system. The models differ on how that power is to be manifested. The trustee model recognizes that the people should have the ultimate say-so in a democracy, but asserts that the people should be kept at some distance from the actual operations of their governing entities and should be allowed to weigh in with their opinions only periodically through elections as mandated by the Constitution. Additionally, as a corollary to this position, if only a relatively small percentage of the population wants to exercise this privilege and vote, that is their right. In any case, only the opinions of those who vote will be taken into account.

The delegate perspective argues that the best possible job of running a society is accomplished by assessing the opinions of *all* of the people who live in that society. The corollary to this position is that the opinions of people taken together provide perspectives and insights that are generally more valuable than any group of representatives acting on their own. Moreover, it is argued, laws and rules that emanate from the people themselves will have a better chance of being accepted and adhered to if their origin is closer to the people who will have to live under them.

The tenets of democracy say that everyone is equal. Adherents of the trustee approach say that while everyone may be equal in some ways and in some situations, only those who are well equipped to make judgments (that is, elected representatives) should have their opinions used for the daily or routine matters of state. This point of view essentially says that the people should be trusted only so far.

This trustee model is to some degree what the Founding Fathers of the United States had in mind when they set up our Constitution (although there has always been great debate among historians concerning exactly what the Founders were thinking as they put the Constitution together). The early constitutional structure of the United States—the world's most famous example of the application of democratic principles—in fact erected a number of barriers between the views of the common people and political decision making. The Founding Fathers embraced in spirit the idea of the value of the collected opinions (as measured by the vote) of the citizens of a country. But the Founders, particularly as represented in the Federalist Papers written in large part by James Madison and Alexander Hamilton, also apparently had quite skeptical views about the ability of the masses to have opinions worth paying attention to on a continuing basis. The Founders were concerned about the passions of the public on a day-to-day basis, the "fluctuations," "violent movements," and "temporary errors and delusions" of opinion. There were other concerns, especially practical ones about harnessing the views of millions of people in thirteen states, but the philosophical questions about letting the people's views have sway over the decisions that would rule the country were paramount.

As a result of these concerns, the Founders put together a plan for policy decisions that embraced the view that the opinions of the people are important, but with severe limits on just how much or how often the opinions should be taken into account. The United States was developed as a representative democracy in which the primary focus of decision making was on two bodies of elected representatives who were designated to serve as surrogates for the people—making decisions in their stead. The Founding Fathers were so concerned that even these representatives might be too susceptible to the whims and passions of the multitudes that they did their best to isolate the upper chamber of the Congress from the people, by giving senators longer, six-year terms and also by removing these senators from the direct election of the public. Additionally, the Founders isolated the president from the masses by creating an Electoral College to make the final decision on electing a new president. In both of these instances, the Founders were in essence saying that stable ways of letting wise and learned individuals make decisions were needed rather than routinely throwing the responsibility for decision making onto the masses themselves. And, of course, the Founders, reflecting the normative patterns of their day, assumed that only certain types of Americans should be able to have *any* type of input whatsoever—white males for the most part, thus excluding any input from over half of the new nation's citizens: women, slaves, and nonwhites.

The early proponents of democracy were, in other words, uneasy about the value of the collective wisdom of the people. They were not at all certain that average Americans were capable of anything approaching direct rule. In the broadest sense, the Founding Fathers instituted two types of barriers between government decisions and the people: (1) representatives, elected by the people to make decisions, and (2) time, reflected in the system by which the voice of the people was for the most part constrained to only periodic formal elections.

These two elements had profound implications on the political dynamic of this country—implications that continue even to this day. They ensure that at the most basic level, the views of the people need be taken into account only on an irregular basis. Representatives do the heavy lifting, making day-to-day decisions as they see fit. As the Founders intended, elected representatives pay some attention to the people, as they do to the opinions of lobbyists, party leaders, special interests, contributors, and a wide variety of other sources. Most elected representatives, of course, want to be reelected. But at a time when the vast majority of representatives (at least at the national level) are routinely reelected, often without having to campaign much at all, the connection between the views of the people and what their representatives end up doing is often problematic.

After the Constitution was ratified, as the decades of the American experience wore on, some of the barriers between the people and their government were lowered. Gradually, the right to vote was expanded beyond just propertied white males. As the nation moved into the twentieth century, minorities and women were finally allowed to have a voice by virtue of an official vote. The direct election of senators was also instituted via the Seventeenth Amendment. But for many, just as was the case for the Founding Fathers, there remained little confidence in the assertion that the views of the people should be of interest or of value in running the country on a day-to-day basis. The United States continues to govern itself by a system in which the power is lodged in representatives, and the debate over just how much these representatives should or do take into account the views of the people continues.

Advocates of the trustee model often like to quote the eighteenth-century Englishman Edmund Burke, one of the most prominent critics of a state of affairs in which representatives are slavishly devoted to following public opinion. Burke advocated the role of some sort of democracy, but he liked having the people exercise their views on only a periodic basis. (Some critics say that Burke was really an elitist who didn't trust the people much at all.) At any rate, Burke felt strongly that representatives sent off to govern should not constantly try to reflect the views of their constituencies. Burke's views live on to this day in part because of his famous statement: "Your representative owes you, not his industry only, but his judgment; and he betrays, instead of serving you, if he sacrifices it to your opinion."[1]

Other Burke-like thinkers have followed. The noted social commentator Walter Lippmann was one of the strongest critics of the value of the general public's views and thoughts. As political scientists Benjamin Page and Robert Shapiro summarize this period of history,

> . . . in the *Phantom Public*, Lippmann declared it a "false ideal" to imagine that the voters were "inherently competent" to direct public affairs. If the voter cannot grasp the details of the problems of the day because he has not the time, the interest or the knowledge, he will not have a better public opinion because he is asked to express his opinion more often . . . [2]

As I will detail later, there was negative reaction to the increasing power of polls almost immediately after they became routinized in the 1930s and 1940s. Lindsay Rogers, a professor at Columbia University, wrote an entire book (*The Pollsters*) lambasting polls, those who conducted them, and those who used them. Critics of the value of continuous measurement of the voice of the people also found support from political science research in the 1950s and 1960s. Analysts of survey results suddenly "discovered" that the public generally did not display high levels of knowledge about specific facts, that there was not necessarily a relationship between a respondent's positions on one issue and his or her positions on similar issues, and that respondents would sometimes express different opinions on an issue when they were recontacted in follow-up surveys. A group of books and articles was published in the 1950s and 1960s that cast doubt on the ability of the public to have a coherent or meaningful input into the political process.

All of this research seemed to underscore the assumption that the average citizen, if not stupid, was at least ill informed and uninterested in the basic goings-on in society. This led to distrust on the part of many observers in the value of attempting to rely on public opinion on a continuous basis—that is, beyond the periodic vote.

## THE REPRESENTATIVES

Now we come to the views of elected representatives themselves, many of whom tend to value their own personal judgments on key issues more than the views of the people they represent. We saw this in particular when members of the House of Representatives and members of the Senate pondered their votes regarding the impeachment of President Bill Clinton in 1998 and 1999. We saw it again when President George W. Bush and his advisers repeatedly claimed that they would not be making decisions on military action in Iraq based "on the polls," echoing Bush's earlier statements while campaigning in 2000 that "I don't need polls to tell me how to think. If elected

President, I will not use my office to reflect public opinion."[3]

These types of views were vociferously espoused by the perennial gadfly and syndicated columnist Arianna Huffington, who at one point in her antipolling crusade argued, "The political landscape today is littered with politicians who never stop looking over their shoulders at the latest polls and whose motto seems to be 'I'm their leader, I shall follow them.'"[4]

In other words, the idea of having wise representatives make the key decisions essentially "on their own" seems perfectly acceptable to many observers. Advocates of the trustee model do not argue for a society that totally disenfranchises the average citizen, but rather for allowing that citizen to have an impact on governing that is *infrequent and indirect* (primarily the vote). Mechanisms that allow much more frequent and much more direct monitors of the will of the people are not highly desired.

As I've noted, some of the most ardent adherents to this trustee viewpoint are the elected officials themselves, who can easily become more and more enamored of their own personal ability to make wise decisions. Relying on one's own judgment is easier than constantly checking with others to discern a course of action, and it is more compatible with a mental image of oneself as brilliant and in possession of supreme reasonableness. Serving only as a messenger/delegate is much less interesting and certainly much less consistent with a healthy ego. It isn't surprising that many elected representatives begin to think that they know best and that the views of the people (between elections) are less relevant. (Still, elected representatives end up responding to a number of other pressures, including in particular lobbyists and special interests.)

Elected representatives sometimes throw up the "but I am in touch" argument and claim they in fact do stay very closely attuned to what their constituents think and feel on a daily basis—and that they certainly don't need polls or other "artificial" systems to augment their understanding of what should be done. A number of studies document the degree to which representatives claim that they enjoy a broad, subtle, and constant "in-touchness" with their people. After all, representatives receive a steady barrage of letters, phone calls, and e-mails in which constituents express their viewpoints. Furthermore, many elected representatives pride themselves on the degree to which they go "back to the district" regularly and maintain the connection with their constituents that allows them to get an almost intuitive feel for what they think and feel.

Those methods of staying in touch are certainly useful and often perform valuable functions. Some elected representatives are indeed quite closely in touch with the views of their constituents. But most don't regularly take advantage of the ability we have today to access constituents' views on a systematic, scientific basis, and many argue that it's not necessary.

Here's a paradox of sorts: elected representatives are both willing and proud to announce that they carefully track constituent calls and letters and take time to hold town hall meetings in order to keep current with citizen concerns. But representatives are much less likely to proclaim proudly that they commission and study the type of scientific polls that would do a more precise job of helping them understand their constituents' concerns and opinions. This doesn't make a lot of sense. Why shouldn't elected representatives take full advantage of the most scientific and demonstrably accurate ways available of understanding their constituencies—polls?

The answer to that question is not totally clear, but we do know that many political elites, in addition to having perhaps inflated conceptions of their own wisdom and value, simply don't have a lot of respect for the people.

This basic disdain for the wisdom of the people on the part of elites was supported by a 1998 poll of elites conducted by the Pew Research Center.[5] The poll asked questions of a sample of representatives, congressional staffers, presidential appointees, and senior civil servants. The poll showed that significantly less than a majority of those in all these groups felt that the public was smart enough to have worthwhile opinions on important matters of policy. (It's interesting that the majority of elected officials use polling in their election and reelection campaigns, despite the fact that they may disdain its use to help guide their decision making between elections.)

This elitist notion that regularly consulting the views of the people is not necessary can be contrasted with what the people themselves say. In poll after poll, the people of the United States affirm that they have more faith in their own collective insights and wisdom than they do in their elected representatives. Two such polls were conducted at times in which public opinion was very important: the months leading up to the Persian Gulf War in 1990 and 1991 and during the Clinton impeachment crisis. In both situations, the Gallup poll asked Americans whether their elected officials should be paying attention to the wishes of the people as expressed through polls in making their decisions, or doing what they (the elected officials) thought was right. In both situations, the public came down firmly on the side of paying attention to the polls. The public, in short, had less interest in their representatives' making decisions on their own, but rather were more interested in the representatives' following the wishes of the people who elected them.

In a September 2003 Gallup poll, Americans were asked to rate how much confidence they had in various components of American society. Confidence in "the American people as a whole when it comes to making judgments under our democratic system about the issues facing our country" was the highest of the eight components tested. Three out of four Americans said they had a great deal or fair amount of confidence in the people. Meanwhile, only 2 percent said they had no confidence at all. The next highest-rated components of society were local government and the federal judicial branch of the government. headed by the Supreme Court.

Indeed, the juxtaposition of the polls of elites and polls of the public tells the story well. The elites in Washington are skeptical of the public's ability to have opinions of value, while the public itself demands that its views be given full attention.

Additionally, regardless of what the elected representatives may think, there are studies that show the degree to which representatives are in reality not highly in touch with what the people feel. Lawrence R. Jacobs and Robert Y. Shapiro wrote an entire book (*Politicians Don't Pander*) on this topic and presented evidence that shows the startling degree to which elected representatives do not vote in line with what the people they represent want them to. The authors start with the fact that in the fall of 1998 members of the House of Representatives voted to impeach President Bill Clinton even as almost every poll showed that the significant majority of the public did not want them to. As the authors put it,

> The impeachment spectacle reveals one of the most important developments in contemporary American politics—the widening gulf between politicians' policy decisions and the preferences of the American people toward specific issues. The impeachment of Clinton can be added to the long list of policies that failed to mirror public opinion: campaign finance reform, tobacco legislation, Clinton's proposals in his first budget for an energy levy and a high tax on Social Security benefits (despite his campaign promises to cut middle-class taxes), the North

American Free Trade Agreement (at its outset), U.S. intervention in Bosnia, as well as House Republican proposals after the 1994 elections for a "revolution" in policies toward the environment, education, Medicare, and other issues. We challenge the long-standing bias among elites against government responsiveness to public opinion. It is the failure of politicians, we argue, to attend to the public's preferences and to encourage public deliberation that is threatening America's democratic system.[6]

Another scholarly book, *Misreading the Public*, by Steven Kull and I. M. Destler, addresses these same issues. The authors point out a wide gap between how well elected officials and policy makers think they understand public opinion on foreign policy, and what is actually the case:

> Although elected officials and those who advise them generally have an incentive to understand the public, this does not mean that they necessarily do . . . There is a significant gap between the dominant perceptions of public attitudes held by the policy community and the attitudes held by the majority of the American public.[7]

This gap that Kull and Destler talk about is not a good thing. Elected representatives self-evidently do not always make wise decisions. The impact of their decisions is not infrequently disastrous, no matter how impressive their credentials. Closing the gap between public opinion and elected officials' decisions can't hurt, and almost certainly will help.

Most important, it is worth reemphasizing that Americans are generally not happy with the representative system of government as they know it. They often feel profoundly distanced from their representatives. Americans' perceptions that their elected representatives are out of touch and essentially ignoring their (the people's) views are no doubt a major cause of low confidence in Congress and low ratings of the ethics and honesty of senators and congresspeople. It has also led to loss of faith in government as an institution and to the widespread embrace of ways to wrest control back from formal legislative bodies, including initiatives and referenda and the type of recall campaign made famous by the ouster of California governor Gray Davis in October 2003.

Ratings of Congress are low, and trust in government generally has been very low for the past quarter century. (This pattern of distrust in government was interrupted by the rally in public positivism that followed the September 11 terrorist attacks, but within a year levels of trust and ratings of Congress had begun to fall again.) Elected representatives at the national level get some of the lowest ratings of honesty and ethics that we measure in our polling—not too much above lawyers and car salesmen. In November 2003, just 20 percent of Americans gave a "very high" or "high" rating to the honesty and ethical standards of senators, and just 17 percent gave a "very high" or "high" rating to the honesty of members of the House. That contrasts, by way of comparison, to the 83 percent rating given nurses, who were at the top end of the scale. The institution of Congress also receives low scores on our measures of confidence in institutions. In a June 2003 Gallup poll, Congress received only a 29 percent confidence rating from the American public, compared to the 82 percent confidence rating given the military, the 61 percent rating given to the police, the 55 percent rating given the presidency, and the 47 percent rating given the Supreme Court. In other words, Congress—designed to be the component of government closest to the people—gets worse ratings than the executive or judicial branches.

The people repeatedly tell us in surveys that they want more input and want their representatives to pay more, rather than less, attention to them. Indeed, this feeling is so pervasive that citizen participation in the political system through voting remains historically low—in part, I am convinced, because people feel that whoever they elect is likely to ignore their wishes and do what he or she wants regardless.

It is perhaps no wonder that Gallup polling finds that the closer the government is to home, the higher its ratings. When asked in which branch of government Americans have the most confidence, local government comes in first, followed by state government and then federal government. And when asked in which branch they have the *least* confidence, the federal government comes in at the top.

People have become so disaffected by the way they are being represented that they are more and more likely to take over the reins of government themselves, short-circuiting the representative system altogether. At least twenty-seven states now have direct initiative and referendum laws in place—laws allowing the people to have their say directly without having to go through their representatives at all. In Oregon, initiatives and referenda have rendered the elected representatives in the state legislature in Salem as secondary actors (much to those representatives' chagrin). Major new laws in California are often made through a direct vote by the people—not by the legislature in Sacramento. Many school districts are set up so that the people, rather than elected representatives, have to vote on the budgets. Even a casual search on the Internet finds an enormous number of sites representing groups dedicated to the direct-democracy movement, which advocates that all laws be made directly by the people.

Perhaps the most vivid example of the impact of citizens' dissatisfaction with the way the representative democratic system is working comes from the California gubernatorial recall that occurred in the summer and fall

of 2003. The chance to throw out an elected governor gal-
vanized millions of California voters to go to the polls in
significantly higher numbers than in a normal nonpresi-
dential election. Voters were fed up with a governor whom
they considered to be out of touch with the people, and
took the opportunity to show their dissatisfaction by voting him out of office. There was a great hue and cry about
presumed negative implications of the recall. Many critics
didn't like the process (for a variety of reasons), but underneath the criticisms was the fundamental fact that
Californians were not satisfied with the way their representative government was working.

Some argued that California voters should have just
shut up and waited for the next election. The fact that they
so willingly embraced the concept of recall, however, represents not the undisciplined actions of immature, unso-
phisticated bumpkins, but the responses of voters who felt
that the incumbent governor was out of touch with the
people he represented. The ousted governor, Gray Davis,
eventually came to agree. Davis told a *New York Times* reporter shortly before Arnold Schwarzenegger took over as
governor in mid-November 2003, "I didn't stay in touch
with the people. That's clearly my biggest regret. Voters
are the source of all wisdom. You have to conduct an ongoing dialogue with them."[8]

The bottom line is clear. California voters felt disen-
franchised with the political system and took action to do
something about it.

My objective here isn't to argue the merits of the initiative and referendum system and the changes it has brought
about in states like California, but rather to highlight
what's behind it: the desire of the citizens to have more
input into the policy decisions that affect them.

All of this isn't necessarily new. Most of us remember
that Ross Perot, in his 1992 campaign for the presidency,
advocated the direct input of the citizens on a regular basis

using new electronic means (which is even more feasible today through the Internet). Perot lost the election, but he got 19 percent of the popular vote and was obviously to a significant degree tapping into the common people's disgruntlement about the way their representative government was operating.

Although some may think it a little disingenuous to be quoting polling results in defense of the whole polling process, I think it is worthwhile here to repeat the conclusions of a major study on what people think their government should do (conducted by the Center on Policy Attitudes in Washington, D.C., in 1999). The study found:

1. "An overwhelming majority of Americans feel that the views of the public should have substantially more influence over government decisions than they presently do, and that the public's views should have more influence than those of elected officials. A strong majority expresses confidence in the public's judgment and says it would give more credence to the decisions of a random sample of Americans informed on all sides of an issue than to the decisions of Congress."
2. "The majority of Americans believe that most of the decisions the government makes are not the decisions that they would make, and an overwhelming majority believes that the government is not being run for the benefit of the public as a whole."
3. "The public's feeling of being marginalized from government decision making has risen dramatically over the last few decades, and on several measures is now at an all time high."[9]

Other polls have found similar sentiments. The people want more input and feel that elected representatives are operating too much on their own.

## POLLING AS THE MECHANISM TO FILL IN THE BLANKS

In the old days, it was much easier for elected representatives to justify a true trustee role because there wasn't an efficient way of staying in touch with the people even if representatives wanted to. Many congresspeople and senators had to travel for days to get to their state capitals or to Washington. Their ability to assess on a continuing basis what their constituents were thinking and feeling was minimal. So representatives truly had to assume they knew their constituents well enough to represent them appropriately in the long periods of absence during which they were away from their districts or states, unable to assess local sentiment on a direct basis at all.

In short, one of the big problems with democratic theory and practice in the past centered on the practical difficulties in trying to measure the public's will in the larger and larger groups that constitute political units. It is one thing to have a group of people in a small community come together in order to hash over the issues of the day and reach collective decisions; it is another to try to have a town meeting when the numbers of people involved begin to reach into the thousands and, in today's situation, the millions. As Robert Dahl summarized the problem in his book *On Democracy:*

> As the focus of democratic government shifted to large-scale units like nations or countries, the question arose: How can citizens *participate effectively* when the number of citizens becomes too numerous or too widely dispersed geographically (or both, as in the case of a country) for them to participate conveniently in making laws by assembling in one place? . . . How best to meet these democratic requirements in a political unit as large as a country is, of course, enormously difficult, indeed to some extent

unachievable . . . Until the eighteenth century, then, the standard view was that democratic or republican government meant rule by the people, and if the people were to rule they had to assemble in one place and vote on decrees, laws or policies. Democracy would have to be town meeting democracy; representative democracy was a contradiction in terms.[10]

As Dahl goes on to point out, the larger and larger sizes of nation-states soon made this assumption untenable. Because it was untenable, the idea of representative democracy gained acceptance. If the people couldn't be involved in every decision directly because there was no practical way of getting together in one place to voice their collective opinions, then they would elect their representatives to do their bidding for them.

But let's follow through on this logic. One of the biggest differences between the time at which the Founding Fathers put the U.S. Constitution together and today is our increased ability to measure and obtain the views of the public on a regular basis. If representatives were necessary in previous times because it was impossible to assess the opinions of large numbers of people on a routine basis, then representatives should in many ways be less necessary now—in a practical sense—because it *is* possible to assess the opinions of large numbers of people, even with the very large populations we are dealing with today.

The ability to measure public opinion on a regular, constant, and in-depth basis is provided by polling. It is thus my belief that polling is a significantly important development in the history of democracy. (Of course, another difference between the late 1700s and now is the increased ability of average citizens to stay apprised of what is happening around them. In other words, the changes in American society over the last two centuries work in two ways. Not only can politicians stay better informed about the views of the people they represent, but people have far more access to news and information than they used to. I think it is reasonable to assume that they are therefore better informed than they were two hundred years ago, although this is difficult to establish empirically.)

It is at this point that I can bring in the views of Dr. George Gallup, who spent a great deal of his time dealing with the issues we're wrestling with here. Gallup was focused on the ideal that having every citizen involved in the political process is the bedrock of democracy. Indeed, I'm told by Gallup's two sons that he loved Switzerland (where he had a second home) because he admired its system of local, involved votes of the people on key issues.

One of the bases for Gallup's beliefs was the thinking of James Bryce, a fascinating figure in American history. Bryce was unabashedly an advocate of the idea that the people in a democratic system should have as much power as possible as quickly as possible.

Most Americans today haven't heard of Bryce, but he was a famous man of his time, a British author, historian, social observer, and at one point ambassador to the United States. He wrote a great deal about his views of the American democratic experiment in the late 1880s and is best known for his big book *The American Commonwealth*. Bryce was an unrestrained advocate of the power of public opinion, "vague, fluctuating, complex" as it is.

Bryce, like other observers, focused on the problems of attempting to allow this public opinion to be measured and expressed in societies larger than small towns and communities. He argued that there were several stages in the process of translating public opinion into action. In the first stage, the ruler of the society merely attempts to take the public's views into account. In the second stage, when public opinion is out of sync with the ruler or ruling class, the differences end up being settled "by arms." In the third stage, public opinion is realized through representatives: "[The sovereign multitude's] will is expressed at certain intervals upon slips of paper deposited in boxes and is carried out by the minister or legislature to whom the popular mandate is entrusted."[11] (This should sound familiar; it is a direct expression of the trustee model discussed above.)

Bryce envisioned the fourth stage as the final one, the stage at which the will of the people could be expressed at all times and in all ways:

> A fourth stage would be reached, if the will of the majority of the citizens were to become ascertainable at all times, and without the need of its passing through a body of representatives, possible even without the need of voting machinery at all. In such a state of things the sway of public opinion would have become more complete, because more continuous, than it is in those European countries which, like France, Italy and Britain, look chiefly to parliaments as exponents of the national sentiment. Popular government would have been pushed so far as almost to dispense with, or at any rate to anticipate, the legal modes in which the majority speaks its will at the polling booths.[12]

Bryce, in other words, recognized that there needed to be a more continuous reading of public opinion than was available just through periodic elections, arguing that voters could well change their views on issues between votes. Bryce was very impressed, as Dr. Gallup emphasized in his writings, with the idea of using a more frequent vote on issues—referenda on key issues, for example, as occurred in Switzerland. But Bryce recognized their limitation:

> The referendum, or plan of submitting a specific question to the popular vote, is the logical resource, but it is troublesome and costly to take the votes of millions of

people over an area so large as that of one of the greater states; much more, then, is this difficult to apply in federal matters.[13]

Note that Bryce essentially skipped right over the delegate model of representative democracy. He was all in favor of the concept of using whatever tools might be available to let the people govern directly. Bryce's hypothesized fourth stage, in essence, was a form of direct democracy in which the role of representative would be done away with altogether.

As I've noted, I don't think removing the representative role from government altogether is reasonable at this point in our history. We need representatives and implementers and those who act as our agents. But Bryce's basic ideas are clear. The ultimate source of wisdom and guidance in a society should be the people themselves, and steps should be taken to ensure that this wisdom is maximally taken advantage of by those entrusted with the power to make decisions in society.

Indeed, Bryce concluded that the governments in democracies like America might approximate his fourth stage of democracy if the representatives acted at all times *as if* they were taking public opinion into account (that is to say, assuming that it continued to be necessary to have representatives at all). In Bryce's words,

The supremacy of their [the people's] will is expressed in the existence of a constitution placed above the legislature, although capable of alteration by a direct popular vote. The position of the representatives has been altered. They are conceived of, not as wise and strong men chosen to govern, but as delegates under specific orders to be renewed at short intervals.[14]

That's as clear a statement of the delegate model of representative government as we are likely to find.

But writing as he was in the nineteenth century, Bryce actually despaired of finding an efficient mechanism for measuring public opinion regularly. As he put it, "The mechanical difficulties, as one may call them, of working such a method of government are obvious. How is the will of the majority to be ascertained except by counting votes? How, without the greatest inconvenience, can votes be frequently taken on all the chief questions that arise?" Bryce pointed out that "the machinery for weighing or measuring the popular will from week to week or month to month is not likely to be invented . . ."[15]

It should be clear at this point why Dr. Gallup found Bryce's writings so appealing. For one thing, Bryce's ideas verified Gallup's faith in the wisdom of the collective views of the people of a society. Second, and more important, Gallup knew that he had at his disposal what he considered to be the Holy Grail, the missing link, the method Bryce was looking for: the poll. "The sampling referendum [the poll], then, is a modern answer to Bryce's problem," Gallup wrote triumphantly in 1941 in *The Pulse of Democracy*.

> Not only have the polls followed Bryce's suggestion that the people should be approached directly; the development of a careful sampling technique has virtually overcome the obstacles of time and expense which caused Bryce to doubt the possibility of continuous nation-wide referendums. By collecting the opinions of a representative sample of voters, they have made possible that week-to-week audit of public opinion, which Bryce himself called the "logical resource."[16]

In short, Gallup viewed public opinion polling as a truly important way in which the voice of the public could be heard more often and in greater depth, thus exemplifying his, and Bryce's, conception of the ideals of a democracy. As Gallup's thinking evolved in the 1930s and 1940s, he became convinced that polls did not just provide interesting information and fodder for cocktail parties, but had the potential to be a major component of a well-functioning democracy. He felt strongly that the more that barriers between the voices of the public and the functioning of government could be erased, the better.

By the 1940s, Dr. Gallup felt that the time had come when the democratic functioning of society could be improved by moving beyond the problems of the past, that polling allowed society to advance beyond "the age like that of the Founding Fathers of the American Republic," when "participation in the basic ideals of democracy" was limited exclusively to the "wise, the rich and the good." "Public opinion is not today, as it was then, the opinion of a small and exclusive minority of educated persons enjoying a monopoly of economic and political power. Nor can we restore the practice of direct democracy which operated in the early town-hall meetings of New England, or revive the political intimacy of the rural corner store with its cracker barrel."[17] Polling, as Gallup said in one of his speeches, is the "chief hope of lifting government to a higher level."[18]

## SUMMING IT UP

The Constitutional system of government in the United States is a representative democracy and is most likely to stay that way for the foreseeable future, despite significant pressures in some quarters to move the system more toward a direct democracy in which the people have their say on every issue as it comes up.

The pressures toward direct democracy are symptomatic of a generalized disgruntlement on the part of the citizens toward their system of representative government. Citizens increasingly believe that their wishes are not being well represented and that the system of government has somehow gotten out of their control.

Polling provides a remedy for some of these problems. Routinized polling can play a variety of functions in a society, but the most important is the fact that it is a proven mechanism for ascertaining and summarizing the collective opinions of the masses of the people. And having the collective wisdom of the members of a society available for use by whoever is making the decisions in a society is absolutely imperative for maximizing the adaptiveness of our society to the challenges of the future. Representatives must and should pay more, rather than less, attention to the collective wisdom of the people. Polling provides them with the means to do so.

As I've pointed out, polling doesn't have to be tied to a process by which the views of the people are taken into account in a society on a formal basis in between elections. Polling is best viewed, I think, as a scientific mechanism for continual assessment of the opinions and thoughts of the people, a mechanism providing a fund of wisdom and guidance that is available to be used—and should be used—by anyone who is making decisions about the society, be that person a king, dictator, or senator.

When the people's voices are not heard, we run the risk of creating significant imbalance and disequilibrium in our society. The rallying cry in the 1770s was "taxation without representation." Now, in the twenty-first century, it may well be "representation without being paid attention to." I'm not implying here that polling is necessary in order to prevent a revolution of the masses (although some forms of mild revolt are already being seen in many places as a result of the perceived political estrangement of the masses). The argument of this book is not based just on a society's need to avoid revolution and to satisfy or cool out the masses. It is based on assumptions about the best way of running a country, the search for a process most likely to produce the actions, decisions, and results that have the greatest evolutionary force, pushing the society forward in the way that produces the best life and best future for everyone involved.

And everything points toward a system in which the collective wisdom of the people is taken into account more, rather than less, often. *In short, I'm arguing that it makes a great deal of sense to take as much advantage as possible of the wisdom bound up in the aggregated views of everyone in a population, via polling.*

In addition to the benefit of using the people's wisdom to serve as a basis for running society, taking the people's views into account in a more direct fashion yields other societal benefits. When people recognize that their views are being seriously considered and that they have the power to make a difference, they may well spend more time becoming versed on the issues than they might otherwise. There is nothing like empowerment to move people to a position where they take their roles more seriously. Businesses across the country have learned that listening to their workers often translates into improved esprit de corps, increased involvement in the workplace, and a renewed level of enjoyment and a sense of importance. Presumably, the more the public realizes that its opinions have a voice in the way in which its government acts, the more the public will take its responsibility as citizens seriously.

1. Peter Landry, "The Political Philosopher, Edmund Burke (1729–97)," http://www.blupete.com/Literature/Biographies/Philosophy/Burke.htm (September 2000).

2. Benjamin I. Page and Robert Y. Shapiro, *The Rational Public* (Chicago: University of Chicago Press, 1992), 4.

3. George W. Bush, "A Fresh Start in America," Delaware Primary campaign material, February 8, 2000.

4. Arianna Huffington, "A Modest Proposal," filed October 3, 1996, http://www.ariannaonline.com/columns/files/100396.html.

5. Pew Research Center, "Washington Leaders Wary of Public Opinion: Public Appetite for Government Misjudged," released April 17, 1998.

6. Lawrence R. Jacobs and Robert Y. Shapiro, *Politicians Don't Pander: Political Manipulation and the Loss of Democratic Responsiveness* (Chicago: University of Chicago Press, 2000), xii.

7. Steven Kull and I. M. Destler, *Misreading the Public: The Myth of a New Isolationism* (Washington, DC: Brookings Institute, 1999), 249–50.

8. John M. Broder, "Term Waning, Gov. Davis Reflects on the Battle Lost," *New York Times,* November 12, 2003.

9. Steven Kull, "Expecting More to Say: A Study of American Public Attitudes on the Role of the Public in Government Decisions," Center on Policy Attitudes, February 9, 1999.

10. Robert A. Dahl, *On Democracy* (New Haven: Yale University Press, 1998), 93–94.

11. James Bryce, *The American Commonwealth* (Indianapolis: Liberty Fund, 1995), 919.

12. Ibid.

13. Ibid., 1003–1004.

14. Ibid.

15. Ibid., 919.

16. George Gallup and Saul Forbes Rae, *The Pulse of Democracy* (New York: Simon & Schuster, 1940), 32.

17. Ibid., 12.

18. "Polls and the Political Process—Past, Present and Future," speech, George H. Gallup, 1965.

# CHAPTER 4

# Don't Pigeonhole Me

Almost from the time polling began to be taken seriously in the 1930s as a mechanism for assessing and taking into account the will of the people, criticisms began to emerge—some of them vicious, emotional, and passionately argued. As Dr. George Gallup said in *The Pulse of Democracy,*

> We are now witnessing a paradoxical but unavoidable phenomenon—the polls of public opinion are themselves becoming an issue of public opinion . . . During the short space of four years a considerable body of criticism has been directed at this effort to take the pulse of democracy. Three main batteries have opened fire on the modern public-opinion poll. The first charge comes from individuals and groups who object to the specific results that a given poll indicates . . . A second type of criticism comes from those who admit the desirability of measuring public opinion, but emphasize defects in the present methods of operation. Finally, there is the argument that polls weaken the democratic process, either by destroying interest in elections, or by creating a "band-wagon vote" among the doubtful voters.[1]

Today, more than sixty years later, the same criticisms are still very much with us. Something about polling—as

Dr. Gallup discovered many years ago—has a special power to trigger intense emotions from the population at large, and as a result, to generate numerous and deeply felt objections from the public. I've already addressed many of these objections, at least indirectly, in discussing the basic rationale for polling, but it is worthwhile to take more of an in-depth look at the reasons that some people seem to object so vociferously to polls.

## I Don't Like Poll Results That Disagree with What I Believe

First, as Dr. Gallup indicated, there are the negative reactions from those people who object to the specific results of a given poll because the results are not in line with their personal beliefs. It is clear that there are at least two sides to almost every issue about which Gallup polls, making it mathematically certain that someone will be put off by any given poll's results.

This is particularly—in fact, almost inevitably—true when a major news event captivates the attention of the country. For example, significant numbers of people often react negatively to the results of polls before presidential elections because they find it difficult to believe that their candidate is not being supported by the majority of the voters. Many reacted negatively to polls assessing public opinion about the guilt of O. J. Simpson, again because they could not believe that Americans did not perceive the Simpson situation the same way they did. Many Americans were distressed by the results of polls on the Clinton impeachment hearings in 1998 and 1999, and the disputed 2000 presidential election results. People also reacted negatively to the results of polls regarding the Bush administration decision to lead the country toward war in the early spring of 2003. In all these instances, people had such negative reactions because the poll results contradicted what they had assumed would logically be the views shared by the majority of their fellow citizens.

Earlier, I talked about my belief that people are interested in poll results because of what psychologist Leon Festinger hypothesized was a basic human desire to compare and contrast one's own attitudes and opinions with those of others. In a sense, Festinger argued that people are driven to measure their own views by those of others as a reassuring and validating reference standard. While this basic part of human nature may well draw people to poll results in general, there is also a psychological *danger* when humans compare opinions and discover they are in the minority, standing alone in their beliefs at the fringes of society. It may be satisfying to compare opinions when other people's views reinforce one's own beliefs, but it is not nearly so pleasant to compare others' opinions to one's own and discover that the two differ sharply.

Festinger also developed a theory focusing on the fact that humans like to be consistent in their perceptions and thoughts and that an inconsistent, dissonant state is one that most humans want to avoid. We humans are in a state of "cognitive dissonance," Festinger said, when one of our cognitions does not jibe with another cognition, or when a belief does not jibe with our own behavior.[2] This sounds simple, but Festinger's theory has many compelling implications, including some for our concerns in this book. As I apply it to polling, the theory predicts that when we believe strongly in a particular position on an issue, and a pollster comes along and tells us that the majority (or more alarmingly, the vast majority) of Americans believe just as strongly in a totally different position, we can quickly slip into a cognitively dissonant state. It is seldom mentally satisfying to conclude that the majority of those around us contradict our opinion. Simply put, our brains have a hard time handling the fact that most people do not share our cherished beliefs.

So when confronted by poll results that differ from our own opinions, what do we do? There are several ways to resolve this type of cognitive dissonance, based on Festinger's theory. One is to change our own views to coincide with the majority opinion (this is unlikely, particularly in terms of firmly held beliefs). A second way is simple acceptance that we are out of step with the majority of our fellow citizens. (Some people actually like to define themselves as being in the minority and may take pleasure in the fact.) A third approach is to decide that the individuals involved are all deficient in some way and to adopt the belief that we are superior to the majority. A fourth way is to deny the validity of the information itself—to assume that the basic process by which the views of the people are measured and reported is flawed. This is what pollsters confront so frequently because I believe it is often easiest for people to deal with a cognitively inconsistent state by denying the underlying plausibility of the poll results. If the poll is invalid, cognitive consistency is restored.

There are many ways people can use to attack the validity of polls, and I think I have heard them all. One way is to argue that only a certain type of person was interviewed in the poll or that all the "educated" opinions were somehow missed in the sampling process. We at Gallup saw this in 1992 when we were besieged by calls from supporters of Ross Perot. These Perotistas were adamant in insisting that our polls were flawed because they were not picking up the large numbers of Perot supporters these people saw in their own life situations. Abortion opponents or critics of George W. Bush also appear to feel the same way when they read polls showing that large numbers of Americans support abortion rights and approve of the job Bush is doing. They just can't believe it is so. Indeed, in 2002 and 2003, Gallup received many calls and e-mails from both sides of the political spectrum, depending on what poll results said about the president. If results were favorable to Bush, Democrats complained, insisting that we interviewed only Republicans or people from Bush's home state of Texas. If the poll results were less favorable to Bush, then Republicans said that we interviewed only liberals in New York City and Hollywood. Evidently, people can't accept that their views aren't shared by others. The following are various examples of this type of disbelief:

- I would like to know where you obtain your "random" samples. I have never been asked to participate, and neither has anyone I've asked (and I've asked quite a few). Quite often the opinions expressed do not match mine or those of the people I know.
- I am surprised at your sampling. Every single one that I have talked to thinks that he [Bush] is doing a very poor job.
- I have conducted an informal poll about Bush's approval rating and the willingness of people to go to war. My results are significantly (statistically) different from your results. I question the validity of your survey.

As can be seen from these responses, it seems quite difficult for many Americans to accept the fact that other citizens don't hold to the same evident truths that they do. The result? Individuals blame the polls and pollsters.

Journalists get the same type of reaction to news stories that contain reporting that is discordant with readers' and viewers' beliefs. Most reporters and editors have firsthand experience with irate readers who insist that a news story is biased or poorly reported because it presents a conclusion out of sync with the reader's own views. But polls

seem to go a little further in fostering this type of dissonance. People who have deeply reasoned and highly emo-
tionally charged beliefs just find it tough to accept the fact
that millions of their fellow citizens—as represented by
polling—hold opposing views.

In many instances, it is important to note, people are
correct in perceiving that the opinions of their friends and
neighbors are similar to theirs. Humans tend to talk and
socialize with those who agree with them, often avoiding
those with whom they disagree. This is no doubt driven by
the human desire to avoid cognitive dissonance and to
enjoy the comfort of knowing that one's personal views
are similar to those of others. Thus, the reality is that we
are often surrounded by people who share our views. It's
no wonder that we find it difficult to believe polls showing that a majority of the broader population doesn't
agree with these views, leading us to convince ourselves
that the polling must be flawed.

Indeed, another offshoot of Festinger's theory predicts
that humans will selectively expose themselves to information that is consistent with their preexisting beliefs and
avoid information that contradicts their beliefs. Conser-
vatives tend to listen to Rush Limbaugh and read conservative columnists; liberals seek out liberal commentators.
This tendency to surround oneself with gratifyingly consistent information also helps explain why certain people
complain that our polls can't be right because no one they
know possesses the beliefs the polls say typify the population.

Perhaps all of this negative reaction to poll results that
differ from one's own beliefs shouldn't be surprising
when we consider how ego-crushing it can be. Certainly
on a one-on-one basis, it is not uncommon to find sharp
arguments and unpleasantness when there is disagreement on a topic or issue. Many a dinner-party conversa-
tion has been interrupted by violent disagreements over

contrasting positions and attitudes. But when just one person disagrees with someone, it is fairly easy to get over it, and the person can be dismissed as deranged, insane, stupid, or ill informed. The problem with being confronted by the results of a poll, on the other hand, is the fact that the poll represents the opinions of *large numbers* of people. It may be easy to accept the fact that one jerk at a dinner party likes the president while you don't, or that one coworker at the office opposes abortion while you are in favor of it. It is another thing to be confronted via polling with the fact that millions of people—a majority of people in some situations—disagree with your opinions. It is much harder to dismiss a poll than to dismiss the opinion of just one person. Thus, a cognitively dissonant state is created when a person confronts a poll whose results are at variance with that person's own closely held opinions.

Some people, in other words, may react so negatively to polls because they represent not the opinions of just a single person or politician or interest group, but of almost everyone! Even worse, poll results make it crystal clear when a person's views are in the minority. Polls receive prominent play in news reports, thus essentially rubbing the opinions of others in one's face.

I'm not sure there is a remedy for the negative reaction that polls create in people who simply find it impossible to think that their personal beliefs are so out of sync with those of the majority of Americans. If we look at the big picture, it is healthy for a society to have widely diverse opinions and population segments whose strongly held beliefs are in the minority. As pollsters, one of our objectives is to convince people that a poll doesn't have to be flawed just because it shows that the beliefs of the majority are different from those of a given person. But we have a long way to go in this regard.

# I Don't Like Being Pigeonholed

In my experience, people often take issue with poll results because they resent being pigeonholed. People don't always like being categorized, typified, or summarized. Journalist Walter Kirn's opinion piece in the Sunday *New York Times Magazine* of April 6, 2003, encapsulates this sentiment in rather poetic fashion:

> No opinion poll, however probing, can drill down into the tar pit of emotions churning and steaming at my core and dredge up a representative sample of anything . . . I don't want to be part of a body of opinion now. I don't want to be lumped with strangers of the same income level, race, locale, sex, party, faith and age. I don't want them to speak for me, or me for them.[3]

Clearly, Kirn suffers from the common, perhaps even admirable—but incorrect—conception that each human is totally unique. Many people treasure this perception of uniqueness and feel that any efforts to typify an individual's specific attitudes and opinions without a detailed, personal interview cannot be accurate. Indeed, all pollsters can testify that the results of polls are frequently dismissed by people who say "I wasn't called" or "They didn't interview me."

When people say "I wasn't called," they are actually incorporating several different types of objections to polls. For one thing, these people may be saying rather straightforwardly that they don't believe in polling methodology. They can't accept the fact that they (and perhaps about 290 million other Americans) weren't called, even though the pollster claims that the poll is representative of the entire society. But I think there may be more to it than this. I think that to some degree, this type of complaint is based on the fact that people resist the idea that their personal views are summarized by a poll, in essence reducing their thought patterns to a number—particularly if they haven't been personally interviewed in some depth.

Humans' egocentric natures lead them to believe that their own particular blend of life experiences, attitudes, and opinions makes them—or any person, for that matter—totally unique. Because polls claim to represent the views of all Americans, doubters cry, "How is this possible? I am a complex person with nuanced, complex beliefs. The pollster didn't interview me. I'm not like anyone else. So don't tell me that your poll represents either me or any of the other millions of those not interviewed." In other words, how can a measurement procedure that doesn't explicitly measure each of us, one by one, accurately represent who we are and what we think?

There are grains of truth in these thoughts. At the most basic level, each human *is* unique. Every person, with the possible exception of newly born identical twins, has a combination of genes and life experiences that at some deep level makes him or her different from everyone else. No pollster or other social scientist can possibly capture the unique essence of a person in all of his or her exquisite intricacies without interviewing that person in great detail. As the television show about New York City used to say, "There are 8 million stories in the Naked City." In other words, there are as many different stories in New York as there are people in the city.

But the truth is that science is all about summarizing and classifying. Most scientific procedures that focus on the human don't attempt to take into account, at one time, the entire array of variables that make up the whole organism. Science attempts in large part to analyze subject matter by generalizing and looking at the entire class of objects under study, not specific plants, animals, or humans one by one.

While each human is in the final analysis unique, each

at the same time is identical to every other human in a variety of ways. We are similar in the most basic sense because we are all mammals. Each of us has a heart and lungs. We share our blood type with millions of other humans, as well as our racial background, our height, and our age. In other words, while any one human is at the deepest level a unique combination of characteristics and qualities, that human also shares characteristics, traits, and interests with millions of others.

Humans also share their attitudes with millions of other people. Humans who vote do so for one of only two or three candidates in the typical election, they are likely to belong to one of only a handful of political parties, and they will agree with one of just a few basic positions on major social issues. These attitudes may be nuanced, to be sure, and finely calibrated in a way that is not exactly like another person's, but one's attitudes can always be lumped into broad categories. I may have subtle, exquisitely reasoned, and fine-tuned attitudes toward the death penalty, for example, but when pressed to do so, I will usually be able to agree with one side or the other of a simple dichotomous question: "Do you favor or oppose the death penalty for murder?" Additionally, although any given voter in an election may have very specific views of individual candidates, in the end he or she has to vote for just one of the candidates.

Again, this is similar to the situation that obtains in much of science: categorizing and grouping the objects under study. All plants and animals can be categorized into phyla and genera. Each plant and animal is unique at some level (most dog owners are convinced that his or her dog, for example, is unique), but at a broader level, each is part of an identifiable type or group. A German shepherd is a German shepherd regardless of the personality and idiosyncrasies that endear one particular example of this breed to his owner. By the same token, although all humans are unique at some basic level, they are *not* unique when it comes to the broad and general characteristics in which pollsters are usually interested.

Polling asks Americans to categorize themselves in terms of very broad values on specific variables. Polling is usually not a highly targeted procedure designed to pinpoint humans on refined levels, but instead lumps humans into much less specific, broad categories. It can do this because humans are *not* unique in many ways, but are similar to others across the country who share beliefs on social and political issues.

Let's look at an example. A March 2000 Gallup poll was able to divide the world rather neatly into categories based on attitudes toward Bill Clinton's job performance as president of the United States. Sixty-three percent of those polled said that they approved of the "way Bill Clinton is handling his job as president." Thirty-four percent disapproved (another 3 percent said they didn't know). Many Americans at that point in history no doubt had fairly nuanced views of Bill Clinton. Americans had been through eight years of exposure to Clinton's complex personality and the widely varied aspects of his personal life, demeanor, scandals, and accomplishments. But the classic Gallup job approval question forces Americans to put themselves into either the "approve" box or the "disapprove" box. Like it or not, this procedure forces poll respondents to summarize their attitudes. Thus, an American who in March 2000 said he or she approved of Clinton's job performance was essentially in the same category as about 126 million other Americans. It is true that a particular person who said he or she approved of Bill Clinton's job performance may well have explained his/her perception of Clinton in a substantially different way than his or her neighbor who also approved. But in terms of this job approval question, it didn't matter. The poll was designed to put people into broad categories and not to pick up nuances.

Now, this is not to say that polling about someone like Clinton can't get a little more complex. When we asked Americans whether they approved or disapproved of Bill Clinton *as a person*, only 35 percent of Americans said they approved, 59 percent said they did not approve, and 6 percent were indifferent. Again, an American who did not like Clinton personally—perhaps because of his behavior or morals—was not alone, but one of 118 million other Americans.

We could have cross-tabulated the responses to the two questions in order to develop a more finely tuned analysis. A certain percentage of Americans both approved of Clinton as a person *and* approved of his job performance. Another group of Americans disapproved of Clinton on both dimensions. Others approved of his job performance but disapproved of him as a person. A very small number approved of him as a person but disapproved of his job performance. But even at this deeper level, an American who thought positively about Clinton's job performance but disapproved of his personal traits was sharing that combination of views with millions of other Americans. This person's viewpoint, in other words, was hardly unique.

Now, the list of questions and various combinations of questions about Clinton could have been longer. If a pollster had asked one hundred questions about Clinton, it is likely that any given American's combination of responses to those questions would indeed begin to move more and more toward uniqueness. After all, even the dichotomous responses to just ten questions could be combined into literally thousands and thousands of different patterns. In this situation, one's more complex patterns of beliefs would be duplicated by only hundreds of thousands of others, rather than millions. If there were one hundred different questions about Clinton, there might be a point at which a particular American's response patterns across all of the questions would not be duplicated at all *by any other* American. (There are 2 to the 100th power different ways that one hundred dichotomous questions could be answered.) In other words, we could ask enough questions and do enough analysis to put each and every human into a category that is shared by very few others. But that wouldn't help us accomplish our objective of understanding the broad sweep of public opinion.

I'm reminded of the 1960s novel *The 480*, by Eugene Burdick,[4] in which a brilliant political scientist used the computer (then a new idea) to classify Americans into one of 480 different categories based on their characteristics and attitudes. The novel's scientist, Dr. Devlin, uses this information to create the perfect candidate to appeal to just the right numbers of people in these categories. The idea of using this type of market research and computers to help design a political campaign has become commonplace nowadays, but what has always intrigued me is the idea that there were actually a meaningful 480 different ways to cross human characteristics relating to a potential presidential vote. That seemed high. But my point here is that even in this (fictional) scenario, each of the people in each of the 480 slots shared his or her classification with hundreds of thousands of other people. It's hard to escape the fact that there are many others who are in numerous ways just like us.

Survey research deals in broad variables and analyzes them either singly or in combination with one or two others. The process is aimed at measuring the relative prevalence of these characteristics across society. An individual may at a deep level have highly idiosyncratic and unique opinions and feelings about social topics or political subjects, but is also one member of a large segment of society who responds to broad questions in the same way.

By way of example, I think it is fair to say that the same

principles hold even with snowflakes, often used as the prototypical example of uniqueness in nature. Even if it is true that no one snowflake is like any other, it *is* possible to classify snowflakes into rough categories based on their broad characteristics or the basic shapes into which they fall. Even though humans are each at some level totally unique, they can be characterized in terms of general physical characteristics and in terms of the broad way in which they respond to survey questions. The fact is, troubling though it may be to some of us, most human characteristics and attitudes, analyzed one at a time, are shared by millions of others. Sampling enables the researcher to represent the prevalence of broad attitudes and opinions in ways that are projectable to the entire population.

Thus, the anger directed at polls from those who don't think they, as individuals, can be categorized or reduced to a number is usually misplaced. People *can* be categorized. People are reducible to broad categories on many characteristics, and it is the measurement of those types of characteristics across broad populations that is the job of the pollster.

1. George Gallup and Saul Forbes Rae, *The Pulse of Democracy* (New York: Simon & Schuster, 1940), 213.

2. Leon Festinger, *A Theory of Cognitive Dissonance* (Evanston, IL: Row, Peterson, 1957).

3. Walter Kirn, "Don't Count Me In," *New York Times Magazine*, April 6, 2003.

4. Eugene Burdick, *The 480* (New York: Dell, 1965).

# CHAPTER 5

# The Tyranny of the Majority?

Some critics argue that relying too much on the will of the people—and, in the same vein, relying too much on polls that represent the will of the people—can lead to a tyranny of the majority. By "tyranny of the majority" we mean the mathematical fact that in a social group governed by democratic principles, more than half the people can effectively make the decision to discriminate against those who are in the minority. Concern over the potential dark side of majority rule goes as far back as ancient Greece. James Bryce discussed its relevance to America in some detail in *The American Commonwealth*, as did Alexis de Tocqueville in his landmark nineteenth-century book *Democracy in America*.[1] To quote Bryce's simple definition, "The expression 'tyranny of the majority' is commonly used to denote any abuse by the majority of the powers which they employ."[2]

The facts are straightforward. The rule of the people, if used in the strict sense in which a majority wins out, can lead to a situation in which a minority is continually oppressed. A situation in which 51 percent of the public is Catholic can theoretically lead to the passage of a law mandating that all non-Catholics be denied citizenship rights or thrown into jail—if the majority Catholic population is so inclined. Or so the argument goes.

This can be perfectly legal. As Bryce points out, "Such abuse will not be tyrannous in the sense of being illegal."[3] In other words, in most democratic systems—everything else being equal—the possibility exists for a majority to be tyrannous and oppressive of the rights of a minority and still be within the bounds of the law. (I'll get into more detail below about possible constraints on this tyranny.)

Bryce, writing in the late nineteenth century, indicated that the concern about a majority in democratic systems using its power to oppress the minority or in other ways engage in tyrannous behavior was not a new concept. He pointed out that Aristotle made the comparison of the potential abuses of a monarch to those that could be made by a majority of the people. Bryce also called attention to America's Founding Fathers' concerns about the tyranny of the majority, sensitive as they were to the possibility that letting the public have its way could ultimately result in an unhealthy dominance of the minority by those with majority control. The Founders worried that the majority of the people would be overcome by "passions" and advocate actions that would harm both the "public good and the rights of other citizens."[4] Indeed, I think it is fair to say that almost anyone who has thought seriously about using the collective power or wisdom of the people as the basis for societal decision making has confronted this issue.

One of the core problems with power and governance is the attempt to make and implement decisions that are maximally beneficial for everyone in the society. It is rarely possible to please all of the people all of the time; someone is always disappointed (if not tyrannized). A society based on the concept of decision making by the collective will of the people (or the majority of the people in a strict voting sense) will always experience situations in which someone or, more particularly, some group of people in that society will disagree or not like the result. A minority can be defined as those whose opinions are not in the majority. Unless there is 100 percent consensus on a given issue, someone will be disappointed. In other words, *tyranny of* the majority is always possible when there is *rule by* the majority. In any presidential election, for example, the minority—those who vote for the losing candidate—have to live under the presidency of someone they did not vote for and presumably do not like. Similarly, a referendum on a specific issue can leave the minority on the losing side in a situation in which they disagree with the legal outcome of the vote.

As a result of the possibility that majorities might make decisions that oppress minorities, most democratic societies have built-in safeguards to avoid blatant legalized tyranny. In the United States, these include most notably the Bill of Rights and the power of the third branch of government, the judiciary, to interpret the Constitution and to overrule laws that might oppress the minority or deprive citizens of basic rights. So the first response to those who argue that a strong reliance on the collective wisdom of the people will lead to a willful repression of the minority is the reminder that, in the case of the United States, the country has a built-in set of checks and balances that helps militate against just that kind of situation.

Perhaps more important, tyrannous opposition toward minorities seems to be an unusual occurrence in contemporary societies with democratic cultures. We just don't have a great number of examples in which the clear and well-measured expression of the will of the people is to oppress and tyrannize those in the minority.

Certainly, it is correct to say that majorities in societies have countenanced tyrannical actions and social systems at many points in the past. The history of mankind is replete with majority agreement with exploitive and oppressive situations that would be considered totally unacceptable today (although we didn't have reliable public opinion polls in Hitler's Germany or in the antebellum United States). But when there was apparent majority agreement with tyrannous policies, these sentiments generally reflected the entire social structure and culture of those times. In other words, laws, rulings by judges, intellectual wisdom, decrees from monarchs, and public opinion all shared common values and assumptions. I'm not at all convinced that making laws by virtue of majority public opinion would have been any different than or any more tyrannical than any other type of decision making in these points in time. Indeed, although it can't be proved scientifically, it may well have been that public opinion—if it had been possible to measure it—could have been *less* in favor of oppression of minorities than the actual leaders and authorities who countenanced it at specific points in history.

Majority sentiment in the antebellum South was presumably overtly tyrannical against blacks. However, although there were no reliable polls in the 1850s and 1860s, the fact that the country went to war over slavery suggests that an accurate poll of the entire U.S. population in 1861 might have shown majority abolitionist sentiment.

National polling in the 1950s and 1960s showed that the majority of the country favored greater civil rights for blacks, although opposition was still evident in the white population in the South. But the whites in the South were a minority of the total U.S. population, suggesting again that majority sentiment—in this situation—was actually *non*tyrannical. Antiblack laws were kept in place more because of the dominance of certain powerful elected representatives from the South than because of the tyranny of the majority of the people of the country.

I'm hard-pressed to find recent examples where public opinion measured by polling data has shown a strong ten-

dency for the majority to oppress the minority or hold
views that strictly benefited themselves (that is, the majority). Public opinion is actually quite eleemosynary. In the
health care debate in the early 1990s, for example, Americans were not only concerned about the impact of new
health care programs on their own health care but also focused on the implications of new programs on the needs
of the minority. Americans in many ways were more willing to adopt a health care plan based on helping others,
rather than one based just on improving their own situations. And a good deal of polling about George W. Bush's
proposed tax cut plan in 2002 and 2003 showed that
Americans were willing to forgo tax refunds (of direct personal benefit) in lieu of spending for government programs such as welfare or Social Security, or federal deficit
reduction. While these results don't deal with tyranny of
minorities directly, they highlight the fact that majority
opinion is often exactly the opposite—that is, supportive
of policies that come to the aid of minorities.

There is no contemporary polling, or voting evidence, to
show that Americans have made the decision to oppress
and take away civil rights from such minorities as
Catholics, Jews, or the elderly. There has been no tyranny.
If anything, acceptance of positions and issue stances beneficial to minorities has increased. The majority of white
Americans now indicate an almost unanimous willingness
to accept a black candidate for president (blacks make up
only 12 percent of the country), and the majority of Americans say they have no concerns about blacks living in
their neighborhoods or going to their children's schools.
Disagreement is evident in the polls on exactly what
should be done in relation to the racial situation in the
United States, but there are no signs of agreement with
any types of direct oppression, tyranny, or discrimination.

To be sure, this whole issue of the impact of majority
rule versus minority freedoms leads to some thorny and

complex issues. Most people would not consider it to be the oppression of a minority to restrict small groups of people from crying "Fire!" in a crowded theater, although the fire-criers conceivably could claim that they are being tyrannized. In the U.S. culture today, some gays and lesbians argue that they are being tyrannized by virtue of the opinion of a majority of the people in the country that there should not be legalized same-sex marriages. On the other hand the vast majority of Americans support laws prohibiting discrimination against gays and lesbians in terms of employment.

Perhaps it is fair to say that the fear of tyranny of the majority often comes back to the more general discussion we had earlier about the wisdom and power of the collective will of the people. Those who worry about the majority tyrannizing the minority presumably worry about all sorts of wild or evil things that the majority could advocate. But at some point, one has to have faith that the collective wisdom of the people is worth paying attention to—or one has to propose an alternative source of wisdom that will be more effective in the long run, which I don't think is possible.

And, in the context of this book, it is important to remember that I am calling for the collective opinions and the attitudes of the public to be used as a *source* of wisdom and guidance for whoever is in power—not necessarily as a strict and binding way of making daily decisions in a formal system. The majority of the people can make mistakes. It is possible that in some situations, they *will* tyrannize the minority. A constitutional framework creates some barriers to tyranny, and in a representative democracy, there is a layer of additional action that has to be taken is the legislative process before a tyrannous majority sentiment can be made into law.

But in the American system, the majority's views will ultimately prevail, and there's no way around that. The majority can even overcome legal or constitutional impediments to tyranny if so inclined. Although votes of two-thirds of the Congress and three-quarters of the states' legislatures would be necessary to do so, the Constitution could be amended to change even the Bill of Rights and deprive minorities of basic rights—if a supermajority of Congress and a majority of the public in each state of the Union were so inclined. In the end, the U.S. Constitution puts the power in the hands of the people, and the people acting together can act and make decisions that are not to the liking of the minority.

All sources of wisdom or decision making have flaws. The alternative to relying on the majority or collective wisdom of large groups of citizens is to revert to the wisdom of single individuals or groups of elites, who—in the long run—have no lesser and probably a greater chance of tyrannizing minorities.

## No New Thinking?

Will a reliance on the collective will of the people mean there is no creativity, no bold leadership, no new thinking? Some critics feel it is dangerous for the leaders of a country to follow the results of polls too closely because these leaders will then attempt to please the public, rather than do "what is right." Too much of a reliance on the collective opinions of the people will, some argue, have the effect of robbing society of the possibility of moving forward based on vision, innovative leaps of thought, or deep-rooted convictions. If we depend on the collective wisdom of the aggregated masses of the people (for example, as measured by polls) to help guide society, it is argued, there will be no new thinking, no radical departures from what is safe or customary, and no room for the visionary leader and great thinker who stands up for what he or she believes and bucks the tide of public opinion.

This appears to be one of the central arguments of pundit and critic Arianna Huffington, who in arguing for citizens to refuse to answer poll questions, says that "because of public opinion polls, our political leaders have been turned into spineless followers" and that "allowing polling data to become a substitute for thinking has become a very wobbly crutch indeed."[5]

This argument about the impact of polls on leadership is a favorite one for other poll critics as well. The designation of a politician in recent years as "poll-driven" has increasingly been seen as horrific rather than honorable. This is the concern I often hear from talk show callers who express fear that politicians will slavishly read the polls and feed back to the people what they want to hear, rather than what they "should" hear. These critics seem to revere politicians who think for themselves and who make up their own minds about what is best for society, unfettered by having to pay attention to thoughts or whims of the masses.

President Bill Clinton suffered from this type of criticism throughout his administration. Critics noted that his programs and proposed initiatives seemed to be driven by extensive surveys that determined the issues of importance to Americans, not from his personal convictions or grand vision. And this was apparently to a large degree true. Clinton did pay attention to polls. I remember watching his 1996 State of the Union address—which introduced a new emphasis on "values"—from the set of Chris Matthews's television show. My immediate reaction— which I expressed on-air to Matthews—was that Clinton's address seemed to have been lifted from a pollster's notebook (the particular speech called for school uniforms and a list of other relatively nonoffensive proposals that according to our polls Americans favored). Unbeknownst to me at that time, pollster and consultant Dick Morris indeed had been at work behind the scenes doing extensive polling work for Clinton, and the State of the Union address reflected it. As Morris says in his book *Behind the Oval Office*, "The values agenda emerged fully in the president's 1996 State of the Union address. This was a speech that changed everything."[6] Morris, who talks about his extensive polling operation used to uncover the benefits of this value orientation, goes on to ask why Republicans allowed the Democratic president to steal the values position. Morris asks, "Why didn't Republican pollsters tread the same path I did?" He says that Republican consultants were not "accustomed to breaking new ground on issues," and then goes on to point out that Clinton "was not confined by any preexisting dogma and used polling extensively to pinpoint public concerns and test approval for his proposed solutions." Morris said, "I came to love our weekly polls of America. I saw them as a chance to chat with the country. In over a hundred polls, I got to know Americans very well."[7] Presumably, by way of Morris's briefings, Clinton also got to know Americans very well.

The bottom line was that Clinton's job approval rating went up after the January 1996 speech, and later that year he cruised to reelection victory over Republican Bob Dole. By all empirical indicators, Clinton was doing a good job of representing the people of the country. But he suffered mightily in the eyes of critics because he was attempting to understand the people and use his knowledge of what they wanted, rather than valiantly pushing an agenda based on personal convictions.

But I should hasten to point out that Clinton was not the first president to rely on or pay attention to polls. Edmund Wilson's fascinating study of President Theodore Roosevelt, *Theodore Rex*, shows that Roosevelt was paying attention to polls way back in the early 1900s.[8] Lewis and Clark College political scientist Robert M. Eisinger has reviewed the history of presidential use of polls while presidents were in office. He documents in his book *The Evolution of Presidential Polling* how consistently polls have been a part of the White House diet of information for many decades: "With the advent of polls, presidents have found the political instrument that provides them with autonomy, accuracy and power. Archival data demonstrate that Presidents' repeated use of private polls has been a means to gauge public opinion independently and autonomously."[9] I was in fact surprised to find in reading the second volume of Robert Caro's biography of Lyndon B. Johnson[10] just how much LBJ relied on private and public preelection polling in his 1948 U.S. Senate campaign, a prelude to Johnson's focus on the polls when he ascended to the presidency. Biographies of John F. Kennedy and Richard Nixon repeatedly reference these presidents' review of polling data while in the White House. It is clear to historians that Franklin D. Roosevelt was paying close attention to public opinion polls in the late 1930s and early 1940s as he made decisions on how the U.S. should react to the war in Europe before Pearl Harbor pushed the country to a total war footing.

But despite this general pattern by which the occupants of 1600 Pennsylvania Avenue have themselves paid close attention to polls, the negative reaction to the use of polls as part of legislation or executive decision making shows that many perceive it to be an essentially illegitimate procedure. Indeed, when Texas governor George W. Bush began his campaign for president in 1999 and 2000, he took great pains to emphasize the fact that he would not be governed by public opinion or polls were he to take office (although there is no question that Bush's White House advisers very closely monitored polls once Bush became president).

We were particularly exposed to the argument that "leadership means making decisions on one's own" (that is, without polls) during the 1998 and early 1999 Bill

Clinton impeachment hearings. Elected representatives in 1998–99 who were holding hearings and voting for impeachment in the House and on the decision to convict in the Senate were apparently enamored with their pursuit of what they considered to be right and "constitutional," even though polls showed that the majority of the country was opposed to Clinton's impeachment. Some representatives voiced their willingness to go down in defeat when they ran for reelection if that was the result of sticking by their convictions rather than pandering to the wishes of the people.

Indeed, as members of the House and then the Senate faced extraordinary pressures in terms of their votes on the articles of impeachment, the whole issue of the degree to which they should follow the wishes of the public in their deliberations became hotly debated. As the prospect of House and Senate votes loomed closer, politicians and some pundits seemed particularly appalled at the thought that decisions on impeachment might be made by taking poll results into account. At one point in 1998, for example, Nebraska senator Bob Kerrey said on ABC's *This Week with Sam Donaldson and Cokie Roberts*, "I would certainly not make one of the most important decisions a senator can make on the basis of polls."[11] (I would argue that a senator should say exactly the opposite: "I would not make one of the most important decisions a senator can make without finding out what my constituents want me to do.")

An August 18, 1999, column by Walter Shapiro in *USA Today* was headlined "Pollster-Bashing Now a Campaign Trend" and highlighted more examples of these types of attitudes. Shapiro quotes Governor George W. Bush as saying, "I know how to lead. I don't run polls to tell me what to think. The most important, most influential job in America should be the president, not the president's pollster." Shapiro goes on to quote Bush's press secretary as saying, "Governor Bush has never taken a poll to determine a policy matter."

In the same article, presidential candidate Steve Forbes was quoted as saying, "The power of the Washington elites won't be tamed, bent or broken by a candidate who relies on pollsters and tutors to tell him what to think." Former senator and presidential candidate Bill Bradley argued that a major course of public dismay is that "not enough politicians speak from their core convictions, but instead take polls."[12] House Judiciary Committee chairman Henry Hyde said, "We're trying not to be guided by polls but by our instincts and our conscience."[13] Congressman Bill McCollum, one of the House impeachment managers, said that "lawmakers have no business putting a 'finger in the wind' of public opinion to make their decisions ... You're an elected representative, and part of your function is to learn what the general public doesn't have access to and make a judgment."[14]

In a *New York Times* article, McCollum also said, "It [polling] won't affect what we do. We are determined to do this fairly and objectively and not listen to the polls at all."[15] Senator Phil Gramm of Texas said, "I believe in the end that the people of Texas, wise people, fair people of Texas, didn't elect me to read those polls."[16]

What do we make of all of this? I think some of this desire on the part of elected representatives and leaders to be left alone to lead and make decisions on their own is based on ego. Most people think they are fairly smart, and that's particularly true of those people whose self-confidence is strong enough to prompt them to run for office and to withstand the rigors of an election campaign. Naturally, it is easier to convince oneself that it is right and good to make decisions based on one's inner conscience than it is to accede to making efforts to understand and then reflect the opinions of one's constituency. It is also a lot less time-consuming.

But there is apparently a genuine feeling on the part of some that elected representatives—left on their own to do what they think best—will somehow, perhaps miraculously, become innovative, bold, creative, and inspired to the point where they end up leading society in brilliant new ways that benefit everyone concerned. Along with that faith is the fear that leaders, loaded down with too much knowledge of what their constituents think, will get caught in a type of endless loop, constantly changing and adjusting their attitudes and behaviors in an effort to mimic or react to what they know about others. And following that thought is the belief that the process of aggregating the opinions of the masses tends to lead to conservative, traditional, noninnovative thinking. The presumption is that small groups of individuals can come up with more "outside the box" thoughts, ideas, and solutions than a broad cross section of society ever would. In other words, it is argued, relying on the collected opinions of a large number of people has a good chance of resulting in solutions that are near the middle of the spectrum of possible choices, producing mediocre outcomes.

There are problems with this hypothesis. In fact, it is not unusual to find that leaders are the ones taking a more conservative course, while the people are often more willing to take chances. Psychologists call this the risky shift phenomenon. People in groups (albeit small groups) make riskier decisions than individuals do on their own. Take, for example, the war on Iraq as we polled about it in the second week of March 2003. The polls showed that the citizens of the United States were actually more in favor of the risky decision to go to war against Saddam Hussein than many of the leaders of the United States (and leaders of countries around the world). A plurality of Americans agreed that the United States and its allies should be applying more force and power to the war effort, rather than the same amount or less. The aggregation of the views of the masses, in other words, were in favor of pushing the situation beyond what the leaders were doing at the time; the majority favored a risky shift.

More fundamentally, I think some people simply may not like the idea of relying on polls as the basis for decision making because it takes away from their romantic idea of the loner, courageously developing and standing by positions of his or her own. This reflects a particular strain of individualism that pervades the American culture, which to a significant degree reveres the maverick, the loner, the person who travels to the beat of his or her own drummer.

Indeed, Americans seem to love the individual who stands up against the crowd and sticks up for his or her principles. We have a warm place in our hearts for a man like the character played by Henry Fonda in the movie *Twelve Angry Men*—a man who stood his ground even in the face of the eleven other jurors who wanted to convict the defendant (of course, the Fonda character was ultimately vindicated). We revere whistle-blowers. We like stories of iconoclasts who buck the crowd. We have visions of individualists like Ayn Rand's Howard Roark, the character in *The Fountainhead* who went his principled ways, disdainful of the weak, drifting, irresolute ways of the masses.[17] We revere Abraham Lincoln, who stood up for what he believed in, even though historical accounts suggest that he was in pretty bad shape as far as the opinions of the people of the country were concerned—particularly in the early years of the Civil War. I think of John F. Kennedy's Pulitzer Prize–winning book *Profiles in Courage*, which focused on the stories of United States senators who stood up for what they believed in, regardless of the fact that their views did not fit with the prevailing wisdom or the views of the masses.[18]

I well remember talking to a politician who was

appalled by the idea of polls as a basis for his decision making. He had built his self-image around the idea of standing up for what is ultimately right, regardless of the views of the people or the fact that he was in the distinct minority. In fact, I think he rather enjoyed the idea of being on the outside, ignoring collective opinions, fighting the "good" and lonely fight. (Practically speaking, I might add, he had little success in being elected to office.)

Perhaps Americans, especially politicians, are influenced by the literature and filmography of the Old West, both of which underscore the idea that Americans idealize the individual who resolutely goes his own way. Nothing seems to fire up the admiration of Americans as much as a portrait of an individual who sticks to his guns in the face of social pressures—who in essence stands up for what is right even when most around him are saying that it's wrong. Devoted fans of the writings of Ayn Rand will extol at length the virtue of the lonely individualist pursuing what he or she thinks is right and good, despite the attempts on the part of a more evil, conformist society to corral their originality and insights.

It is also worth reiterating that many elected representatives like the "relying too much on the views of the people is dangerous" argument, because they have the tendency to think that they are intelligent and uniquely insightful in their own right. For many politicians, it is very satisfying to be able to make decisions on their own and adopt the assumption that they would be hampered if they had to pay constant attention to the views of the masses. To analyze public opinion, to consider what polls say, or to attempt to feed back to the public what it is that they want done is often considered to be a diminution in the status of the elected representative, an affront to the image of the intelligent, crusading decision maker.

There is a paradox here between the fundamental principle of collective rule that is so much a part of democracy and the idea that once elected, representatives should be left to their own creative and wise ways. As I noted in chapter 3, this paradox was both anticipated and created by the Founding Fathers. They left us with the idea that the majority should ultimately have its say in running a democratic society but that smart, well-informed individuals (elected representatives) should lead the country forward on a practical, day-to-day basis. In other words, we've been left with the concept of majority rule juxtaposed against admiration for individual thought and those who act courageously on their own.

My point of view is that this juxtaposition has gotten out of kilter. We have too much emphasis on the supposed brilliance of those men and women we elect to represent us, and too little on the wisdom of the rank-and-file people who make up the society. There's as much or more reason to fear the decisions of lonely leaders following personal convictions and personal sets of values as there is to fear decisions made on the basis of the collected experiences and wisdom of all the people in the society.

It is important at this point to underscore my belief that leaders and politicians can and do have tremendous insights and innovative ideas. It is important in governing a society, just as it is in business and industry, that these new ways of looking at the world be made a part of the way in which things work. Innovative ideas and creative approaches, whatever their source, need to be made a significant part of the governing process.

However, the problem with governing a large society is balancing the unarguable value of having new and original input from leaders against the power and wisdom of the people. It's one thing to have the intelligent idealist's ideas and convictions put into the societal mix. It's another to have an intelligent idealist whose ideas and convictions are made into law in contradiction to what the broader base of the citizens of a society might agree with.

In other words, I'm not implying that leaders' opinions should be ignored. Rather, their insights and wisdom should be tried out on the public, and the creativity and charisma of the leaders who have great, innovative insights should be used to persuade the public of the power of these new ideas before they are imposed on the public willy-nilly. At some point, if the public does not "get it" and does not agree with the wisdom or ideas of the leader, then the leader must pull back. The idea of a courageous leader persisting for month after month, or year after year, with an idea or an approach that does not meet with favor by the public, works only to a point. After a while, if the idea is well communicated and the public still does not budge, then the courageous iconoclast must retreat and rethink. To persist too much longer turns the tables on the democratic nature of the country and moves it instead to a situation in which there is too much power on the part of individuals or groups of elites.

The origin of thoughts and ideas in the societal mix can and should come from anywhere, including elected representatives. It's just that the collective wisdom of the people must pass judgment on them at some point, or we are back down the road to dictatorship and rule by the elites.

All truth does not have to *originate* from the collective views of the people. In Darwinian evolution, the changes that allow species to adapt and flourish in changing environments and situations actually originate from genetic or mating mutations. But the ability of these changes to provide superior adaptation to the environment ultimately determines their value. In similar fashion, the origin of wisdom and novel approaches to solving problems in human societies can come from any leader, prophet, iconoclastic thinker, kook, congressperson, or author.

Indeed, we should fervently hope that there will never be a shortage of new, revolutionary, radical, and wise ideas in human societies. We all benefit from having a continual infusion of new thinking and radical new approaches. That's certainly one of the advantages provided by young students in contemporary society. Although often misguided in their assessment of the facts and in their visions about the future, students' unattached status, idealism, naïveté, and freedom from responsibility can provide the type of fresh perspective and input that any social system needs to continue to adapt and survive.

Ultimately, however, a society needs some way of making decisions on *which* principles, *which* new ideas, *which* changes to adopt. It is the collective wisdom of all of that society's people that I contend provides by far the best basis for reaching these types of decisions. The long-term value of mutations and new genetic matings is determined by the winnowing process of evolution. It is my contention that the value of new principles and novel approaches to guiding human society needs to go through a similar process of vetting, through the filter of the views and opinions of the collectivity of the citizens of that society. Polling is the tool that makes this possible.

It is a useful exercise when considering criticisms of polling to substitute the word "public" for "polls" in the antipoll rhetoric of politicians and other critics. Those who are saying that polls should be ignored are in essence saying that the people of a society should be ignored. As I noted previously, Senator Gramm of Texas spoke against the use of polls in 1998. Consider the implications of what he said if you remove the word "polls" and replace it with "the people": "I believe in the end that the people of Texas, wise people, fair people of Texas, didn't elect me to *pay attention to* them."

All in all, concern that paying attention to the collective wisdom of the people will stifle new ideas and courageous, innovative thinking is far outweighed, in my opinion, by the possibility that the failure to pay attention to the wisdom of the people will allow societies to run seriously off track.

The criticism that polling robs democracy of its elements of leadership and progress was faced long ago by Dr. George Gallup, who said, "Polling is merely an instrument for gauging public opinion. When a president or any other leader pays attention to poll results, he is, in effect, paying attention to the views of the people. Any other interpretation is nonsense."[19] As Gallup noted, the idea that leaders follow polls is in many ways the very essence of democracy. How, in a democratic society, he asked, could the criticism that "he just follows the polls" be considered pejorative? Would it not be worse for leaders to ignore what polls are saying and hence—by extension—ignore the expressed will of the people?

Politicians should proudly make known the fact that they are continually assessing the views of their constituents and that in turn they are attempting to take into account what the public demands. If a politician doesn't agree with the public's views as represented by polls, then the politician should make every effort to understand the basis for the people's opinions, and then conceivably to go back to the people and argue the politicians' case—taking the public's opinion extremely seriously rather than ignoring it. But the public's opinion in the end has the greatest chance of being wise and just. In Gallup's words, "Throughout history, the most effective leaders have been those who have had a keen understanding of the public—leaders who have known the views and prejudices of their followers, their lack of knowledge and misinformation, their hopes and aspirations. The answer . . . is not that the country will suffer when its leaders begin to pay a lot of attention to public opinion polls. The country will suffer when its leaders ignore, or guess about the public's views and make wrong estimates of their knowledge."[20]

## ENDLESS FEEDBACK LOOP?

Critics of polls also argue that continually feeding polling data back to the public creates a situation in which the people themselves can become thoughtless sheep, mindlessly following the majority rather than thinking for themselves.

This putatively negative impact of the feedback of polling data to citizens becomes a particularly relevant issue during elections. Critics argue that knowledge of how others intend to vote can result in all manner of negative consequences—including the creation of the so-called bandwagon effect. The bandwagon effect occurs when people change their minds from their "true" opinions simply because they know what other people are thinking or planning on doing, based on a desire to jump in and be a part of the crowd. In an election context, it is argued that this results in a downward spiral of loss of support for a candidate shown to be losing in the polls, or an upward spiral of enthusiasm for a candidate who is clearly the leader. Deluged by polls during an election, citizens will change their vote to conform to what the polls tell them the masses are thinking, will write off any thought of voting for a candidate who is down in the polls, or will quit thinking about the race altogether if the polls show that the race is lopsided and that one candidate is prepared to win. Or at least that's the argument.

Presumably, no one expects citizens in a democracy to make decisions on issues and candidates totally in isolation. But observers who criticize the role of polls in this process seem to argue that organized and quantified feedback from other citizens—in the form of poll results—goes too far, and that it encroaches on the ability of individuals to reach enlightened decisions all on their own.

It is unclear, however, at what point the use of feedback from fellow citizens in a democracy begins to go too far.

Many of polling's harshest critics, for example, seem to endorse the concept that it's perfectly fine for citizens to come together in person to discuss issues and hear what one another has to say. For example, a well-known public opinion scholar, James Fishkin, is critical of the ability of average citizens to have opinions worth paying much attention to, but is very enthusiastic about the idea of creating deliberative forums in which citizens meet and talk in a modern-day town hall setting, based on his belief that citizens involved in such discussions might arrive at better, more informed decisions. (More on this in the next chapter.)

But just how much does this in-person deliberating differ from the broader input from friends and neighbors provided by polls? I think not much. They are all part of the same process.

Polls, in fact, are in many ways an extension of a town hall, deliberative process. Polling simply distills the opinions of *all* of one's neighbors in an accurate fashion—an expanded version of what the voter would find out by asking neighbors in the community where they stand on the issues of the day. The idea of town meetings wherein people get together to discuss their opinions is essentially as old as America itself. The idea of polling as an expanded town meeting is much newer, but not categorically different.

There's a broader question here: just how harmful is it in general for people to know how others in one's society are thinking and feeling about the issues of the day? As I've pointed out, most of us pick up a good deal about how those around us are thinking and feeling by virtue of our daily interaction, and as a result of normal family and water-cooler discussions. Polling just solidifies that process and makes it more systematic.

When it comes to elections, it is useful to note that specific, quantified feedback from one's fellow citizens is always made available immediately *after* an election day in the form of the actual election results. Nobody tries to keep this information from the public. Yet it is certainly possible that the mere fact of learning who wins and who loses an election could change people's opinions in the long run. In other words, upon finding out that one's favorite Democratic candidate received only a small percentage of the vote in a given election, one could—in time-honored bandwagon fashion—switch to the Republican party in time for the next election in order to be with the "in crowd." Would this be so bad? No. I think most people would find this to be perfectly acceptable. So it's hard to argue that getting information about how people are feeling *before* an election is any more damaging than getting information about how they felt *after* the election.

There is also little evidence to support the idea that knowledge of how others feel on an issue, or how they intend to vote in an election, affects the recipients of this knowledge. In the election context, for example, there is sparse evidence that preelection polls have an impact on voters' decisions on whom they're going to vote for. In fact, as George Gallup used to point out, if polls created a gigantic bandwagon effect in which citizens changed or formed their opinions in order to go along with the masses, there would eventually be nothing but consensus on every issue and a 100 percent vote for one specific candidate. In other words, if candidate A had 51 percent of the vote in preelection polls, then the bandwagon theory would predict that more and more of the 49 percent of those voting for other candidates would switch over to vote for candidate A. Ultimately, if this process played itself out, no one would want to be in the minority, and everyone would end up voting for candidate A. This doesn't happen, of course. Indeed, in many elections, front-runners lose their front-runner status, and candidates way down in the preelection polls charge ahead and eventually win. In 1992, third-party candidate Ross Perot was not going to win the presidency according to all the polls, yet his percentage of the vote climbed as election day grew nearer, and he eventually claimed 19 percent of the vote—the highest third-party total since Theodore Roosevelt in 1912.

It is also true that the contention that individuals in society are swept along willy-nilly by the views of their fellow citizens embodies a pretty negative assumption about the intelligence of the average citizen. I don't think most of us are that likely to change our opinions based on what we find out other people think and feel. In fact, some of us actually may enjoy—rather perversely—the idea of going against the crowd.

There is also nothing inherently wrong with citizens using polling information as they meditate on issues and candidates—if they want to. To make a decision or cast a vote based in part on an understanding of how other citizens are thinking is just as legitimate as using other sources of information or insight to do so—if not more so. As I've noted, social psychologists have long observed that humans have a social comparison drive based on the need to compare and contrast opinions and attitudes against those of relevant others and relevant reference groups—particularly when we are unsure where we stand on an issue. Using polls as accurate representations of how others feel on an issue helps fulfill this need and lets the citizen be aware of and react to the accumulated wisdom of his or her neighbors. In many ways, this is a quite rational and useful process.

The fear that social comparison leads to robotic conformity is less intimidating if one has an essential faith that the public is wiser and more thoughtful than some would make it out to be. Citizens can and should be presumed to be able to handle polling information in a responsible and reasonable way. To argue that polls are inimical to democracy puts scant faith in the ability of the average citizen to deal with a free flow of information. The public can in fact do a good job of making distinctions and figuring out what polling information it wants to use and what information it wants to ignore.

There's a great example of this from the run-up to the California recall election in October 2003. The CNN/ *USA Today*/Gallup poll came out just after the September 24 debate (the only one in which candidate Arnold Schwarzenegger participated) and showed not only that the recall vote itself was passing but that Schwarzenegger had jumped into a commanding lead over his nearest competitor as the candidate to succeed Governor Gray Davis. The poll redefined the race, which previous to the debate had been characterized as one that was very close. New York City tabloids put the picture of Arnold on the front page, and he immediately became the front-runner.

Was it bad for the democratic process in California that polling showed Schwarzenegger was charging ahead and looked like he might win? Some people thought so. As the authors of the ABC News Web site The Note put it, "We like to let the voters decide, unaffected by endgame media coverage being dominated by the results of polling . . ."[21] But I disagree. I think the provision of the new information in an election context is good, not bad. Voters in California were presented with a great deal of information about the way in which the election was shaping up, and they were able to use it to make more intelligent decisions.

Think about it this way. The object of elections is to elect the best possible candidate, which is much more important than fostering a massive guessing game in which no one knows what is happening until election day is over. The preelection polling in California showed the very real possibility that Schwarzenegger could be elected governor (which he eventually was). Hearing the results of the polls, voters may well have taken the possibility of a victory by Schwarzenegger more seriously. Voters who may have been interested in Schwarzenegger only because of his celebrity status were suddenly presented with cause to think more seriously about the implication of their vote. The preelection polling gave them information they could use, if so inclined, as the basis for changing their vote. The polling allowed voters to ponder, ahead of time, the implications of what was happening—providing, as it were, an opportunity to refine the voting process before the vote became final. And when all was said and done, the prospect of a Schwarzenegger governorship didn't seem that alarming to that many Californians. Knowing full well that he had a very good chance of winning the election (because of what the polls showed), the voters went out in massive numbers and ratified what the polls had predicted by putting him in office. Democracy was well served.

I argue that this provided a better outcome than if the voters in the state had been totally clueless about how well Schwarzenegger or any of the candidates were doing. Moreover, as I've pointed out, the campaigns themselves were running private polls on a continual basis that allowed them to have insights into the dynamics of the election. Why leave the public in the dark? If there weren't well-done, objective polls, there would have inevitably been attempts on the part of both citizens and journalists alike to characterize where the public stood on issues or candidates based on whatever information they could dredge up. These efforts would vary widely in terms of accuracy. California would have been rife with rumors and assumptions about how the public stood without any way of substantiating their accuracy.

In other words, well-done, scientific polls are a plus for society because—at the very least—they provide accurate information about what one's fellow citizens are thinking, rather than just supposition and conjecture.

1. Alexis de Tocqueville, *Democracy in America* (New York: Penguin, 1956).

2. James Bryce, *The American Commonwealth* (Indianapolis: Liberty Fund, 1995), 986.

3. Ibid.

4. Alexander Hamilton, James Madison, and John Jay, *The Federalist Papers* (New York: Bantam, 1982), 45.

5. Arianna Huffington, "The Pollsters Can't Hear the Silent Majority," filed November 14, 2002, http://www.ariannaonline.com/columns/files/111402.html.

6. Dick Morris, *Behind the Oval Office* (New York: Random House, 1997), 218.

7. Ibid., 233.

8. Edmund Wilson, *Theodore Rex* (New York: Random House, 2001).

9. Robert M. Eisinger, *The Evolution of Presidential Polling* (Cambridge: Cambridge University Press, 2003), 31–32.

10. Robert Caro, *The Years of Lyndon Johnson, vol. 2, Means of Ascent* (New York: Knopf, 1990).

11. Senator Bob Kerrey, *This Week with Sam Donaldson and Cokie Roberts*, ABC, n.d.

12. Walter Shapiro, "Pollster-Bashing Now a Campaign Trend," *USA Today*, August 18, 1999.

13. William E. Gibson, "The Deep Divide: Inquiry Becomes a Partisan Feud," *Fort Lauderdale Sun Sentinel*, September 19, 1998.

14. Tamara Lytle, "Insight: Impeachment, the Trial: Free Will or Will of the People," *Orlando Sentinel*, January 10, 1999.

15. *New York Times*, September 27, 1998.

16. Phil Gramm, *New York Times*, January 4, 1999.

17. Ayn Rand, *The Fountainhead* (New York: Bobbs-Merrill Company, 1943).

18. John F. Kennedy, *Profiles in Courage* (New York: HarperCollins, 2003).

19. George Gallup, *The Sophisticated Poll Watcher's Guide* (Princeton, NJ: Princeton Opinion Press, 1972), 3.

20. George Gallup, *Guide to Public Opinion Polls* (Princeton, NJ: Princeton University Press, 1944), 7–8.

21. The Note, ABC News Web site, October 1, 2003, http://abcnews.go.com/sections/politics/thenote/thenote.html.

# CHAPTER 6

# Do the People Know Enough?

Critics of the idea of relying on collective opinions for societal guidance come back again and again to the argument that the public simply doesn't know enough about what's going on to be able to make wise decisions. I've addressed this issue in a general way and have explained how the collection of different individual viewpoints, even when no one person involved is all-knowing or supremely intelligent, provides great insight and coverage of the issues involved; each individual has particular and unique perspectives that no one leader or group of elites could possibly hope to duplicate.

Still, it's interesting to take note of a specific strain of the "people don't know enough" argument that uses public opinion polls to criticize public opinion polls. Critics like to highlight surveys that show Americans are often ignorant of specific facts and figures relating to politics, geography, and historic events. Many Americans can't point to Bosnia or Iraq on a map, don't know who the secretary of defense is, can't name the leader of France, and can't correctly estimate how many Americans are black or Hispanic. If the people lack knowledge, so the argument goes, then how can their opinions and insights be used to help guide the key decisions that face the country today?

The assertion that Americans don't always do extremely

well on tests of knowledge is true. When pollsters ask Americans questions about specific facts and details, the percentage who get the answer correct can be quite low. There's little question that the average American probably wouldn't make a great *Jeopardy!* contestant, as evidenced by these results of a variety of polls conducted over the past several years:

• Just 33 percent knew the name of the U.S. secretary of state in August 2000 (Madeleine Albright).
• Only 6 percent knew that Dennis Hastert was Speaker of the House in 2000.
• Virtually no Americans knew who the prime minister of Japan was in 2000.
• Only 16 percent in 1991 knew that the capital of Canada is Ottawa and not Toronto or Montreal.
• 6 percent of Americans could name the prime minister of Israel in January 2000 (Ehud Barak).
• 40 percent can name the current Russian president (Vladimir Putin).
• 6 percent knew the name of the prime minister of Canada in February 2003 (Jean Chrétien), up from 2 percent in 2000.

At the same time, Americans don't do so badly on other tests of knowledge:

• 64 percent of Americans knew the religious faith of Joe Lieberman in August 2000 (when he was about to become the vice presidential candidate).
• In 1996, a Gallup poll showed that 53 percent knew that Newt Gingrich was Speaker of the House.
• 90 percent could name the vice president of the United States in 2000.
• 59 percent could name the attorney general while Bill Clinton was president (Janet Reno).

- 72 percent knew that George W. Bush was governor of Texas while he was running for president.
- Tiger Woods was correctly picked as the world's top professional golfer by 62 percent of Americans in January 2000.
- 62 percent in 2000 knew that Bill Gates was the chairman of Microsoft.
- 71 percent named Fidel Castro as the leader of Cuba in 2003.
- 51 percent knew that Tony Blair was the British prime minister in 2003.
- 59 percent in 2000 named Jay Leno as the host of *The Tonight Show* on TV. (Many named David Letterman, showing that they were in the right cognitive space, if nothing else.)
- In a 1999 question, less than half could choose the correct description of the geographic location of Kosovo, but many chose a semireasonable alternative out of a list of four given to them:

  a. Kosovo is in the Balkans region of Central Europe, north of Greece: 42 percent.
  b. Kosovo is in Central Asia and was part of the Soviet Union before it broke up: 26 percent.
  c. Kosovo is in Central Africa and was a former colonial possession: 4 percent.
  d. Kosovo is in Southeast Asia, near Burma and Cambodia: 4 percent.
  e. Don't know/can't guess: 24 percent.

All in all, America's knowledge scorecard is not an A+ by any means, but it's one that is not as abysmal as many might think. And keep in mind that these are answers to "on the spot" quizzes stuck in the middle of a Gallup poll. It is probably hard for even the smartest among us to come up with answers to these types of quiz questions, under pressure, within seconds of their having been asked with no warning.

Nonetheless, this Kosovo question is illuminating. The "Central Asia/formerly part of the Soviet Union" alternative was tricky (similar to SAT questions when the question makers put together alternatives that are just slightly different one from the other in order to make it hard for the test taker to select the correct one). Kosovo was part of Yugoslavia and in fact was under Soviet domination. A respondent could be excused, perhaps, for hearing the "was part of the Soviet Union before it broke up" wording on the phone and choosing it as the correct answer. I think it's in fact encouraging that only 4 percent chose each of the two most obviously wrong alternatives (that Kosovo is in Africa or Southeast Asia). Americans, in other words, seem to have at least a vague notion of where Kosovo is.

The other research finding that fuels the criticisms of those who think that Americans are too ill informed and don't have opinions worth paying attention to is the allegation that the public doesn't follow the news on a regular basis. Certainly, it is true that Americans' attention to news stories is on a continuum of sorts. Some people are news junkies and watch, listen, and read about the news on a daily if not hourly basis. Most of us have friends or family who are glued to CNN, take hours each day to read the *New York Times* from first page to last, and get Internet updates on fast-breaking news around the clock. Others of us pay relatively little attention to the news, catching the drift of what is going on, but certainly not following news developments in any systematic way on a day-by-day basis.

Gallup has long asked Americans how closely they are following what's going on in the news. The responses show that the public's attention to some important news events can indeed be quite low.

To be sure, the percentage following such dramatic and sharply focused news events as the death of Princess Diana or the death of John F. Kennedy, Jr. is very high. But other less specific but no less important events certainly don't receive the same level of attention. Less than 50 percent of Americans in November 1999, for example, said that they were closely following news of the budget battle between the Republican-controlled Congress and President Clinton, despite the fact that the debate had lasted more than a month into the new fiscal year and the government was being kept running only by virtue of a series of continuing resolutions. In May 2000, only 7 percent were closely following the issue of China being let into the WTO, despite the fact that some observers felt that this was one of the most important news stories of the year.

On the other hand, in the months leading up to, and during, the Iraq war in 2003, the average American was following the news of the war quite closely, and the public was indeed picking up on the nuances of the situation. In February 2003, for example, we asked Americans to rate a series of countries on a favorable/unfavorable scale, as we had done the year before at about the same time. There was no change in the American public's rating of Spain compared to the year before. But ratings of France fell precipitously. This was quite reasonable based on current events. Between February 2002 and February 2003, France had failed to support U.S. efforts to go after the regime of Saddam Hussein. Spain, on the other hand, had been our ally. The fact that the American public's ratings of these two countries diverged so sharply made it obvious that the American public had indeed been paying attention to what was going on in the world around them. In fact, when we again asked the public to rate countries in March 2003, France had fallen even further, as had Germany and Russia, two other countries that did not support the Bush administration's push to go to war against Iraq.

In similar fashion, we found strong evidence once the 2003 Iraq war began that the public was attuned to progress on the battlefield. There was a dramatic drop in the American public's perceptions of how well the war in Iraq was going over the period of just one day between Saturday and Sunday, March 22–23. The war had started on Wednesday. For the first couple of days news reports seemed to suggest an easy victory. Then, by Sunday, the news became grim. The U.S. Army was stalled. Americans changed their evaluations, virtually on the spot. By Monday, perceptions of how well the war was going in our polls got even worse. But by the next weekend, American troops began to move into Baghdad and progress became much more apparent. Simultaneously, perceptions that the war was going well jumped back up again, and estimates of how long the war was going to take and how many casualties would be sustained fell sharply. In short, the public was following the news closely and calibrating their perceptions of U.S. military progress accordingly.

And it was obvious that the residents of California were paying attention to politics during the run-up to the October 7, 2003, recall election in that state. Our polling in late September found that Arnold Schwarzenegger had moved to the top of the list of the candidates vying to replace Governor Gray Davis. But in the same poll, respondents indicated that it was State Senator Tom McClintock who had performed best in the widely viewed televised debate held the previous Wednesday. This demonstrated two things. First, Californians paid attention to the debate and made independent judgments about it (or otherwise they would have just assumed that Schwarzenegger had done best, since they were most interested in voting for him). Second, along these same lines, the voters were easily able to discriminate between debate performance and their choice for governor, making the kind of mental differentiation that some critics assume that average citizens are incapable of carrying off.

So it's a mixed bag. Few Americans know the names of foreign leaders. But most quickly reject the idea that Kosovo is located in Southeast Asia or in Africa. Few Americans can name the prime minister of Japan. But the majority were paying close enough attention to the news in March and April 2003 to be able to distinguish between Spain's and France's attitudes toward the United States vis-à-vis its involvement in Iraq.

This focus on the implications of Americans' level of knowledge of facts and figures was at the heart of the influential 1991 book *The Rational Public*, by political scientists Benjamin Page and Robert Shapiro. In many ways, the book was written to respond to the fact that "it is common to express skepticism about, even disdain for, the knowledge and the reasoning capacity of the public." The authors spend a good deal of time reviewing data relating to this alleged lack of knowledge and reasoning capacity. They came to the conclusion that the public is in fact rational, well informed when it matters, and quite stable in its views on the key issues of the day. I'll discuss *The Rational Public* in more detail below.

But is it really necessary to have high levels of factual knowledge or a Ph.D. for one's opinion to be valuable? It would, in fact, be quite easy to hire Ben Stein, members of MENSA, or university professors as our leaders, entrusting our decisions only to those with demonstrably high IQs and/or a great deal of factual knowledge. We could establish knowledge tests or use SATs, GREs, or IQ tests as screens to ensure that it's only the smartest and the quickest of mind that we entrust to guide our societies. Or, as I will discuss below, we could establish screening tests within our polls and pay attention only to the opinions of those who demonstrate a great deal of knowledge and interest in a topic. Or we could value only the opinions of those who have gone through a deliberative process in which they have been exposed to arguments and debates about specific issues.

But I'm not convinced of the benefit that would accrue from this attempt to isolate (or create) smart people, with its concomitant assumption that average people are too stupid to pay attention to. There is just not a lot of evidence that conventionally defined smart people will do all that much better than the rest of us in making decisions. Very smart people have been entrusted with making very important decisions down through the years, and there is no consensus that this has worked out so very well.

Jimmy Carter was universally recognized as being quite intelligent, but no one contends that his presidency was outstanding or that his insights were revolutionary or dramatically insightful. On the other hand, in November 1999, we saw then presidential candidate George W. Bush fail to provide the correct names of the leaders of a number of foreign countries when asked to do so by a reporter for a Boston television station. Did this mean he would be a bad leader? Not necessarily. Ronald Reagan continues to get very strong retrospective presidential job approval ratings from the American public, even though there is little doubt that he would not have done particularly well if he had been challenged while in office to rattle off the names and specifics of facts about the world and foreign leaders.

David Halberstam christened the group of highly educated and experienced men who made the decisions that led the country into Vietnam as "the Best and the Brightest." President Lyndon Baines Johnson had served in Washington as a congressman, senator, and vice president for well over two decades before he became president and was an extremely bright and obviously very experienced politician. Johnson's top advisers included Harvard M.B.A. and former president of Ford Robert McNamara, former Harvard dean McGeorge Bundy, and former

Rockefeller Foundation president Dean Rusk. Yet the whole Vietnam situation into which these men led us is now considered one of the biggest foreign policy blunders of the last half-century. All of the high IQs, experience, and book learning didn't seem to do much good in this situation.

Hillary Clinton assembled a "dream team" of bright academics and experts to help fashion her health care reform plan in 1993, but the plan failed politically at least in part because it appeared to many to be fundamentally lacking in common sense and practicality. What if she had paid more attention to an extensive review of polling data on health care, analyzing the problems and projected solutions from the perspective of the people of the country? There's every reason to believe that this might have helped her group develop a plan that was accepted by both the Congress and the people in addressing what remains one of the nation's top problems to this day.

There is no indication that colleges and universities are run in unusually brilliant fashion, even though their administrators and faculty are all very well educated and undoubtedly scored at the top ranges on standardized testing. Most bankrupt companies are run by very intelligent people, and many of those formerly associated with failed dot-com companies were graduates at the top of their classes at the best colleges and graduate schools.

I love Roger Lowenstein's book *When Genius Failed*, which recounts the fascinating history of the Long-Term Capital Management Company.[1] This firm was started in the 1990s by two certifiably intelligent Nobel Prize–winning economists who were convinced that their theories for hedging the financial markets would allow them to make money in any financial environment, at any time. The economists were surrounded by some of Wall Street's most brilliant and experienced talent. Although the company's business plan worked for a while, it began to fail spectacularly after a set of unusual occurrences in the real world. The company ultimately lost billions and almost brought the world's financial markets to their knees. All that brainpower brought about disaster.

There simply isn't proof that smart and well-informed people or even small groups of smart people always make the best decisions. Traditional "intelligence" and the status of possessing great knowledge are limited concepts that address only part of what's important. No one person can be smart across all areas, have knowledge of all issues, have had experience across all aspects of life, and have the ability to make sound decisions in response to all questions.

We may like to assume that extremely well educated people are in the best position to pass judgment on important issues, but I don't think that's always the case. Among other things, having a great deal of book knowledge does not mean that one has good judgment or common sense. (As a former college teacher, I can testify to the fact that many learned members of academia have little feel for the practical implications of their sphere of knowledge. Many brilliant professors bump into walls and have difficulty figuring out how to change a lightbulb.) And, even those who study a topic at great length would no doubt be the first to admit that there simply is no way that any one person can know everything there is to know about the issue from all perspectives.

Some people know where Bosnia is, while others know what it is like to care for an ailing elderly parent, or be dependent on the government for prescription drugs. Some people have seen crime in their neighborhoods for most of their lifetimes, others have lived in integrated areas, while others served in Vietnam and the Persian Gulf War. Even if some Americans don't know where Iraq is at a time when U.S. troops are being committed there, they may well remember personal experiences with Vietnam. If some Americans don't know the name of the secretary of health and human services, they may have had to spend months attempting to get payment for prescription drugs out of a recalcitrant HMO. Put it together and you have the mix of perspectives through which wisdom accrues.

I often hear the greatest objections to using polls to help guide government decision making when it comes to foreign policy. The usual objection is that international relations is simply too complex an area for the average American to understand. (Again, before going on, I need to call attention to the less-than-stellar U.S. foreign policy record created over the years by the leaders and experts who presumably *do* understand foreign affairs.) Of course, there are most certainly cases where the decision making has to reside with experts, such as support of a particular regime in Chad or Ukraine, or the specifics of economic sanctions against Iraq. There is a good rationale for having a State Department with its various agencies and sections devoted to studying the details of what is happening in specific areas of the world. But for decisions dealing with the broader scope of foreign policy, the ability of average citizens to contribute wisdom increases.

Let's look again at the mix of respondents who might be included in a typical poll. There are people who (a) lived through appeasement and World War II, (b) lived through the cold war, (c) lived through the U.S. involvement in the Korean conflict, (d) lived through and served in Vietnam, (e) lived through the Reagan years, (f) came of age in a world in which communism ceased to be a threat, (g) traveled extensively around the world, (h) grew up surrounded by immigrants, and (i) were themselves born or raised in foreign countries. Thus, the people included in this type of random sample, when polled about the broad parameters of foreign policy questions, bring to bear a distillation of perspectives on the world that is in many ways more well rounded than any panel of elites or experts could possibly duplicate.

In the fall of 2003, the Bush administration did its best to convince Americans that the intricate and involved situation in Iraq justified spending tens of billions of dollars there. Gallup found a growing perception on the part of the American public that it didn't make a lot of sense to spend this much money in Iraq at a time when there was a crying need for economic progress at home. Many Americans may not have known the nuances of what was happening in Iraq (and many would not have been able to point out Iraq on a map), but they did know enough to question involvement in that country on more general grounds. Americans wondered about the value of spending hundreds of billions of dollars in a country when there was no ready explanation of why the money was being spent, why other nations were not joining in the effort, or what this expense meant in terms of investing money to solve problems at home. In other words, having a meaningful broad perspective on the value of U.S. involvement in Iraq was not necessarily directly dependent on having a great deal of specific knowledge about Iraq and its history.

Think about the perspective that is brought to bear on the thorny problems of race relations by the typical random sample of Americans, which could include: (a) whites who grew up alongside blacks in the South before the civil rights movement and who have watched the enormous changes since, (b) whites who live in urban areas alongside blacks and other minorities, (c) whites and blacks who have come of age recently and remember nothing about the earlier days of the civil rights struggle, (d) blacks who have lived and worked extensively among whites, (e) whites who work alongside blacks every day, (f) parents of both races who have kids who go to integrated schools, (g) whites whose kids at some point were bused in the attempt to bring about school integration, (h) and those who have seen affirmative action programs at their place of employment and in their local school districts. From all of this blend of experiences and real-world learning comes a distilled wisdom about how to handle relations between the races that simply cannot be duplicated by a group of elite experts, no matter how much empirical data on race issues they possess.

In other words, because the great dilemma of race is played out in the lives, schools, and workplaces of average Americans on a daily basis, it is to their insights and various perspectives that we can profitably turn when we are seeking solutions to race-related problems.

All in all, it is probably too much to ask Americans to hold *Jeopardy!*-style bits of knowledge and facts in their heads at all times. It makes perfect sense, in fact, that most of us are selective in terms of what we retain about the specifics of the world around us, or we would fast become cognitively overloaded. The equally important point is that even those individuals who do attempt to cram a great deal of specialized knowledge into their brains still can't know it all. But by combining the views of all of the people in a society, we tap into such a wide range of experience and knowledge that we come at a problem with accumulated insights much more difficultly gained from any one person or small group. It is my contention that Americans have solid, basic perceptions of broad principles and a feel for the direction in which they want their country to go. It is this wisdom that can be so valuable for a society's progress.

There is also an essential illogic in the idea that in a democratic society the people are too dumb for their insights and attitudes to be given merit. If the people are too ill informed to take their views into account as measured by polling, then why let them have their input at the time of the vote? If the principle of democracy states that ultimately the people should have the power in a society, then why shield daily decisions made by elected representatives from the input of these same people?

## DELIBERATIVE POLLING

Over the years, various people have focused on the idea of looking independently at the opinions of those citizens who know a lot about or who have thought a lot about a topic or issue. They are responding to the assumption that these informed citizens have more worthwhile opinions on issues than those less knowledgeable. Dr. George Gallup pioneered a method, still in use today in one way or another, that focuses on separating out the views of those people who can be identified as knowing more about a topic than others, and seeing how the groups created by differing levels of knowledge vary in their opinions. I'll discuss this later in this chapter.

Another advocate of the idea of paying attention just to those Americans who can be shown to have knowledge about a topic is James Fishkin of Stanford University. He set about to attempt to change things by creating situations in which individual citizens become more knowledgeable and more involved in the news and issues of the day—and then are asked about their opinions after this transformation has taken place. Fishkin argues that the average person in society, although ordinarily inadequate to rely on for societal direction, can provide wisdom if he or she is transformed into something akin to a knowledgeable elite.

Let's slow down a bit here and go over this, because I think it illustrates an interesting point. Dr. Fishkin champions the elaborate idea of what he calls a deliberative poll. The deliberative poll as he envisions it has three steps. First, a random sample of average citizens is selected just as would be done in a typical poll. Second, these citizens are flown to a central location, usually for a week-end, and educated and informed about the key issues of the day. The participants also debate, argue, and deliberate. Third, the organizers measure the opinions of these "informed average people." As a consequence of the deliberations, the argument is made that the results represent a purified and refined essence of what democratic guidance should be all about.

Fishkin, in other words, argues that a sample of average Americans should be transformed into an informed elite by giving them new information, allowing them to discuss and deliberate the topics of the day, and including them in elaborate weekend briefing programs. Then, he argues, their opinions become more worthwhile and more valuable. As he says in his book *The Voice of the People*,

> The deliberative poll is unlike any poll or survey ever conducted . . . A deliberative poll attempts to model what the public would think, had it a better opportunity to consider the questions at issue . . . The resulting survey [after deliberation] offers a representation of the considered judgments of the public—the views the entire country would come to if it had the same experience of behaving more like ideal citizens immersed in the issues for an extended period.[2]

Fishkin's original thought was to duplicate the process that goes on (or went on in the good old days) in very small communities and societies that hold town hall meetings that involve discussion and debate among all of the citizens in the area. The society today is too large to conduct town hall meetings, so Fishkin advocates combining the random sample survey (so that the results are generalizable) with deliberation and thought. Out of this deliberative process, he argues, comes a refined and valuable consensus of opinion.

Fishkin's ideas produced a brief flurry of attention in the election years of 1996 and 2000, but the central assumption behind his thoughts was of concern to some pollsters and, indeed, some students of democracy. One issue is that Fishkin's deliberative polling contains a strong strain of elitism. His program of transforming common citizens into deliberating elites imbued with new and enlightened ideas and ideals implies that the opinions of the regular, nondeliberative public are not valuable. (Fishkin doesn't just imply this, he states it outright, and spends a good deal of time in his books pointing out how ill prepared the average citizen is to pass judgment on many of the important issues of the day.) Fishkin argues that the opinions of the average people in a society should be valued most when these people cease to be average and are transformed into a special class of more informed citizens. Only after the educational process takes place, he asserts, can citizens' opinions be taken seriously. Fishkin is, essentially, creating an artificial group of people, a "vanguard" of the masses, to help guide the direction of the society for the uninformed population left behind.

I have two problems with Fishkin's ideas. First and foremost, as noted, he is skeptical of the value of average citizens' opinions on the issues of the day, a skepticism with which I disagree. Second, he assumes that one or two days of briefings and deliberation can provide a quantum leap forward in the insights citizens can bring to bear on issues, and I'm not convinced that's true.

Don't get me wrong. Fishkin's basic proposal that citizens come together and deliberate the great issues of the day is an excellent one in a broad sense. I wish we had more of this kind of thing. Any society should welcome the input of groups of its citizens who band together and carefully deliberate policy questions and the moral dilemmas confronting society. New information, ideas, and strongly held positions are the mother's milk of democratic society. Ideas generated by groups of deliberating citizens can be a fine addition to the democratic process. Indeed, from a slightly different perspective, it's clear that a lot of this already goes on. We already have hundreds of think tanks and institutes and commissions in the United States today that do just that: bring people together to contemplate and deliberate policy issues and push the results back out to the society at large.

The wrinkle for Fishkin is his assumption that the views of those citizens who have not come together to deliberate are unworthy of consideration. This is where I take issue with his concept. Most average Americans will never have the opportunity to "deliberate" and read special position papers, but I don't think that invalidates their opinions. The information gathered in daily life and the deliberation that takes place around the water cooler are reflective of the real world. And we need to obtain our societal guidance from that world, where real people are living out their lives.

I also think there are real practical problems to what Fishkin advocates. His typical deliberative poll experiment involves bringing a random sample of people together for a weekend of briefings, discussion, and debate. But no one can argue that a few days of discussion makes someone a true expert in an area or on a topic. Why not bring the sample together for six months of deliberation, or even ask the sample to go to college for four years doing nothing but focusing on the area under consideration? Additionally, the weekend's presentation of position papers and briefings on a topic are by necessity selective and certainly can't represent all perspectives and all relevant knowledge on an issue. There's no way of determining if the deliberation will cover enough of the widely varying nuances of an issue to ensure that the participants are truly informed. Indeed, many times the wisest input on a decision comes from someone who is thinking totally outside the box and is bringing to bear some information or training or experience that is only tangentially related to the topic under consideration. Briefing and deliberation won't in and of themselves ensure that this type of perspective is presented. (In reality, it is interesting to note, the people who come together in Fishkin's deliberations often end up having opinions that are not much different from the opinions of general population surveys of the entire, nondeliberative population. If this turned out to be the case across a number of deliberative poll experiments, it would render the discussion about the merits of the concept moot.)

As I mentioned earlier, George Gallup advocated a process by which the opinions of those who were more knowledgeable about a topic were differentiated from those who were less knowledgeable about that same topic. He called this the quintamensional approach. His method consisted of asking the respondents a series of questions about the issue under consideration and then filtering the opinions based on what they said. Gallup pointed out that this method measured five aspects of public opinion:

1. The respondent's awareness and general knowledge about the topic
2. The respondent's overall opinions about the topic
3. The reasons why the respondent holds his or her views
4. The respondent's views on specific aspects of the problem
5. The intensity with which the respondent holds the opinion

As Gallup said, "Through the use of filter or information questions, the opinions of persons representing all levels of knowledge on an issue can be ascertained. The opportunity to correlate opinions with the extent and type of information possessed by those included in the survey opens a new door to the study of the factors which influence public opinion on important issues of the day."[3]

We at Gallup don't often go through these five steps in our polling today, partly because it is too time-consuming. But we use a shorthand method and ask respondents in our polls how closely they have been following particular issues. As Dr. Gallup advocated, we often break out the sample in ways that allow us to look at the opinions of those who are informed about an issue separately from those who are not.

This is of interest to us analytically. There are situations in which it is important to know how those who have closely followed a situation differ from those who have paid less attention, allowing us to approximate what would happen if all of the people in the society focused intently on an issue. But we never look *only* at the opinions of the informed group. There are several reasons for this. For one thing, those who are following a situation closely and are most informed are often not at all typical of the general population. It is quite common that people who have the most information about an issue are those who are strong advocates of a particular position on what should be done about the issue. Their data are thus skewed in one direction or the other.

For example, those who know the most about abortion and the nuances of what is involved in the various legal, ethical, and medical ramifications of pregnancy termination may well be those who are either very strongly pro-life or very strongly pro-choice. Looking just at the opinions about abortion of the informed segments of society would not necessarily provide the insights and wisdom we are after; it would instead provide a sense of the distribution of highly emotional opinions on the issue. It is not uncommon, additionally, that opponents of a particular policy are the most well informed, thus creating even more possibility that the opinions of those who know a lot about an issue present a highly skewed portrait.

Moreover, all of these efforts to separate out the opinions only of those who have great knowledge about an issue flounder when it comes to the specification of the exact cutoff point for the informed versus the uninformed groups. It is easy to envision the range of knowledge of an issue as stretching along a continuum that includes those with virtually no knowledge on the one end to those with "perfect knowledge" on the other. But there is no such thing as perfect knowledge. There is no point at which a person can be said to know everything there is to know about an issue. Any attempt to separate out the knowledgeable from those who are not knowledgeable is stymied to some degree by the key question of where to draw the line. Exactly how closely does one have to be following an issue to be considered knowledgeable? What types of tests might be necessary to separate out those who can be classified as truly informed on the issue and therefore able to give an opinion worth paying attention to?

So I think it is most appropriate to look at knowledge about an issue as a *variable* to be included in polling analysis, much as we look at the relationship between position on an issue and such things as age, education, and region of country. It is interesting to know how an informed group thinks about a policy position (whether or not the informed group comes about "naturally" in the real world or is created by an artificial deliberative process). But the value of the group's opinions is one that has to be viewed in context. In other words, the type of well-done analysis of polling results that I'm advocating will pay attention to the levels of the public's interest in a policy topic and how closely the public has been following the topic. If there is a relatively new issue that has just come to the attention of the public, we acknowledge as much and indicate that public opinion on that issue is based on initial reaction to a new topic. We can then monitor changes in opinion that might occur as the issue becomes more prominent. In essence, as Daniel Yankolovich has called it in his book of the same name, we can follow what happens in the process of "coming to public judgment." And, as I've noted, we can carefully look at the differences between those who have followed an issue carefully and those who have not, and use that as an input into our decision making. People who haven't been following an issue closely are responding in terms of their first impressions, and that type of reaction—although not based on careful deliberation of all of the complexities involved—can be an informative one, if and when it is put into the right context.

But underneath it all, it is extremely important that we not lose sight of the fundamental point that the mix of the views of all of the people in a society has the significant benefit of allowing a wide variety of insights and experiences and attitudes to be focused on an issue—a mix that is impossible to duplicate by determining a priori whose opinion should or should not be paid attention to.

These types of considerations bring us right back to the problems associated with the assumption that it is possible and/or desirable to look just at the opinions of those "in the know" on a topic. There's simply too much involved to eliminate the responses of those who don't pass some litmus test of knowledge about a particular issue.

## ARE THE OPINIONS OF THE PUBLIC STABLE ENOUGH?

I have often been startled and puzzled as I come across the unsubstantiated comments of pundits and critics who assert that public opinion wildly fluctuates. The opinion piece by Walter Kirn in the April 6, 2003, *New York*

*Times Magazine* included this commentary about what he alleges is an instability in the views of the public about the war in Iraq:

> The "numbers," as pollsters like to call them . . . have been all over the place since the [Iraq] war started. It's not worth citing any particular numbers since they probably did a back flip yesterday evening depending on the news from the front lines, but the overall trend has been toward volatility and away from settledness.[4]

And at just about the same time, in a March 28, 2003, recounting of a Dartmouth College speech by pundit and columnist Arianna Huffington, the student newspaper, the *Dartmouth*, reported the following: "Huffington cited the wildly fluctuating approval rating for the war as proof that the public opinion changes every time a news story breaks."[5]

Other critics over the years have joined these two in arguing that the public's view is fickle and will change rapidly from poll to poll. They complain that the views and attitudes and feelings of people are fleeting and changeable and too likely to shift with the wind. Indeed, a whole school of thought critical of the use of public opinion to help guide policy decisions sprang up in the 1950s and 1960s, fueled in part by political scientists who were surprised to find that the opinions of some respondents who were asked the same questions at different points in time seemed to change.

But, as scholars have pointed out, the overall distribution of the opinion of Americans on key issues stays remarkably constant. It's unclear exactly where Kirn, Huffington, and other critics of polls were getting their information. But the truth about the stability of public opinion is essentially exactly the opposite of what they assert.

An analysis of polling results on some of the more newsworthy and important issues of recent years suggests that stability is the norm. Huge, quick shifts in public opinion on issues and policy are rare. There is, in fact, considerable evidence that public opinion on major issues is rational and stable. The public's overall views on important social issues do not flip-flop back and forth and are not, as Founding Father James Madison feared, subject to the momentary "impulse of passion." Instead, public opinion is more often than not coherent, steady, and clear. This assertion about the instability of public opinion was addressed in *The Rational Public* by Benjamin Page and Robert Shapiro. In fact, their chapter 2 is aptly titled "The Myth of Capricious Change" and begins with the statement "It is widely believed that the American public's policy preferences shift frequently, rapidly, and arbitrarily."[6] After a careful review of evidence, the authors conclude, "Our data reveal a remarkable degree of stability in Americans' collective policy preferences, clearly contradicting any claim of frequent changes or wild fluctuations in public opinion."[7]

Let's look at the issue of opinions about the war in Iraq in 2003—the ones that Kirn and Huffington contended were so wildly flipping and flopping about. Gallup conducted twenty-eight polls prior to the beginning of the war on March 19, 2003, in which we asked Americans about their basic views on taking military action against Iraq in order to remove Saddam Hussein from power. There was extraordinarily little variation in the responses, with the one exception of the period immediately after the September 11 terrorist attacks when sentiment to go after Iraq shot up along with many other measures, as part of a general rally effect. In fact, support for military action against Iraq was in the low 50 percent range as far back as 1992 and—lo and behold—was still in the same general range twelve years later. Furthermore, when we began asking Americans if they favored or opposed the war after it had started, poll after poll showed that support was extremely steady at around 70 percent. In fact, support levels for the war were almost exactly the same across seven different Gallup polls in which a basic "favor or oppose" question was asked between March 22 and April 23. Even when we asked about the war in a different way ("Was the situation in Iraq worth going to war over?"), we got about the same 70 percent agreement. In other words, despite all of the dramatic events that transpired once the war got under way, the public's sentiments on the war stayed remarkably constant.

Two additional points are worth noting here. First, support for the idea of going to war did vary if pollsters put different stipulations within the questions: for example, with or without the support of allies and the United Nations, if it were certain that a specific number of Americans would be killed, and so forth. Second, it is remarkable that basic levels of support in the first several weeks of the war stayed constant even as other polling showed that the American public knew that things were not going smoothly for the coalition forces.

Another interesting example of the relative maturity and stability of the public's attitudes comes from the study of Americans' reactions to the issue of tax cuts, one variant or the other of which has been offered by Republican presidential contender Bob Dole in his campaign in 1996, by the Republican Congress in 1999, and by President George W. Bush in his 2000 presidential campaign. Polling suggests, as does common sense, that the idea of tax cuts in general is very appealing to Americans. Americans have long felt that they pay too much in taxes. It follows that in the most general sense, questions that ask the public if they favor a cut in their federal income taxes are met with positive responses. One might suppose that a purely self-interested public would therefore be thrilled with tax cut proposals, which would, after all, put money in their pockets.

But the public fairly consistently throughout the 1996 campaign seemed to put tax cuts into a relative framework and did not overwhelmingly endorse them. In 1999, when poll questions gave the public alternatives of tax cuts versus spending the budget surplus money on such things as Social Security and Medicare, the public was able to put into perspective long-term gains versus short-term gains, and opted for the latter. And, as noted, these views were fairly consistent and did not change from week to week or even from month to month.

Another example of the restraint of the public is evident from an examination of attitudes toward gun control throughout the spring and summer of 1999, as highly publicized school and business shootings created extraordinary attention on the role of the availability of guns as a causal factor in violent deaths. Americans throughout the decade had favored stricter gun control laws, and it might have been hypothesized that in the wake of the shootings, the percentage supporting still more draconian laws might have increased significantly—that is, demands for even stricter gun control laws. But the poll results reflecting gun control attitudes stayed remarkably constant. Americans' views were stable and not subject to short-term fluctuations, even after the hue and cry of supporters of gun control after the tragic events.

Some offer the O. J. Simpson case as an example of the stability of the attitudes of the American people, if not their insights. After the celebrated car chase and subsequent arrest of Simpson for the murder of Nicole Brown Simpson and Ron Goldman in 1994, the average American quickly came to the belief that the murder charges against Simpson were true. There was, of course, an enormous amount of publicity and visibility to the charges and to the trial itself during the months and years that followed, and it might have been expected that a fragile public would have changed its mind frequently as new evidence and accusations and developments and court testimony unfolded. Instead, the polls showed that Americans stuck to their views of the case without much change in the months leading up to the famous criminal trial, during the trial, and in the immediate aftermath when Simpson was found not guilty.

One of the best-known examples of the relative stability of the public's opinion over the course of a major, highly publicized issue came during the presidential impeachment crisis of 1998 and early 1999. The public did not vacillate much at all during the months in which the case unfolded. Shortly after the possibility of a relationship between President Clinton and a White House intern became public in January 1998, polling established that the majority of Americans thought that the president had had an extramarital affair (later changed to reflect the wording "sexual relations of any kind") with Monica Lewinsky. When Clinton made his infamous declaration "I did not have sexual relations with that woman, Miss Lewinsky," accompanied by his wife's statement on the *Today* show that he was the victim of a "vast right-wing conspiracy," the percentage disagreeing with him and saying that the charges were true went down slightly. But then it quickly rebounded and stayed well above the 50 percent level throughout that spring and summer—until Clinton's stunning confession on national television and in his legal deposition that he had indeed had an "inappropriate relationship" with the woman.

This situation leads us to two key conclusions from a public opinion perspective (and obviously a whole host of conclusions from a more general perspective that we will not get into in this book!). First, the public very quickly ferreted out the truth in the situation. Americans knew Bill Clinton, knew human nature, and quickly (and accurately) saw through the president's obfuscatory responses. Americans figured that it was probably true that Clinton had strayed from the marital bed. Second, despite the incredible publicity and hue and cry on both sides of the issue as the drama unfolded, the American public stayed remarkably constant in its attitudes. Americans also made the decision early on that the president should not be impeached (and if impeached, that he should not be convicted by the Senate and removed from office). That conclusion on the part of the public changed very little even as the story with all of its ramifications dominated news coverage for months on end.

The stability of the public's perception of issues is particularly noteworthy when the issues involved are emotional and deeply felt. Gallup's tracking of Americans' attitudes toward abortion, for example, reflect a very steady pattern wherein the majority of the public says that abortion should be legal in some circumstances, while minorities say that it should be either legal or illegal in all circumstances. These attitudes have moved very little over the past ten years.

Similarly, attitudes about the death penalty in cases of murder in the United States do not surge up and down capriciously. They stay generally stable for long periods of time. From the mid-1990s to 2003, for example, there was a great deal of focus on the death penalty in the United States. There was the escalating level of attention paid to the possibility that innocent people were being falsely sentenced to death, only to be found innocent based on DNA identification. The state of Illinois imposed an embargo on the use of the death penalty until further study could be made to answer the question of why it seemed to be applied so unfairly. The sentencing to death and ultimate execution of Timothy McVeigh in 2001 (for his role in the 1995 Oklahoma City bombing) brought out strong emotions about the death penalty, both pro and con. Yet through all of this, there was little abrupt change in the overall level of public support for the death penalty. Support rose slightly in the mid-1990s, then fell back down, but generally within a range at or above the 65 percent level.

To be sure, there have been some changes in these attitudes toward the death penalty over longer periods of time. Support waned in the 1960s during a period of time in which there were no executions in America, only to jump up again as executions were reinstated in 1976. But I think it's fascinating to note that when Gallup first asked about the death penalty in 1936, 59 percent said they supported it, not that far off from the 64 percent support we find today.

Those who contend that public opinion is fickle and wavering should also examine the early results from pre-election polls leading up to the 2000 presidential election. As early as May 1998, more than two years before the election, Republicans indicated in polls that they preferred Texas governor George W. Bush as their candidate. Although there was the usual intense campaigning in the run-up to the election, including the entrance into and the exit from the race of a number of candidates, these perceptions did not vary significantly right up to the nominating convention in the summer of 2000.

The list goes on and on. I spend a good deal of my time at Gallup measuring and monitoring trends in public opinion, and I'm constantly amazed at how much attitudes and opinions about major issues do not change over time. Every month we ask Americans a series of questions in our Gallup Poll Social Series about various important issues of the day (education, crime, governance, health care, etc.). We rarely see major shifts up and down in the responses to these questions, and opinions on core issues are often within just a few percentage points of where they have been for years. When we do see changes, they are usually explainable by real-world events. For example, the American public's attitudes toward France have over the years generally been positive—that is, until the early months of

2003 when France chose not to support the United States, and in fact publicly chastised President Bush's justification for war. We then noticed the big shift I discussed earlier: Americans became more negative toward France. But then, lo and behold, these newly negative attitudes remained quite stable months after the war was over.

Benjamin Page and Robert Shapiro's aforementioned book *The Rational Public* presents chapter after chapter of analysis of social issues, economics, and foreign policy, showing that the trend lines of public attitudes toward each issue has been remarkably and dramatically consistent. As Page and Shapiro summarize, "Public opinion about policy does not by any means undergo incessant change . . . Furthermore, when opinion change does occur, it is usually modest in magnitude."[8] The public's views on issues are more often than not a stabilizing influence in society, solid and slow to change—providing an important context for debate on the important issues of our time.

1. Roger Lowenstein, *When Genius Failed: The Rise and Fall of Long-Term Capital Management* (New York: Random House, 2001).

2. James S. Fishkin, *The Voice of the People* (Binghamton, NY: Vail-Ballou Press, 1995), 162.

3. George Gallup, "Qualitative Measurement of Public Opinion: Quintamensional Plan of Survey Design," speech.

4. Walter Kirn, "Don't Count Me In," *New York Times Magazine*, April 6, 2003.

5. Tim Mosso, "Huffington Decries Lack of Leadership," *Dartmouth*, March 28, 2003.

6. Benjamin I. Page and Robert Y. Shapiro, *The Rational Public* (Chicago: University of Chicago Press, 1992), 37.

7. Ibid., 45.

8. Ibid., 65.

# CHAPTER 7

# Behind the Curtain: How Polling Is Done

We now come to the most important of the objections to polls laid out by Dr. George Gallup sixty years ago: the fact that people, as he put it, "emphasize defects in the present methods of operation."[1]

This is an understatement if there ever was one. It is apparent that many people just don't understand how polling works, thus providing the basis for the bulk of the objections to polls that we receive here at Gallup. The basis of these objections is straightforward. Polling uses small samples (what seems to be *very* small samples to most people) to represent the views of very large numbers of people. And it is difficult for many people to believe that this process provides a true understanding of what everyone in the larger society thinks.

That skepticism is evident when we survey people about polls (something we do from time to time), and I certainly hear it when I am on radio talk shows or after making a speech. I get bombarded with questions about the credibility of our polls. Again and again, people question how the views of a few hundred people can possibly be representative of 200-plus million adult Americans.

As I noted earlier, this skepticism about polls is nothing

new; Dr. Gallup ran into disbelief about the process almost from the first day he began to release his polls in the
1930s. He spent a good deal of time attempting to explain
his techniques in articles, books, and speeches up until his
death in 1984—something most other survey researchers
and pollsters have continued in the years since. As Dr.
Gallup said, "Unless the poll watcher understands the nature of sampling and the steps that must be taken to assure
its representativeness, the whole operation of scientific
polling is likely to have little meaning, and even less sig-
nificance, to him."[2]

Exactly how does polling work? How do we know for
sure that the results of polls are representative of what
they are supposed to measure? These are good questions,
and there are legitimate answers for them. There are
mathematical and logical reasons why the random selection process that is at the heart of polling does in fact
allow us to use a carefully selected sample to represent
millions of people in the population from which that sample is drawn. I'll get into those a little later in this chapter.
But there is also the simple proof that comes when we
have the opportunity to compare survey sample results to
events in the real world, most notably in preelection polls.
On the night before an election, polls tell us how the people in a small random sample say they are going to vote.
By the end of the next day, the voting decisions of millions
are known, and the two can be compared. Elections, it
turns out, provide a perfect opportunity to test just how
well a small sample does in estimating the behavior of the
population from which it is drawn.

Most pollsters recognize that a major function of preelection polls is to validate for a sometimes skeptical public that the process of random sampling can work. That's
one of the reasons why we at Gallup put so much emphasis on horse race polling before major elections. It's a great
test laboratory.

With that in mind, let's look at an example from the November 5, 2002, midterm congressional elections. These elections were important because they provided the first major test of the coattails of President George W. Bush, who put his reputation to a significant degree on the line, publicly and vociferously campaigning for Republican candidates across the country in the weeks leading up to the November 5 vote.

There isn't a nationwide vote in midterm elections; there are typically a variety of governors' races and about one-third of U.S. Senate seats up for grabs. But every American who goes to the voting booth in a midterm election has the opportunity to vote for the representative from his or her congressional district. (As we all remember from high school civics classes, every member of the House is up for reelection every two years, so every American except for those living in the District of Columbia gets to vote for Congress in each midterm election.) We can treat these congressional races as a national election by asking a random sample of all Americans whom they are going to vote for in their congressional district. We then aggregate the results and come up with a composite portrait of the total vote for Congress across all 435 congressional districts (for example, 50 percent of the American public is going to vote for the Republican candidate in their congressional district and 50 percent is going to vote for the Democratic candidate). The next day, we can compare the results of the preelection sample to the overall aggregated vote total of the millions of Americans who went to the polls in all of the 435 congressional districts. Comparing the results of a poll of 1,000 or 2,000 people to the actual voting results of millions provides an excellent test of the ability of surveys to use small samples to predict the behavior of a large population.

Here's how the process worked in 2002.

On the nights of October 31 through November 3, we

at the Gallup poll talked with exactly 1,221 Americans on the telephone and asked them to indicate for whom they planned to vote in their local congressional race in the November 5 election. But these weren't just any 1,221 Americans. They were selected by using a process called random digit dialing, or RDD. RDD is fascinating and complex, and I'll explain it in some detail in the following pages. But, for the time being, let's accept the fact that a computer is loaded with every residential phone exchange in the nation and then selects phone numbers on a purely random basis until the desired sample size is reached.

The 1,221 Americans interviewed just before the November 5 election were thus contacted because their phone numbers were part of a true random sample of all adults in the nation with access to a residential phone line. To make sure of this, after interviewing was completed, the computer cross-referenced the major demographic traits of this group against census estimates for the nation. The percentage in the sample from each major geographic region of the country, and the age, gender, and race, were adjusted slightly to be in line with known population parameters.

All of the 1,221 Americans in the sample were told they were a part of a Gallup interview, were reminded about the coming election, and were asked a series of questions about their voting status and their vote. Exactly 1,061 people in the sample professed to be registered voters and said they were going to vote in the election. (The remaining 160 people were asked a series of demographic questions to help us weight the overall sample as one of the final stages of the process.)

We knew that not all of the 1,061 people who said they planned on voting would actually do so on election day. The respondents didn't realize it, but a set of questions they answered was designed to estimate their likelihood of voting. (Gallup analysts have developed and fine-tuned these questions over a sixty-five-year period.) Respondents were asked whether they happened to know where people vote in their neighborhood, about their voting habits in the past, about their interest in the election, and so forth. Each of the 1,061 Americans who said they were going to vote was then asked the key question about their intended congressional vote the next day.

Interviewing was over at about 4:30 p.m. on Sunday, November 3. A computer program at Gallup's headquarters then began its work. The responses of the 1,061 interviewees who claimed they were going to vote were carefully analyzed. Gallup's analysts and computer programmers gave each of the 1,061 people in the sample a score. Those with the highest numbers had the highest probability of voting. These people answered almost every question in a way that indicated a strong likelihood of voting. They had voted in the past, knew where to vote, and had a high degree of interest in the election. Those with low numbers had a low probability of voting. Despite their professed voting intentions, they didn't know where to vote, hadn't voted in the past, and had a lower level of interest in the election. Our experience suggested that they probably wouldn't show up at the voting booth.

The computer was programmed to separate out a smaller subset of people in the sample at the high end of this "probability of voting" scale—in this instance 715 of them—that would be most representative of the subset of people in the real world who would end up voting. We call these people "likely voters," and their answers were given full weight in the final sample. The answers of a second group were included, but given a smaller weight because their probability of voting, although high, was slightly lower than that of the top group. And the responses of a third group of people—those who had the lowest probability of voting—weren't considered at all in the final analysis. We estimated that the chances that this group would actually turn out and vote were so low that they should be totally excluded from our final sample.

It is important to keep in mind that this final sample of likely voters maintained the basic assumption of randomness that had guided the entire sampling process and were thus a randomly selected subset of likely voters in the real world. They became a very valuable group of people. Based on the mathematical properties of randomness and probability, it was almost certain that their responses would be representative of the responses of the huge group of all voters across the country.

The final step was to look closely at what the people in this carefully selected random sample said they were going to do on election day, based on their responses to the "money" question: "If the elections for Congress were being held today, which party's candidate would you vote for in your congressional district—(1) the Democratic Party's candidate or (2) the Republican Party's candidate?" If voters were undecided, we followed up with, "As of today, do you lean more toward (1) the Democratic Party's candidate or (2) the Republican Party's candidate?"

We found that 51 percent of the 715 people in our "likely voter" sample said they were going to vote for the Republican candidate and 45 percent for the Democratic candidate, with 4 percent undecided. Of course, any or all of these voters could change their minds between Sunday night and the Tuesday vote. Experience indicated, however, that this usually didn't happen. By this point—just days before an election—what people tell a pollster is very likely to be what they do when they enter the voting booth a day or two later. Thus, the 51 percent and 45 percent figures were highly likely to be representative of the vote of the large group of likely voters who would turn out on election day.

All of these computations took place within about an

hour late on Sunday afternoon. By six o'clock that night, the data had been transmitted to CNN headquarters in Atlanta and to *USA Today* in Virginia, and by midnight had been placed on Gallup's Web site. By Monday morning, the estimate derived from the sample of 715 likely voters formed the basis for the front-page headline in *USA Today*: "Late Shift Appears to Favor GOP."[3]

Then came Tuesday. By the time the polls closed, more than 75 million Americans had showed up to vote. By the next morning, the votes in the 435 congressional districts across the country had been tallied. The results: about 51.7 percent of the vote went to Republican candidates; 45 percent to Democratic candidates.

A remarkable (but familiar) scientific feat had occurred. The theory of random probability sampling had allowed a random sample of 715 voters to reflect almost precisely the actual behavior of the more than 75 million voters who voted on election day:

| THE CONGRESSIONAL VOTER, NOVEMBER 5, 2002 | | |
|---|---|---|
| Political Party Affiliation of Candidates | Random Sample of 715 Likely Voters Interviewed October 31–November 3 | Actual Voting Behavior of More Than 75 Million Voters on Election Day, November 5* |
| Republican | 51% | 51.7% |
| Democrat | 45% | 45% |

*Based on totals as of November 7, 2002.

This whole process is a refinement of something that has been going on for more than sixty-five years. Back in 1936, a young Iowan, George Gallup, startled the world when he declared that Franklin D. Roosevelt was going to be reelected as president of the United States. Gallup based that prediction on a small sample of only several thousand people. At the same time, the *Literary Digest* magazine had a group of several *million* people in its famous poll that had been running for a number of years. The *Literary Digest* said Roosevelt would go down to defeat. The *Digest*'s editors laughed at Gallup. How could this man's small group of people possibly be as accurate as the magazine's own huge sample? Gallup stuck to his guns. His predictions were published before the election in the *Washington Post* and many other newspapers. A major showdown was in place.

Gallup had a secret weapon. His polling provided what he called "the first real test of scientific sampling in a national election."[4] The *Digest*'s sample, although massive, was essentially a convenience sample—based on gathering people's names and addresses from subscription, telephone, and automobile registration lists. It made no pretense of following any type of scientific sampling procedures.

Gallup's theory of sampling won the day. Roosevelt won the election (and two more after that). The *Literary Digest* sputtered, but couldn't explain away its miscall. Coincidentally, a few years later it folded. Gallup, on the other hand, is still very much with us, and George Gallup's basic principles of sampling are still the basis for ours and almost all modern-day polls. There are a host of new complications that we face today, and many procedures we use are significantly improved over those used by George Gallup in the 1930s. But, as we saw in the November 2002 midterm elections, when sampled and measured accurately, the opinions of just a small number of Americans can and do accurately represent the opinions and actual behavior of millions.

It's not just this one election. Most preelection polls end up providing accurate predictions of the actual election results. The National Council on Public Polls has compiled lists of polls and compared them to the outcome results across a number of elections in recent years, and has concluded that they indeed do an accurate job of sampling, as validated by the close correlation between the results of the sampling and the actual vote on election day.

Despite all of this evidence, though, there is no way around the fact that many skeptics don't believe that polling small numbers of people can accurately represent the views of millions. Yet it does. How does this process work?

## PROBABILITY SAMPLING: THE SCIENCE OF PROJECTING FROM A SMALL SAMPLE TO A LARGE POPULATION

Polls are based on a process by which small samples are used to project to large populations. The terms "sample" and "population" are used fairly precisely by statisticians. A *population* is a large group of elements that is the primary focus of an investigation (residents of the United States, for example, or voters in California). A *sample* is a smaller group of elements taken from that population. The whole process of sampling and polling and calculating the "margin of sampling error" you hear so much about is focused directly on the relationship between these two entities: the sample and the population from which the sample is taken. Selected correctly, the sample becomes a surrogate for the population, thus saving the investigator the time and trouble of having to measure each element in the (often) extremely big population.

Gallup liked to remind audiences that this whole idea of using a small sample to generalize to a larger entity is not confined to polling. He was famous for his "blood" example. He pointed out how it was unnecessary for a doctor to withdraw all of the blood in a patient's body in order to check that patient's blood type or white cell count. The sample comes out of the patient's finger or arm and usually suffices as an accurate indicator of the condition of all of the blood throughout the patient's body.

Similarly, Gallup used to say, it is not necessary for a housewife to eat all of the soup in a bowl in order to see if it is too salty. All she has to do, he said, is "stir the tomato soup thoroughly in order to be certain that the various components are well mixed before she tastes it. After the soup has been stirred, she can take a spoonful at random from any part of the bowl and be reasonably sure that it will contain the same mixture of ingredients as the contents of the entire bowl."[5] Along the same lines, it is not necessary for an environmental scientist to test millions of gallons of water in a lake to see if it is contaminated with bacteria. A small sample or set of samples taken from randomly selected points will usually suffice.

The population of interest to pollsters is usually all the people who live in a specified metropolitan area, a state, or a country. The pollsters' key objective is to avoid the time and cost that would be involved in interviewing each and every person in that large population in order to get an estimate of the general levels of support or opposition to a policy, approval of a governor or president, or—more prosaically—the percentage of that population that prefers football to baseball as their favorite sport. A well-collected sample can provide estimates of these types of population characteristics that are quite accurately representative, just as a blood sample or a water sample gives an accurate representation of the condition of the larger entity from which it is taken.

There are two underlying assumptions in this process of sampling from populations: (a) it is important to be able to investigate and understand an entire population, and (b) it is difficult to measure everyone in a large population, so some type of very specific, precise sampling procedure is necessary in order to ensure that the sample represents the whole.

The basis of the first assumption may not be as obvious as it seems. Random sampling is based on the bedrock assumption that we absolutely need to understand the *entire* population of interest, that it is worthwhile and important to go to the time and trouble to either take a complete census of that population or design a sample using the types of procedures we are talking about here in order to make sure that it is representative of that entire whole.

We've talked in previous sections of this book about the importance of understanding the collective opinions of large groups of people rather than relying on the opinions of small groups or elites. But when you stop and think about it for a moment, *why* is it necessary or important to understand or measure an entire population of humans— say, all adults living in the United States? Isn't it just as useful to study small groups of humans wherever they can be found? Can't we find some people—wherever we can— and figure out what they feel?

That is certainly what a *New York Times* reporter did on February 15, 2003. The *Times* was interested in how people were reacting to the fact that France and Germany were defying the recommendations of the Bush administration vis-à-vis invading Iraq. The reporter, Felicia R. Lee, simply went to the Times Square subway station in Manhattan (conveniently located just a block or so from the *New York Times* headquarters building) and stopped random passersby and asked them questions. The reporter then followed up by reviewing the letters to the editors in a couple of newspapers and—bingo—she had her story on the attitudes and reactions of the people to the France and Germany situation ("Americans Turning Eagerly to Gibes at the French").

The responses of the people this reporter talked to were used to make inferences about what all Americans were thinking or feeling about this issue. She had no way of knowing how correct her assumptions were. (And this made the validity of the conclusions in the article doubtful, an issue to which we will return below.) But, again, did the *New York Times* reporter really *need* to understand all Americans' views on these issues? Why wasn't it okay just to look at the views of the few people she happened to run across? The answer in this case revolves around the fact that attitudes toward France can vary widely from person to person and from region to region, and the reporter has no necessary reason to believe that people in New York's Times Square are just like all other people across the country. She needed a way to talk to everyone in the United States or a sample of everyone in the United States, as we will discuss below.

This whole question of the necessity of measuring each and every element in a population is more compelling than you might imagine. Many scientists who are interested in studying something make no effort to attempt to measure or understand the entire population of whatever that entity happens to be, but are happily content to study any examples that are handy. This is sometimes the case even when it comes to the study of humans. I have stressed in this book the need to be able to measure or estimate the opinions, attitudes, and behavior of entire populations. But not all scientists and others who study humans have found that this is necessary. Sigmund Freud did not use surveys, but depended on what he gleaned from his very limited number of patients to develop his theories of human mental functioning. Medical scientists often use available patients, cadavers, and any other available human beings to test their theories. Many of us are familiar with the use of sophomores on college campuses as subjects for psychology experiments.

All of these scientists work under the assumption that the processes they study are universal across the human species and that the type of confirmation available from investigating an entire population is not necessary. Many journalists often seem to operate under a similar assumption when it comes to their efforts to report public reaction to news events. Hence they seem content to grab any available group of humans as opposed to taking very careful steps to make sure that the humans being studied are randomly selected and representative. The example of the *New York Times* article in which the reporter used the classic "man in the street" journalistic technique is just one of many; this technique is extremely common in both print and broadcast journalism. Indeed, the ease of use of the Internet today allows researchers or journalists to take the opinions of any group of humans who happen to sign on and take a poll to assume—erroneously—that they in some way have reflected the opinions of the entire society.

We're really dealing here with a fairly straightforward and important question: just how necessary is it to focus on the need to understand an entire population as opposed to examining any members of the population that happen to be available? It is almost always easier and cheaper to use *available* humans rather than going to the time and trouble of figuring out a way to interview all humans in a population or to use the types of sampling techniques we are talking about here to estimate the results that would have been obtained had it been possible to interview each and every human in the population. So it's very tempting to grab whoever happens to be available.

Here's a way of looking at this, using CNN as an example. CNN has bureaus in many cities across the country (and around the world). Suppose there is a major news event and CNN producers want to get the people's reaction to that event. Fair enough. But if the producer calls up the CNN New York bureau and tells them to go outside in order to get some "person-in-the-street" reaction, you are going to see how a group of New Yorkers who happen to be walking near Penn Station are feeling about the issue. If the CNN producer tells a reporter in Atlanta to do the same thing, you are going to get the reactions of a different type of person who happens to be walking the streets in that southern town (reactions that could be quite different from those found in New York City). And finally, if the producer calls out to the CNN Los Angeles bureau, which happens to be located on Sunset Boulevard in Hollywood, the type of people stopped are going to be quite different in still other ways. All of this is okay so long as one is interested only in the reaction from people in these specific areas, but it tells us little about the views of the 99 percent in the rest of the country.

Now, if the CNN producer had a really big budget, then he or she could start sending reporters out on the street in many, many different locations across the country. And if the producer picked those locations randomly, and did some other things right, he or she would slowly but surely be approximating exactly what it is that CNN does when it commissions a scientific poll: gets a random sample that is generalizable to all of the people in a specific or given population.

## WHY DO WE NEED TO STUDY ALL OF THE PEOPLE?

At this point, it is useful to return to our basic question. Why do we need to generalize to *all* of the people in a population? Why not just be content with the kind of man-in-the-street type of examples I gave above—grabbing anybody that happens to be available?

One answer is that we don't *always* need to be able to generalize to a large population. We want to measure all of the members of a large group primarily when we are focusing on the distribution of specific widely varying characteristics. We don't need to look at all the members of a large population when we're only interested in studying characteristics shared by everyone in that population.

The scientist interested in the breathing patterns of fish will feel comfortable grabbing any available fish because he or she assumes that breathing occurs in generally the same way across all members of the category. In similar fashion, a characteristic is universal across the human species, there is less need to investigate an entire population. Any available specimens will do.

For those interested in studying human life at its most basic, the patterns of interest are those that involve DNA, chromosomes, genes, and basic physiological processes. Scientists interested in these aspects of human beings do not need to study every human or to randomly sample humans from a broad population in order to understand or investigate these aspects. They don't need polling techniques. The basic characteristics being studied can be assumed to exist within *all* members of the species. Freud did not study an entire population of individuals living in Austria. He studied, intensely, a selected few patients and extrapolated the principles he discovered to all humans (although it is not at all clear that Freud was correct in his assumption that he had stumbled into some universally applicable principles). As I mentioned, psychologists often use college students as the subject of their study, without any pretense that their campus's sophomores are precisely representative of all college students, or all adults living across the country. These psychologists are interested in observing experimentally how the subjects respond when subjected to certain experimental conditions. They make the assumption that the patterns they detect are so general and so basic that it is not necessary or important to use a sample or an entire population of humans as the subject of study.

Medical doctors study the homeless and others who are

available and willing to come in off the streets to participate in medical experiments. Medical students study
anatomy using cadavers that are in no way selected to be
representative of all humans in any particular population.
Many studies reported in medical journals are based on
experiments conducted with totally nonrepresentative
groups of patients who happen to be available at larger research and teaching hospitals for participation in such
studies. These doctors assume that there are very basic
processes and physiological structures that are the same
across all humans.

On the other hand, there are many situations in which
the scientist is not interested in studying characteristics
that are essentially the same across all members of a
species, but rather characteristics that vary widely. In these
instances, it is the *pattern* of variation that matters, and
this pattern can be ascertained only by targeting the entire
population under investigation.

To return to my fish example, if the objective is to analyze the distribution of types of fish species within a large
body of water, then the scientist must either (a) measure
the species of every fish in the body of water or (b) randomly sample fish in such a fashion that the measured distribution of fish species across the sample can be
generalized to the entire body of water. It simply wouldn't
be useful for the scientist to grab a few fish in one small
inlet of the body of water and assume that this sample represented the distribution of types of fish across the entire
entity. Many fish may only swim in deep waters, or stay
far away from shore, or may not be easily caught—meaning that a group of fish caught near the shore may bear little resemblance to the fish population across the entire
body of water.

Similarly, the work of Princeton University biologists
popularized in the book *The Beak of the Finch* focused on
an entire population of finches occupying some islands in

the Galapagos.[6] In this situation, the scientists did not want to study *any* finches available—something they could have done back home at a zoo. Instead, the interest of these scientists was the distribution of external characteristics of the entire population of finches living on the islands, and how these characteristics varied or evolved based on the environment in which the finches found themselves. The scientists needed to understand the distribution of the birds across the entire population area.

In similar fashion, pollsters are almost always interested in studying the distribution of such things as presidential job approval, ratings of the economy, and vote intentions across all of the people in a state or country. These measures vary widely, and are distributed unequally across regions and subgroups. Thus, some way of measuring all the people, or coming up with a sample that represents all the people, is required. That's what polling is all about. Stopping a few people on the street and asking their opinions does little good in reaching this objective.

The key here is the *homogeneity*, or sameness, of the characteristics or processes under investigation. The more something is the same across all members of a population, the more generalizable are the results taken from any subset of that population no matter how that subset was obtained. All members of a population don't need to be studied if the researcher is investigating regularities and persistent patterns that are found across the entire population; the study of *any* member of that species is in general just as rewarding as the study of any other—or all of them. There is, in short, no need to study all the elements in a population or to develop precise random samples taken from that population when any subset of the members of the population will do just as well. This is most often the case when the object of the scientist's study is basic processes, relationships, and ways in which behavior or other variables play out.

On the other hand, if the scientist is interested in the ways in which characteristics are *distributed* across populations, then using available samples won't work. If characteristics are *heterogeneous*, or varied, across the members of a large group, then the way in which the small group being studied is selected matters a great deal. If a group or sample selected for research is not representative of a larger population, then the characteristics or processes that are uncovered in the research will not necessarily reflect the distribution of characteristics or processes at work for the entire population, and as such are usually of much less interest.

There are many instances in which a particular human characteristic is not uniform across a population of interest, but takes on a number of different *values*. Approval of the job being done by the president is a variable, with "approve" or "disapprove" constituting the two values. Presidential vote intention is a variable, and the candidates in the election are the values. Feelings about the state of the U.S. economy is a variable, while "excellent," "good," "fair," and "poor" are the values. Going to war against Iraq is a variable, while approval and disapproval constitute the values. We don't care so much what a handful of people we meet in a bar or stop on the street think about the president or the economy or the war. We want to know what the *distribution* of opinion on these key issues is across the entire population.

And, central to the focus of this book, if the study of the entire population is not possible, then employing some type of precise sampling procedure allows us to generalize to that population. That's where polling comes in. Polling is the process that is appropriately used when it is assumed that the characteristics or processes under investigation may vary across a broad population, and when we are interested in exactly what that distribution is.

## POLLING IS A PRACTICAL SOLUTION TO THE PROBLEM OF STUDYING ENTIRE POPULATIONS

One doesn't necessarily have to conduct a poll and rely on a sample to study the distribution of values on variables across an entire, broad population. It is much more straightforward to measure *every* member of the population of interest. This is what is accomplished when a researcher conducts a *census*, a common term that has a fairly precise meaning. A census of the U.S. population is conducted by the federal government every ten years, as required under the terms of the Constitution.

There are two major problems with censuses. When the population under investigation has 290 million people (as is the case with the United States), it is extraordinarily expensive to attempt to measure each and every person. In fact, the budget for the U.S. census in 2000 was over $7 billion, and even with this huge budget, experts claim that it is impossible to find and measure everyone.

A second problem relates to the first. Given the enormous cost of conducting a true census, it is impossible to conduct them very frequently or to include large numbers of variables when they are conducted. In the United States, the major census is conducted only once every ten years, and every resident is asked only a handful of questions. In fact, the "true" census in which every person in the population is counted is so limited that the Census Bureau does a large amount of augmentation by using—you guessed it—sampling.

So the attempt to study everyone in a population that has a size above a few hundred members typically must involve some cheaper and more convenient method. It was the attempt to find this more practical and cheaper method of studying all the members of a population that led researchers to look at ways that a small group of elements could be selected from a large population and mimic or accurately represent that large population.

There are basically three ways to sample: haphazardly, using quotas, and randomly.

*Haphazard sampling* involves grabbing any group of people that happen to be convenient, such as stopping people on street corners, calling the first one hundred numbers in the phone book, or asking people to respond to a poll based on a notice posted on the Internet.

Haphazard sampling is extremely common. I can't tell you how many times I see people attempting to generalize to an entire population by using a group of people who bothered to pick up the phone and call an 800 number; a group of people who bothered to do an online poll on the Internet; a few people on the street; reporters who fly into a state or region and interview a few dozen people.

A survey of U.S. military personnel published in the *Stars and Stripes* newspaper in October 2003 provides an interesting example of a study based on a haphazard sample.[7] Reporters for the publication were sent out into the streets of Baghdad with instructions to find any American soldiers they could and ask them to fill out a survey questionnaire. The results, while of some interest, had no necessary mathematical relationship to the opinions of *all* of the military personnel stationed in Iraq—because the sample was haphazard. The opinions of the soldiers interviewed were no more representative of all the soldiers in Iraq than were the people interviewed by the *New York Times* reporter at Times Square representative of all the people in the United States.

In almost all these situations, the assumption of generalizability doesn't hold. You can't take any group of people who happen to be available and assume that the distribution of the characteristics of interest within that group is anything like what you would get if you were able to measure the entire population from which they come.

*Quota sampling* is a little more sophisticated and is in fact the first method used by a number of the early pioneers in polling, including George Gallup. Quota sampling attempts to use prior knowledge of how many people should be in each of a number of demographic groups that comprise the population and to select respondents in order to fill quotas for each such group. For example, we can look at the census and see that about 12 percent of Americans are black and then try to make sure that 120 of the respondents in a sample of 1,000 are black. If half of the people in a population are women, then we make sure that half of the respondents in a sample are women. And so forth. We can use fancier and even more complex procedures. Some quota samples set up elaborate tables with individual cells based on combining variables of interest (for example, X percent should be black females fifty and older, Y percent should be white males eighteen to twenty-nine years old, and so forth). The researchers then go out and look around until they find the right types of people with the right characteristics to interview and thus fill up each of these cells.

This type of quota sampling is an improvement over haphazard sampling but still isn't guaranteed to be representative. Quota sampling assures that the sample has proportionately the same characteristics as the population, on selected variables. The problem, however, is that the people selected to fill each quota group aren't necessarily representative of those portions of the underlying population. It is all well and good to force 12 percent of a sample to be black, but if those blacks are a particular or unusual segment of the black population—say, they were all selected from and interviewed in South-Central Los Angeles—then the sample loses its representativeness. Similarly, it's good to control a sample so that it is half men and half women, but if these men and women are all selected haphazardly from just one state or one region of the country (or in suburban shopping centers), then they won't be representative of all of the men or all of the women throughout the nation.

There's another problem with quota sampling. It is impossible to divide a population up into quotas based on *every* conceivable characteristic that might be important— including such things as race, age, education, income, gender, height, weight, marital status, political leanings, newspaper reading status, and so forth. It's just too much to try to handle ahead of time.

So we come to the heart of the matter. We can select the people to be in our sample randomly. *Random sampling* is the core of the way most polling is done today. It has a beauty and scientific robustness that makes it one of the most important techniques in all of social science.

In the context we're using here, the word "random" has a very special meaning. The concept of randomness is one of the key underpinnings of sampling theory. When we say that we draw a sample randomly, we mean that every member of the population from which it is drawn has an equal chance (or a known chance) of falling into the sample, and that who gets into the sample and who doesn't are purely a function of chance. This equal-probability-of-selection method, or epsem, is the key to most sampling theory. It means that no one person has a greater or lesser chance of being selected than any other person. This in turn means that the mix of the people in the sample has an excellent chance of reflecting the mix of the people in the large population.

Let me repeat. Statisticians long ago discovered that if each element of a sample could be drawn on a totally random basis from a large population, the resulting sample would generally reflect the characteristics of the members of the population within known statistical tolerances.

I like to use a big bowl of marbles as an example (George Gallup liked the marble example as well). Suppose that half of these marbles are white and half are black. Then suppose that the bowl is opaque and we can't look into it. We don't have time to take out every single marble and note whether it is black or white. So we decide to draw out just a relatively few marbles to use as our basis for estimating the proportion of black and white marbles in the big bowl. We mix up all of the marbles and begin to draw them out one by one, totally on a random basis. If we have truly mixed them up, each draw of a marble is truly random and every marble has an equal probability of being selected. And if we do this correctly, and draw out, say, fifty marbles—the distribution between white and black ends up being pretty close to the fifty-fifty split within the bowl itself.

Obviously, if we drew every single marble, the split would be exactly fifty-fifty, since we would have the entire population of marbles laid out in front of us. If we had lots of time on our hands, we could draw hundreds of samples of marbles, putting the marbles back in each time when we are finished. We could graph out the white-black distribution from each sample. We would note that the percentages of black or white marbles would fluctuate with the small sample sizes (say, just six marbles), but as we drew out samples with larger and larger numbers of marbles in each, the percentage breakdown within the samples would be closer and closer to 50 percent white and 50 percent black. We could do this thousands of times and graph out how much the breakdown varied across all of the samples. Using these data, we could then begin to calculate how much variation there was around the true population parameter of 50 percent white and 50 percent black in the groups of samples.

The key to all of the above is that the marbles be drawn totally randomly. Each marble needs to have an equal chance of falling into the sample each time one is drawn out. If all of the black marbles are at the top of the bowl and you simply reach in and get only the marbles on the top, then the equal-probability-of-selection assumption will have been violated, and the sample will no longer be a good estimator of the distribution within the entire bowl.

Some examples from the real world can help us understand this principle. Perhaps the best-known application of random sampling today is the lottery. Almost everyone who buys a lottery ticket accepts the fact that he or she has the same chance of having his or her ticket selected as the next person (although that chance, of course, is minuscule). How is this done? By using a process of random selection in which, figuratively, all of the lottery numbers are thrown into a giant bowl, and a blindfolded person shakes them up and then reaches in and grabs one. (In fact, many televised lottery drawings involve a person drawing one of a group of Ping-Pong balls with numbers on them.) This same process was used in the late 1960s and early 1970s when the U.S. military draft was switched over from local selective service draft boards to a nationwide lottery based on random selection of birthdays, in which every eligible male's birthday was supposed to have about the same chance of being selected. (There were complaints at the time that the process had mechanical problems and was *not* purely random and that birthdays in certain months were more likely to be selected than others.)

Suppose a pollster is interested in estimating the job approval rating for the mayor of Gotham City among all of the residents of Gotham City ("Do you approve or disapprove of the job being done by the mayor of Gotham City?"). If a pollster grabs people who are walking through a Gotham City shopping mall and asks them questions, he or she has violated the equal-probability-of-selection assumption. This sample is not randomly drawn from the total population of the city. Now, you might say, "Doesn't every citizen of Gotham City have a chance of being in the mall at the time when the people are stopped?" The answer to that is no. Gotham City residents who never shop, or never go to that particular mall, or who only go to the mall around Christmas, or who are handicapped and can't get out have no chance of falling into the sample. Furthermore, there are no doubt different malls in Gotham City. A mall on the rich side of town would produce a different sample than one on the poor side. A mall with mostly outdoorsy and recreational stores would produce a different sample than one that had mostly upscale women's clothing stores. So a convenience sample done at a mall would be biased, and worthless in terms of estimating how the total population of the city feels. The pollster needs to find a way of ensuring that every citizen of Gotham City has a full and equal chance of being in the sample.

A sample based on people who hit a particular Web site and vote online is not random because many people have a zero chance or probability of falling into the sample. These include those who don't have a personal computer, those who don't have access to the Internet, those who don't ever go to the particular site in question, and so forth. A mail sample based on all subscribers to a magazine is not a random sample of the entire adult population because nonsubscribers have no chance of falling into that sample.

These examples highlight the differences between true random sampling and other types of sampling. Some of these bad samples are the haphazard or convenience samples I talked about above, meaning that the individuals selected to be included are picked nonrandomly and based on no coherent pattern. Indeed, any sample in which a sizable percentage of the population doesn't have at least a theoretical chance of falling into the sample is simply not useful for estimating the values of that population.

Let's look again at quota sampling. As you will remember, this involves building a sample with the correct proportion of people in each demographic category based on known population figures. In other words, if we know that the population of Gotham City is 60 percent female, 20 percent black, 35 percent over sixty-five years of age, and 40 percent college-educated, we can fish around until we have enough people in the sample in each of these categories to match the population characteristics. Or in other words, we fill quotas. This may sound good, but it doesn't work well, as I've discussed. People in samples will not be representative of all females or all blacks in the population unless they themselves have been randomly selected such that everyone has an equal probability of being selected into the sample.

The use of the word "randomness" in a sampling context is sometimes confusing because it implies a lack of order or systematic process. But "random sampling" is not done in some chaotic, nonthoughtful way. In fact, randomness refers to the way in which respondents are ultimately selected using a very tightly controlled process. As we noted above, randomness in this context is very much like the randomness employed in a state lottery: the process is very exact and precise, with the final selection of the winner done on a basis that ensures that every ticket holder has an equal chance of selection. In similar fashion, a well-done survey sample is conducted such that every member of the population in which the interest lies has an equal chance of falling into the sample.

Let's look at another example. Suppose for a moment that on a fall day in Ann Arbor, there is a stadium full of 100,000 football fans. Some are Michigan fans and are wearing blue. Some are Ohio State fans and are wearing red. The rest, not affiliated with any school, are wearing white. The task is to figure out exactly how many of each of these three categories of fans are in the stadium. Since there isn't time to count every single person, it is decided to take a sample and use the sample to estimate the distribution within the entire stadium.

A lazy researcher starts by walking up a stadium entrance ramp and taking a sample of the first 500 people he or she finds, marking down their clothes color. If it so happens that the researcher stumbles into the middle of the Michigan section, the researcher ends up estimating that 100 percent of the fans are wearing blue. In this procedure, the fans sitting across the field in the Ohio State section had zero probability of falling into the sample, since the sampler was tallying only those close to the portal on the Michigan side of the stadium. This sampling procedure violates the principle of randomness, since not everyone had an equal, and random, chance of falling into the sample. The results are worthless. The same would happen if the lazy researcher stopped everyone going into a portal on the Ohio State side of the stadium.

How could we improve on this process? One way would be to get a list from the Michigan Stadium management of every single seat in the stadium and then employ a purely random selection process in choosing 500 of the seats. Let's assume that the stadium management gives the researcher a long (very long!) piece of paper with 100,000 seats listed one by one down the paper ("section A, row 45, seat 23," etc.). The researcher could choose some random starting point and then select every hundreth seat going down the list, marking each one selected with a pen. When finished, the researcher would have 1,000 of the seats marked. The researcher could then go out into the stadium, with the list of the 1,000 randomly selected seats in hand, go to each seat on the list, and mark down the color of the clothes of the occupant of each. This would work well. Every occupant of every seat in the stadium would have an equal chance of being in the sample selected. Why? Because the pure randomness of selecting the 1,000 seats from the list meant that no one seat was any more or less likely to be chosen than any other. As long as each and every seat was on the list, as long as each seat in the sample was chosen randomly, then each seat is just as likely to be in the sample as any other.

In real estate, the mantra is "location, location, location." In polling, it's "random, random, random." It's hard to emphasize the word too much. Randomness is the key to everything a pollster does when it comes to successful sampling.

## THE LITERARY DIGEST DEBACLE

Let's look back at the example of the *Literary Digest* and Gallup polls in the 1930s because it highlights some of the problems that can occur if the pollster is not extremely careful to use principles of random sampling. The 1936 presidential election also provided the first powerful example of the accuracy of a scientific approach to sampling.

At that time, the *Literary Digest* magazine had been using a polling technique for a number of years that was built on the concept of accumulating very large samples. The magazine's polls had achieved near mythic status because they had been accurate in predicting the winners of the 1928 and 1932 presidential elections. But that was primarily luck. The magazine's samples did not even begin to approximate random sampling techniques. Indeed, the *Digest* allowed people into its sample if they were included on any of a number of lists of people with telephones and automobiles, or who were subscribers to the magazine. This meant that the large group of people in the 1930s who did not fit these qualifications (poorer people, farmers, and so forth) had zero probability of selection into the sample.

The *Literary Digest* distributed ballot cards to more

than 10 million people in the months prior to the 1936 election. Of these, according to George Gallup's report in his book *The Pulse of Democracy*, 2,376,523 were returned and tabulated. The two primary candidates for the presidency in that year were the incumbent, Franklin D. Roosevelt, a Democrat, and Alf Landon, the Republican candidate. The final *Literary Digest* report "pointed to a resounding Landon victory. The poll indicated that Landon would get some 54 percent of the total vote."[8]

At the same time, George Gallup, along with several other pollsters and market researchers, was involved in developing uses for the power of scientific sampling. Gallup intended for his samples to be truly representative of the population of all citizens of the country. (In truth, there were limitations in Gallup's 1936 sampling methods, some of which came back to haunt him in the now infamous miscall of the 1948 presidential election. But Gallup's foundational assumptions remained sound.) He selected only a few thousand people into his sample—a sharp contrast to the millions in the *Literary Digest* sample. Gallup persuaded a number of newspapers around the country, including the *Washington Post*, to publish his results.

Gallup's samples, which gave many lower-class working people and farmers the type of chances of falling into the sample that the *Digest's* lists did not, predicted that Roosevelt would win. Gallup, of course, was right and today the Gallup poll and others like it that are built on scientific sampling are at the core of the multibillion-dollar polling and marketing research industry. The *Literary Digest*, on the other hand, fell into disrepute and went out of business a few years later.

One of the most important points that came out of the 1936 "dueling polls" was the finding that it is the *method* of sampling rather than the size of the sample that matters. The "piling on" of respondents in the *Literary Digest* did no good because the method by which they were sampled was not random. It didn't matter if there were hundreds of thousands or millions of individuals included in the sample if they were selected incorrectly. Not every voter had an equal chance of falling into the *Digest* sample, so the end result was a sample that was not representative of the population from which it was drawn.

This same principle of the primacy of the method of selection over the size of a sample holds today, particularly in light of the ease with which samples of individuals on the Internet can be compiled in large numbers. It is nothing to have tens of thousands of individuals "voting" on the Internet, and these large numbers are often used, as they were in the *Literary Digest* example, to justify their accuracy. There was then, and is now, an appeal to large numbers that has nothing to do with their accuracy. *Big numbers of people in a sample mean very little.*

How large do samples need to be, then, to accurately represent the population from which they are drawn? Assuming that a sample is drawn randomly, its chances of accurately representing the population from which it is drawn does increase as it (the sample) becomes larger. At the upper extreme, if a sample consisted of all the elements of the population, it would reflect perfectly the characteristics of the population because it would consist of each and every element of the population. At the other extreme, the characteristics of a sample of five elements drawn from a large population would have a very low probability of accurately representing the characteristics of the population from which it is drawn.

Still, very large samples are for the most part not necessary. Statisticians have shown that sample sizes of 1,000 or even smaller—if drawn randomly—have quite high probabilities of representing the population from which they are drawn accurately, regardless of the size of that population. Above a certain point, the increased accuracy that results from the time and expense of increasing sample size is minimal. Doubling the size of a randomly selected sample from 1,000 to 2,000, for example, would essentially double the sampling cost and time, but would decrease the margin of error associated with such a sample only minimally (from a 3 percent margin of error to 2 percent margin of error). This is why most national polls in the United States are based on samples of sizes between 1,000 and 1,500. Samples of this size represent the most efficient trade-off between the need for accuracy on the one hand and time and expense on the other.

The key to sampling is the development of a procedure that allows every element in the population of interest to have an equal chance of being selected into the sample. If this procedure is followed, the resulting sample can be generalized to the population within known margin-of-error limitations.

1. George Gallup and Saul Forbes Rae, *The Pulse of Democracy* (New York: Simon & Schuster, 1940), 213.

2. George Gallup, *The Sophisticated Poll Watcher's Guide*, rev. ed. (Ephrata, Pa.: Science Press, 1976), 45.

3. *USA Today*, November 4, 2002.

4. Gallup and Rae, *Pulse of Democracy*, 49.

5. Ibid., 57.

6. Jonathan Weiner, *The Beak of the Finch: A Story of Evolution in Our Time* (1994; repr., New York: Vintage Books, 1995).

7. "Stripes Reporters Visited Nearly 50 Camps in Iraq to Gauge Sentiment," *Stars and Stripes* Web site October 15, 2003, http://www.stripes.com/article.asp?section=104&article=17458&archive=true.

8. Gallup and Rae, *Pulse of Democracy*, 43.

# CHAPTER 8

# Lists and Elections

When pollsters talk about sampling, they have a special place of reverence in their hearts for lists. Lists, more technically called sampling frames, are everything to a sampler. In general, at some point in almost every situation in which a sample is developed to represent a population, there is a list involved. If there is a good list of the entire population to which the researcher wants to refer, then the sampling comes easy. When there is no known list of elements (people, households, areas, times of day, locations, phone exchanges) that relate to the population being studied, then the sample usually becomes haphazard rather than random, and loses its ability to be statistically representative of the population from which it is drawn.

The most accessible lists are those that include every member of the population under consideration. This dream situation (a dream situation for the survey sampler at any rate!) occurs, for example, when the population being studied consists solely of employees at a company, or customers of a company, or students at a school, or registered voters in a specific voting district. For example, in the case of surveying people in the Michigan football stadium, one would need a list of every person in every single seat. If a researcher has a list, then the sampling task becomes relatively straightforward. The sampler selects an appropriate number of people from the list using a random selection procedure and gets started.

How does such a random selection procedure work? The researcher can use what is called a systematic random sampling technique and select every tenth or twentieth or hundreth person on the list. Or, if every person on a list is represented by a number, the sampler uses a random number table or random number generator to select numbers one at a time, each number representing a person, until the requisite number of individuals have been chosen to be in the sample. (This is similar to how state lotteries work when balls are selected randomly.) These procedures give every person on the initial list an equal probability of falling into the final sample as long as every person's number is as likely to be chosen as any other. (Random number tables are just what the name suggests—a long list of randomly selected digits. Believe it or not, statisticians spent a great deal of time in past years figuring out ways to select numbers randomly. Most statistics textbooks have tables of purely random numbers in the back. Now computer programs easily accomplish this procedure, and many pocket calculators have random number generators.)

The element of randomness is valuable to the survey researcher for a couple of reasons. First, it ensures that there is no bias or tilt of the selection procedure such that one type of person is more likely to be selected than another. This is a real key; random sampling means there is no human intervention in the choosing process, no subtle efforts to "balance" a sample. Everything is done by chance. Second, randomness places the relationship between the sample and the population from which it was drawn into the realm of a specific set of mathematical relationships that have been very carefully studied over the years by statisticians. Entire classes of statistical theories have been developed to describe the *sample to population* relationships when the principle of randomness is employed. Because a sample is randomly selected, its relationship to the population from which it is drawn shares mathematical properties with all other samples that are selected randomly using an equal-probability-of-selection procedure. These shared characteristics allow the statistician to estimate how representative the sample is of the population from which it is drawn, using probabilities. These theories, applied to a specific situation, are what enable the statistician to make the "margin of error" estimates that are so often associated with samples (for example, plus or minus 5 percent). These are not guesses, nor are they estimates derived solely from the specific sample under consideration. Rather, they are estimates based on mathematical theory.

This famous margin-of-error figure is probably one of the most common uses of statistics seen by the average American, and I'm often asked about it. Here's a good way to look at it. When statisticians practice by drawing samples from populations using random sampling procedures over and over again, they discover that sample proportions are representative of the population proportions most of the time—but not all of the time. For example, if the female proportion of a population is 50 percent, random samples will usually be *about* 50 percent female— sometimes a little more, sometimes a little less, but usually within a range that can be quantified. That normal error range is what is encapsulated in the margin-of-error statistic. A margin of error of 4 percent associated with an estimate of the percent female in a survey sample, for example, means that the proportion of females in the actual population should be within plus or minus 4 percent of the sample proportion most of the time. Technically, we're saying that the population percentage (if it had been possible to interview everyone in the population) would usually be within a specific range around the estimate provided by the sample. In some aberrant cases (usually five out of one hundred), the sample, even though it is drawn using epsem, will be off more than 5 percent compared to the population from which it is drawn. The calculations of these margins of error are associated with sample size (although a variety of other factors go into the calculation as well). The larger the sample, up to a point, the higher the chances that the sample will be representative of the population from which it is drawn.

## WHAT IF LISTS AREN'T AVAILABLE?

All of this calculating is based on the principle of drawing a simple random sample from a population using a list of all elements of the larger population. Alas, sampling is often not that easy. Many public opinion projects focus on the general population of the United States. There are more than 200 million adults (eighteen and over) living in the country today. Unfortunately for those of us in the polling business, there are not, even in this age of computerized databases, good lists of every citizen in the United States. This lack of a list of every adult (perhaps a good thing for those who worry about privacy and a Big Brother government) was true some sixty years ago, when survey research first started, and is still the case today. There is simply not one easily available registry of every adult American.

The next best thing to a list of every single citizen of this country is a list of every single dwelling unit in the country. If such a list is available, pollsters can randomly sample dwelling units and then select people to interview within each. As long as most citizens live in dwelling units (as opposed to living in the woods or on the street) and as long as the list of dwelling units is complete, then the sampling process works.

Dwelling units in the United States typically have at least two unique identifiers: a street address, including place-name and zip code, and a telephone number, including area code.

Most poll interviewing today is done via the telephone, and use of the telephone number is thus the most common method of sampling households. When survey research began in the 1930s, most researchers were smart enough to realize that telephone lists, even if available, would not follow true epsem principles because a significant proportion of the country did not have individual residential phones. The type of error associated with a sampling frame that does not include all of the elements of the population helped cause the problems with the *Literary Digest*'s estimates in the 1936 election. Thus, when polling started out in a big way in the 1930s, pollsters eschewed the phone and primarily used face-to-face interviews conducted within people's houses. The initial goal of survey researchers became, therefore, figuring out ways of sampling dwelling units. What pollsters really wanted was a simple list of every single American household in the country, which would have allowed them, in some theoretical sense, to select 1,000 or 2,000 of these at random.

However, such a list did not exist. No one had (or even has today, for that matter) a complete list of every dwelling unit in the country, including all houses, apartments, condos, and farms. Furthermore, using a simple random selection procedure with such a list, even if it did exist, would create significant logistical problems for the researcher doing in-person interviews. A random sample drawn from a single (very long) list of all households in America would result in a list of selected households spread out all over the country, from coast to coast and from border to border. The process of sending interviewers to each of these locations (a farm in Iowa, an apartment in Manhattan, a house in Phoenix, etc.) would be daunting, requiring interviewers to drive hundreds of miles in order to find each individual household that fell into the sample. So pollsters in essence killed two birds with one stone by developing ways of approximating a comprehensive list by breaking the country into chunks and then sampling randomly from each.

Pollsters started with the assumption that every person in the country lives in an exhaustive and mutually exclusive geographic unit of some kind. In other words, each person lives in a geographic unit that does not cross with any other geographic unit, and all of these geographic units ultimately cover the entire country. One example of such geographic units would be states, which are exhaustive (every square inch of the country is in some state or in the District of Columbia) and mutually exclusive (no state is part of any other state). Another set of geographic units would be counties (or parishes in Louisiana). With rare exceptions (such as St. Louis and cities in Virginia), every dwelling unit in the country resides in one and only one county, and the counties are not part of other counties. In fact, the county is an excellent choice for use as the beginning, or primary, sampling unit in survey research. There are about three thousand counties in the United States and it is easy to obtain a list of all of these counties and then to select randomly from them. Although there are other geographic units used as the basis for sampling systems (townships, census enumeration districts, etc.), I'll use the county as the basis for the discussion that follows.

As a starting point, the researcher would randomly select a set of counties from the list of all counties in the U.S. Because counties vary widely in terms of population, most statisticians vary the probability of a county being selected based on its population. But, in the end, if done correctly, each and every county would have a known probability of falling into the sample. Since every person lives in a county, then every person has an equal or known chance of having his or her county selected.

Once this smaller random subset of counties has been selected, the researcher is faced with the problem of sampling *within* the county. If Loving County, Texas, were selected, this would be an easy chore, since there are less than one hundred people living in that entire West Texas county. One would simply get the address list of these one hundred residents and sample from that. If Harris County, Texas, were selected, on the other hand, there would be problems, because there are more than 3 million people living there (Harris County includes Houston and its suburbs). For this reason, most researchers using face-to-face interviewing continue the process by subdividing counties into smaller exhaustive and mutually exclusive geographic units that can form the basis for additional random sampling. These are usually census tracts or rural farm units.

At this last stage, there are usually additional problems, because there may not be lists of every household within a selected geographic unit. Here, researchers in the beginning days of sampling became creative. In some instances, the researcher sent out enumerators to create lists of every household within the geographic unit, often by actually walking the streets and drawing maps showing the location of every unit. The sampling was then conducted based on these maps. Sometimes the researcher used some type of "on location" random selection procedure to sample a specific household within the universe of all households within a geographic unit. For example, interviewers were sometimes told to go to a certain street corner and select the houses in which the interviews were to be conducted based on the directions of the compass (for example, the first house on the southwest corner of Elm and Main Streets).

In fact, much of the interviewing at Gallup through the 1980s involved variations of these procedures. Samplers would labor long and hard over maps, randomly selecting what they called primary sampling units (the census tracts or farm units) to which they would send their interviewers. Gallup interviewers could be seen on street corners around the country, figuring out how best to randomly select a house or apartment in which to conduct their assigned interviews.

It is interesting to note that Gallup's major study of the residents of Baghdad in the late summer of 2003 used these same sampling techniques. Baghdad was divided into a series of exhaustive and mutually exclusive *gadha*, which in turn were divided into neighborhoods called *nahiyas*. Gallup ended up randomly sampling 122 *nahiyas*, and interviewers were assigned to conduct interviews in randomly selected dwelling units within each.

These sampling procedures all involve at least three stages: selecting a big geographic unit from all geographic units in the United States, selecting a smaller geographic unit randomly from within the big geographic units sampled, and finally, randomly selecting households within these smaller units.

Statisticians document that as long as each step includes random selection, the end result is a random sample. The use of randomness as the basis for individual selection means that the probabilities associated with getting a sample that is representative can be calculated, which therefore allows the social scientist to better estimate the sample's accuracy.

These procedures were used—albeit in some cases in rough form—by George Gallup and others who did the in-person samples that formed the basis for polling done from the 1930s through the 1980s. At that point, operational procedures changed as most polls made the transition to use of the telephone.

## ENTER THE TELEPHONE

The movement to telephone sampling marked the biggest change yet in modern polling. Although everyone involved in survey research had recognized the potential of telephone samples almost from the beginning of the active use of polls in this country, researchers began to contemplate telephone surveys seriously only after the penetration of phones into the homes of Americans reached a reasonably high percentage. This occurred in the 1960s and 1970s. By the 1980s, telephone surveys became the most prevalent form of survey research in the United States.

One seemingly significant advantage of telephone surveys would appear to be the fact that telephone books provide lists of telephone numbers. This works well up to a point. But it was quickly brought to the attention of samplers that the use of telephone books as the basic list or sampling frame for polls had one major flaw: a good percentage of telephone numbers were unlisted, either because the households paid to have their numbers kept out of the books or because persons moved or missed out on the telephone book publishing deadline. In fact, unlisted phone numbers are remarkably prevalent in the United States today. Survey Sampling, Inc., a firm that provides samples for market and public opinion research companies, suggests that up to 30 percent of households in the United States are unlisted in the white pages of their local phone book. To make matters worse, the distribution of unlisted telephone numbers varies significantly across geographic areas. At one point in the late 1990s, Survey Sampling estimated that well over half of all residential phones in a number of cities in California were not listed in the local white pages. This included an unbelievable 72 percent of all households in Sacramento, named by Survey Sampling as having the highest unlisted percentage out of the country's top one hundred metropolitan areas. At the other end of the spectrum, Sarasota, Florida, was listed by Survey Sampling as the major metropolitan area with the lowest percent of households with unlisted numbers— only 7 percent. Other metropolitan areas with very low unlisted rates are Minneapolis–St. Paul, Little Rock, and Providence, Rhode Island.

Any sample that uses only listed numbers will be significantly skewed toward those areas with the highest percentage of listed numbers. As the figures listed above attest, using listed numbers would give residents in an area like Sarasota or Minneapolis a high chance of falling into the sample. Residents living in Sacramento would have a much lower chance. In fact, based on the above, about 70 percent of the residents of Sacramento would have a zero probability of falling into the sample. There are also issues relating to the fact that people with unlisted numbers might have a different socioeconomic status than people with listed numbers (research suggests that unlisted households tend to be more downscale than listed households).

The use of telephone book lists, in short, violates the epsem rule because people with distinctive geographic or demographic characteristics could have unequal probabilities of falling into the sample.

All of this left samplers in a quandary. Although listings of phone numbers are easily available, there is no published or available list of all residential phone numbers *including unlisted numbers*. (Phone companies will not release unlisted numbers.) What to do?

A solution was soon forthcoming. Innovative statisticians knew that every residential phone number is composed of three parts: the area code, the exchange (the three digits that follow the area code), and the four digits that finish out the number. (Each area code in a phone exchange can have ten thousand numbers associated with it, starting with 0000 and ending with 9999.) For example, the phone number 212-555-1234 has a 212 area code, a 555 exchange, and 1234 as the final digits.

All area codes and exchanges are in the public domain. In other words, it is easy to find every area code in the United States and every phone exchange assigned to that area code. Using that information, it is possible to sample all area code/exchange combinations, which if specified correctly would include the first six digits of every phone number in America. By definition, every household has to have a phone number that is built off of one of these area codes and exchanges. Even if a phone number is unlisted, its area code and exchange are known. (The phone company assigns unlisted phone numbers within "blocks" of residential phone numbers and does not "reserve" area code/exchange combinations just for unlisted numbers— at least not yet.)

Statisticians figured out that within any given area code and exchange combination, there are only ten thousand possible combinations of the last four digits, ranging from 0000 to 9999. Take the area code 212 and the exchange 555 within that area code, for example. Ten thousand possible numbers could be assigned to that exchange within that area code, beginning with 212-555-0000 and ending with 212-555-9999. A computer can thus create a simple listing of every possible phone number in every exchange. More broadly, it follows that the computer can create a listing of every possible phone number in every area code/exchange combination in the country. This provides the researcher with the basis for an equal-probability-of-selection procedure, since—if a random sampling procedure is used to select numbers from this very long list of all possible phone numbers—every existing residential phone would theoretically have an equal probability of selection into the sample. Using the example above, even if the 212-555-1234 phone number was unlisted, it would have the same probability of being selected into a sample as any other phone number because its 212-555 area code/exchange combination would have the same probability of being selected as any other area code/exchange combination. If the 212-555 combination were selected randomly, the computer would randomly generate the final four digits, thus giving the 212-555-1234 number a random one in ten thousand probability of selection. Of course, many of these "created" phone numbers would not be working numbers, but that wouldn't matter. Each live number would still have an equal chance of falling into the sample.

This basic procedure, now used in one way or the other to create most telephone samples, has come to be called random digit dialing, or RDD, because the digits that form the last part of the phone numbers in the sample are selected randomly. There are complications, of course. The procedure allows unlisted and new numbers to be selected with the same probability as listed numbers, but it does not distinguish between working and nonworking numbers, or between business numbers and residential numbers. RDD can thus be inefficient, because large amounts of time are spent calling numbers that are not residences or not working at all. Thus, statisticians developed ways of generating phone numbers using RDD that result in a more efficient sample with a higher "hit" rate of real working residential phone numbers.

One of the first things samplers recognized was that the efficiency of an RDD sample would be improved if exchanges could be winnowed down to just those with active residential "blocks" of phone numbers. In other words, if 212-555 is an exchange known to have residential phone numbers attached to it, then attaching random numbers to the 212-555 combination would have a much higher probability of actually coming up with residential phone numbers than would attaching random numbers to other area code/exchange combinations with no (or few) known residential numbers.

The refinements continued. It was found that phone companies will not only provide lists of area codes and exchanges but also provide estimates of how many residential phone numbers there are (out of the maximum of ten thousand) in each area code/exchange combination. Thus, the pollster can refine the sampling a little by assigning each area code/exchange combination somewhat different probabilities of selection based on the estimated number of actual residential phone numbers in that exchange.

Another practice used by pollsters at times in the past was to select a random sample of all *listed* phone numbers and then to drop the last two digits from the "real" phone numbers and add two new digits, thus creating a new number with randomly assigned final digits. This procedure helped increase the chances that the randomly generated number would be a working residence rather than a nonworking number. As late as the 1980s, many research firms bought telephone books from the telephone company and had huge stacks of them in their sampling departments. These firms determined the percentage of interviews that needed to be completed from various geographic areas (using data from the U.S. census), randomly selected phone numbers from the appropriate area's phone books, and added two "new" digits to the end of the selected phone numbers. I can remember samplers sitting in rooms surrounded by phone books, randomly selecting pages from the books and then randomly selecting listings from the pages, patiently writing the selected numbers down on their sample sheets.

Firms that prepare and market telephone samples also attempt to keep the sampled numbers as close to real residential exchanges as possible by using ways of "cleaning" or purging nonresidential numbers before the survey interviewers actually begin calling them. In some instances, automatic dialers call every number before it is released to be in a sample in order to eliminate those that the computer picks up as being nonworking.

There is little question that these procedures have allowed statisticians to do a surprisingly accurate job of generating samples of residential phone numbers that represent, within known error limitations, the entire population of all residential phone numbers in the United States. RDD procedures are fascinating and complex; they work extremely well and have become the backbone of survey research today.

There are other methods of sampling and polling that are used with some frequency. One of these is the old standby the mail survey, and the other is a newcomer to the field, the Internet survey.

## Mail Surveys

Mail surveys are straightforward. A survey is sent in the mail, the respondent fills out the survey in the privacy of his or her own home, and mails it back. Mail surveys are considered useful when the researcher needs to get a great deal more information in more precise ways than might be possible with the traditional telephone survey. Questions and complex concepts can be presented visually, and the pollster can get answers to questions that might take a while to answer or require looking up data.

Many readers of this book may recall getting very long mail surveys that ask the respondents to enumerate their use of a long list of services and products. I received a long mail survey from *Consumer Reports* that not only asked me to list all of my cars and household appliances but also to rate each one in terms of satisfaction, reliability, and so forth. This type of detailed information would generally be impossible to obtain by phone, unless the respondent was willing to spend hours carrying a portable phone around the house and going from room to room, finding the relevant data.

But the advantages of mail surveys have to be traded off against some major problems. For one thing, they take longer. We routinely conduct telephone surveys in three or four nights. There is relatively little preparation time, since the questionnaire can be put up on the computer screens of the interviewers as soon as the final questions are determined. Once the interviewing is completed, the data are available within minutes. Mail surveys, on the other hand, require a lot of preparation. Even after the questions are finalized, the survey has to be laid out and typeset, the documents have to be printed, the surveys have to be mailed, and respondents have to be given a reasonable amount of time to fill them out and mail them back. Then the usual mail survey involves several follow-up steps in which postcards and other reminders are sent out to maximize the number of surveys returned. All in all, it usually takes months to complete a mail survey, as opposed to days for telephone surveys.

There are also problems of interview control. One advantage to a telephone survey (or the old-fashioned in-person survey, for that matter) is that the respondent can ask for questions to be repeated. Interviewers can also make sure that the respondent is answering the correct question at the right time. Mail surveys, on the other hand, are completely under the control of the respondent, and if he or she doesn't want to fill in half of the questions, there isn't anything that can be done about it at the time. And if the respondent has a problem, there's no one to ask about it, unless he or she calls an 800 number.

Another problem with mail surveys that are used to represent all of the people in a given population area revolves around the difficulty of getting a full sampling frame (list) that gives every residential household within the United

States an equal probability of falling into the sample. This is the same problem that plagued in-person surveys earlier in the last century. There is no shortage of mailing lists, including many lists that contain millions of names. These lists are collated, merged, and cherry-picked in great detail. There are lists of almost every type of person imaginable, sometimes culled down to extremely precise categories. A business interested in selling expensive fruit-cakes through the mail, for example, might merge and purge lists until it had developed a list of high-income households that had previously purchased food by mail. But the pollster is more usually interested in a list of *all* households, not just the ones with particular characteristics. The best list available of all mailing addresses in the United States comes from—not surprisingly—the U.S. Postal Service. It claims to have a list of most postal addresses in the country but acknowledges that the list is probably short about 10 million households out of the 100 million or so in the country.

There's still another problem with mail surveys, and that's low response rates. I'll talk more below about response rate issues as they relate to telephone surveys, but mail surveys are, generally speaking, easier to throw away and ignore than phone surveys. The researcher has to mail out many mail surveys to get back the number needed. That's why some mail surveys include cash or prize incentives to try to increase cooperation.

Researchers interested in conducting mail surveys to represent the general population of America sometimes use what we call a multimode procedure. Samplers generally agree that telephone sampling is the best way to make sure that all households in the country have an equal chance of falling into a sample. And, as I noted, response rates are generally higher. So alert pollsters sometimes conduct a telephone sample first and then use it as the basis for a mail survey, as a second step. This procedure uses two modes of sampling; hence the name "multi-mode." I've used this procedure in conducting research projects for major-market newspapers that wanted to capture a great deal of specific information.

All of the various polling methods attempt to generalize to all Americans. If one has a more defined population, such as all subscribers to a magazine, or all members of an organization, then mail surveys can work very well, since the sample can be derived from randomly selecting from these total population lists. The *Consumer Reports* survey, for example, was sent to me because I subscribe to the magazine. I wasn't selected randomly; I was a part of a total census mailing of all subscribers to *Consumer Reports*.

## INTERNET SURVEYS

Many see the Internet as the great hope for the future of polling. Everyone agrees that it has tremendous potential. Pollsters look covetously at the Internet because of the ease and economy with which it allows surveys to be conducted. Millions of people representing all sorts of backgrounds are online on the Internet every minute, and it seems reasonable that if we can just get some of these people to fill out surveys, we will have an instant (and for the most part free) way to gauge public opinion.

It's no wonder that the past five years have seen a number of polling firms jump into the Internet arena and attempt to develop procedures for sampling on the Internet. Many of these firms claim that it is just a matter of time before the Internet becomes the dominant method of polling around the world, and they may be right. Indeed, the Internet can be a wonderful tool for use in interviewing, but only when two criteria are met. First, every person in the population of interest should have access to the

Internet so that they have a theoretical chance of being selected into the sample. And second, there need to be ways
to sample from the population so that every person in the
population has an equal or known probability of being selected into the sample.

We at Gallup have found that these criteria are met, for
example, when our goal is to interview a particular company's employees. As long as each employee has an e-mail
address and is an active user of e-mail, it is a simple matter either to send the survey questionnaire to every employee or to a random sample of the known list of
employees.

However, it is very difficult to meet these two criteria
when the goal is to generalize to the population of the
United States. One problem is the stark fact that a significant proportion of the United States population does not
use the Internet on a regular basis. Our 2003 estimate, in
fact, is that about 68 percent of Americans have access to
the Internet at home or at work. When we ask Americans
if they have an active e-mail address, the number drops to
48 percent. And we don't know if even those with e-mail
addresses use them regularly. Almost everyone checks his
or her U.S. Postal Service mailbox every day and answers
the phone when it rings. Having an e-mail address, on the
other hand, doesn't mean that a person actually accesses it
every day.

Any attempt to use the Internet as the basis for a sample that is intended to be generalized to the entire United
States population has to reckon with these facts. It would
be comparable to the situation that pertained many years
ago when 40 percent or more of Americans did not have
phones. Pollsters did not use a telephone survey methodology until phone penetration claimed well above 90 percent. Some pollsters claim that the Internet should not be
used for surveys intended to generalize to the entire popu-

lation until active Internet use also climbs above 90 percent.

The second problem with the use of the Internet for polling is just as significant. There is no known list of all e-mail addresses, which in the Internet world are the counterpart to telephone numbers. No one has been able to collect millions of addresses into one big comprehensive directory. The researcher thus has no way of developing a basic list to use for selecting a random sample. (There is no shortage of lists of e-mail addresses available for sale or rent, but most of these have been kludged together from a wide variety of sources and have no pretense of being a total list of all possible e-mail addresses across the country.) Additionally, many Americans have multiple e-mail addresses, and many change their e-mail addresses quite frequently. Our own research shows that 76 percent of Americans who have Internet access have two or more separate e-mail addresses, and 22 percent have five or more. Trying to create a true sampling frame that lists each American's e-mail address only once, so that each person has an equal chance of being selected into the sample, is simply impossible.

Nonetheless, these problems have not stopped some researchers from attempting to use the Internet as the basis for polls of the general population. Some firms simply put together e-mail lists from any available source. It doesn't involve great expense for researchers to ask for the e-mail addresses of individuals prowling the Web who can be persuaded to make themselves available to participate in surveys. But piling up huge numbers of e-mail addresses by trolling around on the Net and asking for participation in no shape or form resembles a procedure that gives everyone with an e-mail address an equal chance of being selected into a sample. The self-selection of individuals onto Internet lists violates the epsem principle because the probabilities of inclusion for any given person are not equal.

Some polling firms have modified their Internet sampling procedures by using quota sampling. We discussed quota sampling in the preceding chapter. In a nutshell, quota sampling assumes that if the numbers of people in various demographic categories are proportionate to the numbers in the general population in those same categories, then the resulting sample is representative of the general population. Given that millions of e-mail addresses are available on the Internet, it doesn't take much effort for researchers to query potential survey participants about their demographic characteristics and then to use this information to fill in a series of quotas. In other words, researchers can select people with specific demographic characteristics and thus create a sample that mimics the characteristics of the underlying population.

The problem is that even though this type of quota sampling can correct some obvious problems with a sample (if a sample is skewed toward the East Coast, for example, or toward younger respondents), the people in the sample within each of the categories still don't necessarily represent all of the people with that characteristic in the broad population. It doesn't do much good to have precisely 12 percent black respondents in a sample if these blacks are not representative of the blacks in the large population. This would be true, for example, if an e-mail sample of 12 percent blacks contained mostly upscale, highly educated black Americans who not only had Internet access but also were willing to volunteer to take part in an interviewing project. The researcher could assert that his or her sample was appropriately balanced because it had the representative proportion of blacks, but since the black sample was not selected so that every black in the country had an equal chance of falling into that sample, the results would in many ways be no more useful than if the researcher had simply gone into one town or one state and selected enough blacks to fill his or her quota in just that location. I've talked about this in previous sections of this book; quota sampling techniques simply do not ensure that a sample ends up being representative of the total population it is supposed to represent.

In many ways, the fact that the Internet allows the researcher to pile up huge numbers of individuals in a sample is reminiscent of the *Literary Digest* debacle seventy years ago. If there is one principle that researchers have learned, it is that the number of elements in a sample is not nearly as important as the way in which those elements are selected. Internet samples of millions of people aren't worth much if they are not representative of the populations they are being used to describe.

There is a method of using the Internet for sampling that more closely follows correct sampling theory. A team of researchers connected with Stanford University in California, Knowledge Networks, Inc., came up with a variant of the multimode method that gets around the problem of excluding households with no e-mail access. They use standard telephone sampling techniques to generate a random probability sample of all U.S. households. Once they obtain this sample, they ask the households selected if they can have permission to install a Web TV operation in their home; that is, install equipment that will enable them to use e-mail whether or not they have Internet access or not. If the household consents, they are given a system that allows the residents to respond on demand to surveys, and this in turn results in a projectable random sample of all households in the country. This method has been used in some European countries, and it mimics the model used by the Nielsen television ratings.

This procedure has significant promise but also has potential drawbacks. There is a great deal of cost involved, which creates very high barriers of entry and limits the number of survey firms that can use the technique. Second, there is a well-known test-retest phenomenon that dictates that the very act of testing someone may have an impact on future results if that individual is retested. If people have an e-mail connection installed in their home purely for the sake of enabling them to answer surveys, and if those surveys deal with current events, then it wouldn't be implausible that these individuals would find themselves boning up on current events, thereby becoming less like the "normal" people they were expected to represent. This would be particularly true if the respondent was a participant in this type of system for a year or more.

Where do we at Gallup stand when it comes to Internet surveys? The Internet obviously has great promise as an efficient and inexpensive way to conduct research, but at this time there isn't a simple way to ensure that every American has a known or equal chance of being selected into an Internet sample. As far as general population studies are concerned, the promise of the Internet is still largely unfulfilled, and Gallup does not use it for our standard national polling.

## RESPONSE RATES

Survey response rates have become a hot topic. A number of articles written after the November 2002 midterm elections focused on Senate races in which preelection polls did not forecast the correct winner, and blamed these miscalls on declining response rates. Columnist, pundit, author, and polling critic Arianna Huffington created a cottage industry of sorts in the late 1990s and early 2000s by "exposing" the low response rates obtained by survey researchers as a fatal flaw in contemporary polling.

A lot of this discussion was and is misinformed and inaccurate. In fact, the preelection polls in 2002 were quite accurate. The issue of declining response rates has been studied and restudied for years by survey scientists, and to date there is little evidence that lower response rates (per se) are having an appreciably negative effect on the reliability or viability of most survey results. Still, I think it is important to discuss this important area of concern and to understand the implications of declining response rates on the quality of poll results.

Let's put response rate issues in the context of the entire survey research process, which, at its most basic, involves proceeding from large groups to small groups in a series of steps. The largest group is the population whose characteristics the process is designed to estimate. The smallest group is the final sample from which interviews are collected. Everything about the poll process involves going from the small sample to the large population. The final sample of interviews that pollsters report is—as we have noted again and again in this book—incredibly small compared to the huge population from which it is drawn. If everything is done right, this small sample does a very good job of representing the big whole. But the research process involves continually shrinking sample sizes.

The first step in the survey process is drawing an initial random sample from a population. This sample is only a fraction of the size of the population and is drawn such that it is statistically representative of the overall population. So at the very beginning of the process, we move from very large to very small, right off the bat. At this point, several additional steps occur that continue to reduce the size of what we are dealing with. The final sample we end up using is almost always a smaller subset of the first sample (which in turn, of course, is much, much smaller than the original population we start with).

We define "response rate," crudely, as the ratio of the size of the initial sample to the size of the final sample. The focus of all the attention has been on this ratio, with the implication that the failure to complete interviews with everyone in the initially drawn sample discredits the final results. But this difference between the number of elements in the initial sample and the number of interviews in the final sample isn't fatal to the survey process as long as the principles of randomness and equal probability of selection are preserved. We've already gone from a very large population to a very small sample when we draw the initial sample. In theory, it shouldn't hurt us to reduce the sample a little more as is almost always necessary.

There are a variety of reasons why an initial sample usually contains phone numbers that don't end up being used in the final sample. For one thing, as I discussed earlier, basic telephone samples often contain nonworking numbers and businesses. Also, in today's environment they increasingly include phone numbers used for faxes and computers and not for general household use. These numbers have to be thrown out. Second, it is often not possible to conduct an interview with every household that falls into the basic sample because not every household can be contacted (for example, the persons who live there may be on an extended vacation during the interviewing period or they may be always on the phone). Third, some individuals contacted in a sample refuse to be interviewed.

Let's look at this process in detail. We assume that a small group (the initial sample) is selected randomly from the large population to which the results are to be generalized. For purposes of illustration, assume that this initial sample consists of 2,000 households, selected using accepted principles of random probability sampling. (Again, these 2,000 are selected to be representative of 100 million households across America.) The next step is to contact these 2,000 households. A percentage of them will fall out of the sample because they are businesses or nonworking numbers. Perhaps we have 400 nonworking numbers, reducing the effective sample size to only 1,600 numbers.

Then, of those 1,600, another 400 households may be un-reachable in the time frame allocated by the researcher. These phone numbers may be busy, may be numbers used for faxes or computer modems only, or may have caller ID or another screening device that lowers the chances that a live person will answer the phone. So now the sample is down to 1,200 phone numbers. Assume that a live person answers at each of these 1,200 households. But perhaps 200 of those live persons will refuse to participate in the interview. This brings the sample down to the 1,000 tele-phone numbers that comprise the final sample.

So we have moved from the target population (which in the usual case for the Gallup poll consists of more than 200 million people) to a sample of 2,000. And from that sample of 2,000, we have moved to a sample of 1,600 be-cause we had to throw out businesses and nonworking numbers. We then reduced that sample even further, to 1,200, as a result of being unable to reach 400 house-holds. Finally, we ended up with 1,000 people with whom we actually completed interviews.

Theoretically, each of these steps is okay. Our goal is to end up with a sample that is representative of the popula-tion, and this can be accomplished by maintaining the ran-domness of the process at each step. Statisticians tell us that a random sample of a random sample is still random.

Our response rate in the situation I've outlined above is 50 percent. Why? Because 50 percent of those in our *ini-tial* sample ended up in the *final* sample from which inter-views were obtained. But remember that our real ratio of the final sample to the total population, of course, is much, much smaller—about 0.0000000006 (that is, the ratio of 1,000 to the 200 million they are designed to rep-resent). Our concern is not the response rate per se, but keeping the final sample representative of the larger pop-ulation from which it comes. A low response rate does not necessarily mean that a survey's results are unrepresentative; the potential problems with survey accuracy are not necessarily exacerbated by low response rates. The fact that a sample is reduced in size in going from an initial sample to the final sample is of little consequence as long as the opinions of those who answer the questions at the end are not systematically different from those who are unavailable or decline to participate.

Arianna Huffington has implied that if the response rate for a typical sample is 40 percent (meaning that 40 percent of the numbers in a sample resulted in completed interviews), this means that only 40 percent of the total population is represented in a typical sample. This, of course, is faulty reasoning. In fact, much less than 1 percent of the total population is interviewed in a typical sample, and this does not mean that less than 1 percent of the total population is represented in the sample. If all of the people in the total population have an equal chance of falling into the sample, they are all represented. Representativeness is maintained as long as at each point in this sampling process the "large to small" reduction is done randomly.

However, potential problems occur if there is nonresponse *bias*, or a failure of the process at each step to include samples that are representative of the ones from which they are drawn. Nonresponse bias can occur, for example, if a certain type of person is more likely to be infrequently at home or refuses to be interviewed. Again, problems don't occur because the final sample is smaller than the initial sample (a lower response rate), but rather because the people who end up in the final sample are somehow different from those in the initial sample (nonresponse bias). This could happen, for example, if older people were less likely to answer the phone, or if certain types of people were most likely to have telephone screening devices.

In theory, it seems logical that one way to reduce the potential for nonresponse bias is to take steps to ensure that more households in a basic sample wind up being included in the resulting sample of interviews. Some pollsters attempt to "work the sample to death" and continue to call and call and call every number in a sample until an interview is completed with someone at that number. By doing this, the possibility that there is bias resulting from a lower probability of selection for those who are infrequently at home can be reduced. To put it another way, with a twenty-callback design (meaning that every number falling into the sample is called back up to twenty times in an effort to complete an interview), the young single person who is seldom at home gets a chance of falling into the completed pool (because with twenty calls, he or she is more likely to be caught at home) that is more equal to the chance of the older person who is almost always at home (and who is reached on the first call).

Additionally, special efforts can be made to "convert refusals" by assigning interviewers to do nothing but work with people who are reluctant to be interviewed. Government contracts often call for making a high number of attempts to complete interviews with every number in the sample. This takes an enormous amount of time and money, however. Some government surveys may be in the field for months in order to allow time for these procedures. That is all well and good for some types of research, but if we are interested in gauging reactions to fast-breaking news events, keeping surveys in the field for three months just won't work.

Most polls are also weighted at the end of the process so that any obvious discrepancies between the sample's distribution on key demographic characteristics and the known distribution of these characteristics in the population can be adjusted for.

But a lot of these efforts may not matter. Perhaps the most important finding to come out of the research on the response rate issue is this: there is not a lot of evidence of response *bias* in the process, no matter how hard survey scientists look. Most current research shows that lower response rates do not have nearly as much of a general effect on survey results as might have been thought. The compromises brought into the process by the need to move quickly, and thus to accept lower response rates, don't seem to seriously harm the quality or the representativeness of the data in most studies. Therefore, what seems like a problem in theory is hard to prove in practice.

Studies have shown that the results obtained from final samples in studies with low response rates are quite close to those in studies with higher response rates. Recent research suggests that the impact of a lower response rate on data quality is also dependent on the particular question being investigated. There is little impact of low response rates in most cases, as I've noted, although there may be for specific types of questions. Additionally, despite the media focus after the November 2002 midterm election on the miscalls of certain senatorial and gubernatorial races, most preelection polls with relatively low response rates are remarkably accurate in their estimates of the final, actual votes.

So while there is a theoretical justification for attempting to complete interviews with as many people in an initial sample as is possible, the practical research suggests that it may not make a great deal of difference in most cases. Pollsters continue to study the impact of differential response rates very carefully, but it is the belief of most professional survey researchers today that the negative impact of lower survey response rates sounds more dramatic than it really is. In fact, I'm willing to say that there is as big a problem with the misunderstanding of response rates and response bias as there is in the actual problem itself.

## WITHIN HOUSEHOLD SELECTION

All of the sampling procedures outlined above deal with the random selection of households. A second-stage procedure in many polls deals with selecting an individual to talk to once the household has been selected. Interestingly, females are disproportionately likely to answer the phone. That means, of course, that if the pollster simply talks to the first person that answers the phone, the final sample will be disproportionately female.

The issue is usually an important one when the object of the study is to be able to generalize to the population of all *individuals* in the sampled population area. That's in fact the case for almost all polls, which measure such things as presidential job approval, support for new abortion laws, feelings about the economy, and so forth. Occasionally, however, the purpose of the study is to generalize to all *households*, such as a study to find out how many televisions there are in an average household, how many households have a septic system rather than sewer, and so forth. In these studies—in which the characteristics of the household rather than the individual are the objects of attention—it is less important to have one particular individual selected from all eligible individuals in the household. In these situations, any individual who answers the phone can be considered a spokesperson for the household.

When individuals are the focus of a study, on the other hand, the randomly selected household becomes only the first step in a multistage sampling procedure. The next step becomes one of selecting an individual to interview within that household.

The most effective and scientifically reliable way to select one individual from a household is to use what is called a grid system. One famous example is the so-called Kish grid, named after University of Michigan sampler

Leslie Kish, who wrote the definitive textbook on sampling, called, appropriately enough, *Survey Sampling*.[1] (Kish, one of the giants of the polling field, died in 2000.) The Kish grid requires that the researcher ask whoever answers the phone in a household to list every adult in the household by age and by gender. The researcher then quickly uses a random selection device and designates one of the individuals to be the selected respondent who is to be interviewed in the survey. If that person is not home, the interviewer calls back and attempts to schedule an appointment with that person.

As one might imagine, the Kish grid procedure is cumbersome. Its most severe handicap is the fact that it is intrusive and often increases the number of contacted households that refuse to cooperate. Thus, other, less complicated within-household selection procedures have been developed. Most involve shortcuts for selecting an individual randomly, such as asking for the person in the household with the most recent birthday, assumed by statisticians to be a randomly distributed variable.

To further enhance (or complicate) the procedure, the total number of individuals that end up being listed can be used by the researcher to weight the data in the analysis phase, since a household with more than one person in it reduces the probability that someone from that household is selected. In other words, an individual who is the only person living in a household has a 100 percent chance of being selected to be interviewed if that household is chosen randomly. An individual living in a household with two adults has, theoretically, only a 50 percent chance of being selected if his or her household is chosen. Assuming that the two households have an equal probability of being selected, the person living in the two-person household does not have an equal chance of being selected with the individual in the one-person household.

## LISTS AND SCREEN-DOWNS

Most of my discussion here has centered on the attempt to generate a sample that is representative of a general population, such as all of the people who live in a particular state or all of the adult population of the United States. The researcher's task is more challenging when it involves the attempt to obtain a sample of individuals who represent a more specific and tightly delineated population. Members of niche populations are often important to market researchers, whose products are usually targeted at specific types of consumers, but public opinion pollsters in some circumstances also want to focus their interviews on a particular group. In these situations, the sampling process can be daunting.

The big deal, as is the case for any sampling situation, is finding a list. If there is a comprehensive list available, random sampling becomes quite easy. But it's hard to get good lists.

A researcher quickly discovers that there are some lists available for almost every group imaginable: lists of investors with more than a million dollars in the stock market, lists of gay men, lists of individuals who have ordered clothes through catalogs, lists of widowed women, and so forth. Most of these lists have been developed in the world of direct mail and are designed for mailing purposes, containing the names and addresses of people who share specific characteristics, assembled from many different sources. (In fact, the list of potential voters assembled by the *Literary Digest* in the 1920s and 1930s gathered together the names of individuals from a variety of places.) A list of senior citizens, for example, might be developed by using driver's license records in states where these are publicly available, combined with subscribers to *Modern Maturity* magazine, product registration cards, and so forth.

These lists are not usually exhaustive, which means they don't cover every possible person who fits the category of people being analyzed. Indeed, many available lists are useful tools for direct marketers and others who want to target specific types of people, but they are not intended to be statistically representative. In most of these situations, every person in the population under consideration does not have an equal probability of being on the list. Thus, the researcher who wants to generalize to a specific population can't simply obtain such a list and claim that the results can be generalized to the total population the list was designed to represent.

So a problem with attempting to reach specific subgroups of the population (teenagers, seniors, Hispanic women, gay men, citizens who have traveled outside of the country within the past year, and so forth) is the lack of sampling frames (lists) that in theory contain the name and/or phone number of every single person who meets those qualifications.

But statisticians have determined that there are—at least in theory—several clear-cut ways to use a basic household list even when the target is a smaller subpopulation. Most of these are based on the fact that a random sample of a random sample still equals a random sample. That's a mouthful, but it's really quite simple: as long as every member of a small subgroup has an equal chance of falling into a large sample, and if these subgroup members can be randomly selected from the large group, the resulting sample will consist of a random sample of the population in which the pollster is interested.

The simplest way of proceeding along these lines is as follows: The researcher begins with a random sample of a general population and then asks each member of that sample if he or she meets some additional qualification. The resulting group of those who meet the qualification will constitute a random sample of all individuals in the total population who meet the qualification. This works because the basic criterion of sampling—that every member of the target population has an equal chance of falling into the sample—is met.

Suppose the researcher is interested in sampling Americans eighteen to twenty-nine years of age. The researcher first obtains a sample of the general population. If it's a telephone survey this will most likely be based on the RDD procedures I outlined earlier. So far, every eighteen to twenty-nine-year-old in the country has an equal chance of falling into the sample as a derivative of the fact that every individual of *any* age has an equal chance of falling into the sample. Those who are eighteen to twenty-nine constitute roughly 15 percent of the adult (eighteen and older) population. Thus, the assumption is that, everything else being equal, about 15 percent of the sample of the general population is eighteen to twenty-nine years of age. This 15 percent of the sample is a random probability sample of the 15 percent of the *total* population that is eighteen to twenty-nine. Then, if the researcher simply separates out this 15 percent from the 85 percent who are thirty or over, we're left with a true random probability sample of the target population.

This separation process is usually very straightforward. Everyone in the basic sample is simply asked their age, allowing the researcher to separate them into two groups: those who meet the criterion (the 15 percent) and those who don't meet the criterion. This is called a screen-down sampling procedure and is very commonly used.

The one major problem associated with this procedure is the cost involved. A screen-down sampling process involves initial interviews with large numbers of individuals who do not ultimately make it into the final sample. Sampling efficiency is low. The cost of reaching the desired population can be very high. In some situations, it becomes akin to searching for a needle in a haystack. When the subpopulation has what researchers call a low incidence in the general population, it is extremely time-consuming and inefficient to screen through large groups of people in order to find a sample of those with the relevant characteristics. This time and expense increases geometrically rather than arithmetically.

For example, screening for a sample that has a 10 percent incidence in the general population means that one out of every ten individuals spoken to will meet the qualifications, and nine out of ten have to be discarded. Screening for a sample that has a 5 percent incidence means that one out of every twenty people spoken to will meet the qualifications, an increase in effort of a factor of two. Screening for a sample that has only a 2 percent representation in the country means that only one out of every fifty individuals contacted will meet the criteria. This gets extremely expensive.

Researchers interested in asking a sample of Jewish Americans questions about their views on U.S. aid to Israel, for example, would find themselves expending an extraordinary amount of time and energy to winnow down an initial RDD sample to obtain the 2 percent of a national sample who are Jewish. Researchers who are doing a lot of interviewing sometimes "ride" a question at the back of the survey asking if the respondent meets some rare incidence qualification. The sample of those who do meet the qualification can be combined across a number of surveys until a sample of sufficient size is reached. For example, in a typical Gallup poll of 1,000, about 20 individuals will be Jewish. If this religion question is asked at the back of twenty Gallup polls, a sample of 400 Jews would ultimately be developed. If the pollster is able to call them back—which can be a problem in and of itself—you end up with a random probability sample of Jews.

Generally, the screen-down mechanism will work when the incidence of the subgroup being investigated is relatively large, and/or when the researcher has a sufficiently large budget and time frame to work through the necessary screening process.

## HIGH-DENSITY SAMPLING

There are other, more complicated ways of sampling rare populations. The Census Bureau and other research sources indicate that individuals with specific characteristics are often geographically homogenous (they tend to live in the same places). In other words, birds of a feather flock together. Since the coin of the realm in most contemporary sampling is the telephone, another way of saying this is that individuals who share certain characteristics also share phone exchanges. It is known, for example, that blacks tend to be highly represented in some telephone exchanges, while hardly represented at all in others. The same residential segregation also occurs in terms of income or socioeconomic status: certain telephone exchanges across the country (for example, those in Beverly Hills) have high concentrations of those with higher incomes or higher net worth, while other phone exchanges (for example, those in rural Mississippi) have very low concentrations of higher socioeconomic status households.

Statisticians have attempted to work out ways of incorporating this knowledge into their sampling procedures. At its most simple level, samplers can—using census and other data sources—separate out the telephone exchanges known to cover areas with high concentrations of the special population under consideration. When numbers are generated using RDD procedures from these exchanges, the probability of finding individuals with the desired concentrations are high, and the efficiency of the sampling procedure is increased.

In other words, if our object is to sample blacks, we can assemble a sample of certain phone exchanges across the country that are known to have high proportions of blacks in them, and generate the phone numbers we call from them. If our object is to reach high-income households, then we can assemble a sample of phone exchanges that are known to have high proportions of wealthy people in them. And so forth.

The problem with this approach is that individuals with the desired characteristics (in the above example, blacks and those with high incomes) who don't live in homogenous areas have low to zero probabilities of falling into the sample. This can be a particularly critical flaw when the fact of living in homogenous areas is related to the attitudes that are being studied. Blacks living in phone exchange areas with high densities of other blacks may have significantly different life experiences and attitudes than blacks who live in more integrated areas. If we use high-density sampling, then the blacks living in areas in which blacks are not concentrated will have a lower chance of being in the sample.

Pollsters often attempt to overcome these flaws by designing complex two-stage samples and weighting the data. As is often the case, pollsters' decisions to use these procedures come down to trade-offs between money and efficiency on the one hand and the need for adherence to the epsem sampling doctrine on the other.

## OTHER SAMPLING CHALLENGES

The interesting examples of the challenges faced in sampling go on and on. In some polling situations, for example, the target population can become very narrow indeed. That's okay if there are lists readily available to serve as good frames from which potential interview subjects can be selected randomly.

I worked for several years on projects involving a large bank in which we randomly sampled from complete lists of all of the customers of the bank. Thus, our sample representativeness was very good, since we knew that every person in the target population was on the basic list and therefore had an equal probability of falling into our sample. We were thus able to use our samples to generalize to all customers within that particular banking system.

In many situations, there are no lists available. This occurs, for example, when a business does not maintain a record of its customers by name, as is often the case for small-transaction retail businesses such as fast-food restaurants, grocery stores, and gas stations. In these situations, the researcher searches for another sampling technique. For example, if the researcher is interested in reaching a sample of the entire population of individuals who have purchased fast food at any restaurant across the country within the past month, then a screen-down from the total national population may work. If such a class of customers in the overall population is relatively rare, or if the researcher is interested in generalizing to the customers of just one particular fast-food chain, then the screen-down procedure becomes less reasonable. The researcher has to find other ways of obtaining a sample of customers.

One way that researchers obtain such samples is to begin by envisioning the population not as cross-sectional lists on paper, but in terms of a population doing certain things at certain *times and locations*. If every member of a target population under consideration is at a specific location (or set of locations) within a specified time frame, then the sampling frame can become the list of relevant *times* at the specific locations, rather than lists of names, addresses, or phone numbers.

Let's take a situation in which the researcher is interested in reaching customers at a specific fast-food chain, which I'll call, Burger Joy. Most customers of the Burger Joy pay in cash and do not appear on any list. The researcher thus has to look elsewhere for a suitable sampling frame. A screen-down is deemed too expensive, since it is calculated that the incidence of Burger Joy customers in the general population is too low to be efficient. The researcher moves to a time and location grid, realizing that all Burger Joy customers share a common trait: they physically go through the doors or the drive-through of the Burger Joy restaurant. Thus, in terms of physical location, the sampler realizes that the population of all Burger Joy customers within a given time period—one month—were in a specific place by definition: a Burger Joy restaurant. The sampler can easily obtain the total population of Burger Joy restaurants in the United States and can specify a time period. He or she can say with certainty that the entire population of Burger Joy customers for a given month will physically be at a Burger Joy restaurant within that time. If the researcher wants to capture that total population, then he or she could send interviewers to each of the three thousand Burger Joy restaurants twenty-four hours a day (or during the hours the restaurants are open) and interview each and every customer who walks through the door.

Capturing the total population of Burger Joy customers is clearly not feasible, but the conceptual idea provides an excellent starting point for a sampling frame. In this situation, rather than selecting a random sample of all of the customers provided on a list, the researcher would begin by randomly selecting a sample of all of the three thousand Burger Joy restaurants. Since more customers come into some restaurants than others, the sampler would probably employ complex procedures that allow the chances of a restaurant being selected to be weighted by its customer count. Then, once this geographic sample was obtained, the researcher would sample according to a time period, assuming again that it would be impractical to station a researcher at each of the sampled Burger Joys for an entire month. The researcher would lay out on a grid all of the hours during which the restaurants in the sample were open, and then sample from those time periods. At this point, the researcher would have a sample of time periods from a sample of restaurants. Then he or she would show up at the sampled restaurants at the sampled time periods and obtain a sample of the customers coming through the door or the drive-through during those periods—for example, every tenth customer. The result would be a solid random sample of the total population of Burger Joy customers. Why? Because, by following the trail, it can be seen that each and every Burger Joy customer during the specified month had an equal chance of falling into the sample, assuming that the restaurant was chosen randomly, that the time periods during which interviewing was conducted were selected randomly, and that the respondents were selected using a random sampling procedure at the specified hour.

I was once involved in the use of this type of sampling procedure in the context of a start-up airline in Texas. The airline was interested in flying between Dallas's Love Field (an airport popular with short-haul passengers in Texas) and a new suburban airport outside of Houston. What was needed was a sample of passengers who flew between Love Field and Houston. The decision was made that a screen-down method would be much too inefficient, in part because there is no specified geographic limit to the areas from which such passengers could originate. As a result, we decided to create a time sample at the one place where each and every member of the target population had to travel: Love Field in Dallas. Researchers calculated a time grid with every time period during which customers flew through Love Field, sampled from it, and then sent interviewers to stop individuals at specified time periods in order to screen down to those who indicated they flew into Houston. Rather than interview them on the spot, however, the researchers obtained their names and phone numbers so they could be interviewed later, in less hectic circumstances. Essentially, this study provided every traveler who went through Love Field during a specified time period an equal chance of falling into the sample.

An important example of this time and place sampling procedure is the well-known *exit poll*, which became so controversial after the 2000 presidential election. Exit polls are designed to represent all voters on election day. They are used to predict who has voted for whom and to explain what is behind the vote. Exit-poll sampling procedures have developed from election to election over the years, have become enormously sophisticated and complex, and are usually reliable (despite the Florida exit poll debacle in 2000).

The process begins with a list of each and every polling place in a given jurisdiction. If the exit polls are being conducted for a presidential election, then every election polling place in the country is listed. Polling places are selected by using random sampling procedures from these lists. Then, once polling places are randomly sampled, the hours during which voting can take place are listed, and specific time periods are selected randomly (in some instances, the entire universe of voting time periods is used). As a final stage, interviewers with clipboards or computer-assisted personal interviewing devices (handheld computers) stop voters during the specified time periods and ask the relevant questions, including the key one: "For whom did you just vote?" Stopping a random sample of voters is a challenge in and of itself, and interviewers have to be carefully trained to stop every tenth or twentieth voter coming out of the voting place, rather than just selecting voters who appear most interested in being interviewed. If done correctly, these exit-poll interviewing procedures yield a sample in which every voter in the United States has an equal chance of falling into the sample. (Of course, enormous controversy erupted in 2000 when the exit poll in Florida ran into a host of unprecedented problems.)

It is tempting for business researchers to try to short-circuit elaborate sampling mechanisms. One of the most common research practices used by businesses is to put out survey forms for customers to pick up and complete. These return cards provide valuable information for businesses, but they cannot be used to generalize to the total population of customers of the business. Quite obviously, not every customer had an equal chance of falling into the sample because of unequal variations in motivation and in the location and visibility of the cards. In fact, it is most likely that customers with strong opinions in either a positive or a negative direction will bother to pick up the cards and respond, while those customers with neutral opinions will often ignore them.

## PREELECTION SURVEYS

One of the most vexing problems for researchers is the attempt to find a way of sampling from a population where the dimensions have not been determined at the time of the interview. This is most often the case when the researcher is interested in talking to a sample in order to generalize or infer what they might be doing at some point in the future. The most common such situation revolves around elections. (I'm talking here about the time before election day, not after voting has taken place.) This just happens to be, of course, one of the most important types of surveys that many pollsters conduct.

The population in which the researcher is interested in preelection polls is the group of individuals who are going to vote on election day. The challenge: this population is not known ahead of the election itself. What is known is that only a subset of the total population of adults will vote in any election, ranging from about 35 percent in midterm elections to about 50 percent in presidential elections. So it's fair to say that elections pose special problems for pollsters because the population is moving and unknown. This has led to more than sixty years of work by researchers trying to perfect the process of creating a sample ahead of time that is representative of the population of those citizens who will vote on election day itself. The basic process is one of attempting to winnow down the broad general population to what we call likely voters.

As I've noted, a much-reduced percentage of all eligible voters will actually end up voting on election day. Those who vote can also vary widely across geographic units and across other variables such as age, education, and party affiliation. The population of voters on election day is difficult to specify precisely ahead of time. The researcher is left with the task of attempting to find the best procedures or mechanisms to use to estimate who will be in and who will not be in the population of voters, and then to find a way of sampling from that estimated population pool.

The starting point for the researcher is to examine specific, known requirements for voting that help narrow down the population. For example, voters must be eighteen years of age or older in most jurisdictions. Most important, the fact that voters must be registered before they can vote has provided a starting-point screening mechanism for pollsters, enabling us to reduce the total population of Americans eighteen and older to a smaller group of eligible voters.

But how do you obtain a sample of all registered voters?

Some pollsters obtain and sample from lists provided by registrars. There are problems with registered voter lists, however. In some states, registration to vote continues right up until election day itself. Thus, any list of registered voters can quickly become outdated. Historically, there have also been problems with the attempt to bring together lists that contain all of the names of all registered voters in an entire state or the entire nation, because this involves putting together a patchwork quilt of information from thousands of different jurisdictions. Certainly, the advent of computerized databases in recent years has made this less of a problem, but there is as yet no one available list of all registered voters across the country. Another problem with registered voter lists is that most do not contain the phone numbers of all of the registered voters. The names and addresses can be matched to obtain listed phone numbers, but those voters with unlisted numbers have to be left out.

A more typical procedure for survey researchers interested in obtaining a sample of election day voters at the state or national level has been to use a screen-down process. That's what we do at Gallup. We begin with an RDD sample of the general population and ask the sample of those reached on the telephone whether or not they are registered to vote. Gallup poll experience indicates that about 80 percent will say yes. Then the challenge becomes one of thinning the sample down to a sampling frame of all *actual* voters. Not all registered voters vote. In fact, in this country, only about 60 to 70 percent of registered voters will vote in any given election, a number that is somewhat higher in high-profile or hotly contested elections, and lower in off-year races or in elections without much interest or specific publicity hook. Identifying likely voters ahead of time when each voter's real probability of voting is unknown is a daunting process.

Actual voters can and often do differ in significant ways from all eligible voters. Mathematically, as the turnout rate increases, the probability that the pool of actual voters resembles all registered voters increases. The limiting point is reached when there is 100 percent turnout and registered voters are exactly the same as actual voters (that is, everyone votes, so analyzing the total population of registered voters works just fine).

In lower-turnout elections, however, the *bias* in the relationship between actual voters and registered voters can be significant. This bias is usually the result of two factors. First, there are demographic characteristics that have traditionally been associated with the propensity to vote. Everything else being equal, certain types of people are more likely to vote than others. The most important of these are age and socioeconomic status. Older and better-educated individuals are in general more likely to vote than younger and less well educated individuals. Republican voters tend to be better educated than Democratic voters, which means that the likely voter pool tilts toward Republicans. This in turn helps explain why in some elections the actual vote on election day can be more Republican than preelection polls predict.

The relationship between these background or demographic variables and actual turnout can be modeled statistically and can be used to help guide sampling or to weight or adjust the results of interviews with a sample of registered voters. This assumes, however, that the patterns that pertained in the past elections continue to pertain in each future election. Additionally, this type of procedure assumes that there are demographic data available—data that contain information on the voting probabilities of individuals based on their demographics. This is often the case for national presidential elections, but the relationship between demographic variables and voting in other, smaller jurisdictional elections is often not known.

The second set of factors involving voter turnout are idiosyncratic and relate to one of a hundred characteristics that can come into play in any one election. In most elections, there are certain factors that activate or excite certain groups of voters and cause them to vote at higher proportions than their proportions in the general pool of registered voters might predict. An election that has racial overtones, for example, might stimulate more minorities to vote than is usually the case. An election that has hotly debated labor-related issues might activate union members. The impact of such background characteristics varies from election to election. The challenge is to find ways of predicting who is most likely to turn out in any specific election. The best way to do this is to use the views and opinions and self-perceptions of the voters themselves, leading to procedures in which the researcher "bootstraps," or attempts to isolate the voters who are going to vote in an election from those who are not, based on what the voters themselves tell the researcher during the survey interview.

The first reaction of many at this point is to suggest that we simply ask those we contact, "Are you going to vote on election day?" and use those who say yes as the sample. The major problem with this procedure is that many more registered voters have all the good intentions in the world about voting than actually make it to the election booth on election day. There is a social desirability and self-perception effect at work, such that the natural inclination of the majority of registered voters who are interviewed before an election is to say that they intend to vote on election day. In fact, Gallup research indicates that on a routine basis, more than 90 percent of registered voters will tell an interviewer that they are very likely to vote on election day, when just about 60 percent actually vote. So just asking people a simple straightforward question about their voting intentions doesn't work well. But we've discovered that if we ask a set of more indirect questions, we can begin to develop an effective way of predicting who is likely to vote and who isn't. These questions have been developed over the years by Gallup, as discussed in chapter 7. When we combine the answers to the questions, we have a good prediction of the probability that an individual will end up voting.

In general, it is fair to say that these procedures work quite well. Preelection polling has been extremely successful over the years, providing pollsters with an important source of information and also one of the most important ways of verifying that polling is an effective way of representing the attitudes and future behavior of millions of people.

1. Leslie Kish, *Survey Sampling* (New York: John Wiley & Sons, 1965).

# CHAPTER 9

# The Elusive Attitude

Random sampling is nothing more than a tool to allow us to short-circuit the time and expense involved in conducting a complete census of all of the people in a population of interest. It facilitates our larger purpose, which is to understand and measure human attitudes and opinions. This latter process is not as easy as it sounds. In some ways, it is the most difficult part of polling. Regardless of whether we end up interviewing everyone in the population in which we are interested or whether we use a random sample, the tricky problem of measuring human attitudes remains.

## ATTITUDES AND PROJECTED BEHAVIOR: WHAT IS IT POLLSTERS ARE ATTEMPTING TO MEASURE?

Let's back up for a moment and look at this from a broader perspective. In no science is the challenge of measurement more daunting than in those that focus on humans. Even Edward O. Wilson, a hard-nosed biologist, admits as much when he says, "Everyone knows that the social sciences are hyper complex. They are inherently far more difficult than physics or chemistry, and as a result they, not physics and chemistry, should be called the hard sciences."[1]

The measures we'll discuss in this chapter are for the most part humans' self-reports of their thoughts, judgments, and past and future behavior. But I think it is worth noting that it is not absolutely necessary to ask humans questions in order to study them. Indeed, "questionless" studies may become more and more prevalent in the future, and the challenge of measuring characteristics of humans will be in some ways simplified if we avoid having them articulate their feelings or write down answers.

Medicine provides a good example. It is fair to say that doctors like to study humans by recording data that can be observed directly (temperature, blood counts, MRIs, X-rays, biopsies, etc.), thus avoiding what is often perceived to be the patients' less-than-precise verbal utterances. Indeed, when a doctor does need to ask the patient for an assessment of his or her own body, the doctor often relies on such evidence warily and keeps looking for "hard" evidence for a diagnosis. (The doctor says, "I know you say you feel pain in your leg, but all of our tests show that there is nothing wrong.") The medical scientist almost always puts more faith in hard data than on data that come from the verbal or written output of the patient. (That may be changing; medical schools are now recognizing that there is value in teaching doctors the skills of listening to their patients.)

Even those scientists usually associated with attitudes and opinions (sociologists and psychologists) have developed a number of methodologies for studying humans without asking them questions. These include watching and studying humans in their native habitats, analyzing population and demographic measures such as migration, births, and deaths, the use of simple unobtrusive measures such as how worn the floor is in front of pictures in a museum, and—perhaps most intriguingly—physiological measures.

Like doctors, social scientists, if so inclined, can treat humans very much as they would treat primitive human cultures where the language is unknown, or as they would treat the study of chimpanzees or baboon cultures. Historically, a lot of anthropological research has involved field observation of cultures without verbal interaction. Scientists can rely strictly on observation by watching members of the species, agreeing on protocols of descriptive terminology, and reaching conclusions based on this "outside" perspective. This observational technique has been used widely in social science (and in journalism).

This "observation only" approach can even carry through to surveys. Sociologists can use standard survey sampling techniques to select respondents on a random basis, go to the homes of those randomly selected members of the population, and spend time engaging in pure observational measurement, as would anthropologists lurking on the fringes of a newly discovered primitive culture. For example, I've always been fascinated by a study conducted by sociologist Edward O. Laumann, who once had interviewers unobtrusively record the living room styles in the homes of the individuals randomly selected to be in a survey. (He noted, among other things, that lower-class homes were more likely to have wall clocks in them, and upper-class homes were more likely to have separate rooms for television viewing.)[2]

Along the same lines, there has been a trend in marketing research wherein researchers spend time in consumers' homes observing the occupants much like anthropologists would study primitive cultures. These researchers watch how people go about their daily business and how they perform tasks that relate to specific products. The intrepid investigators sometimes follow the consumer around with a video camera, rarely asking questions; they are interested in analyzing the actual behavior relating to products rather than what people say about them.

Additionally, although social and psychological science does not yet have a widely available way of peering directly into the human brain, there appears to be a general hope that someday soon the brain can be routinely mapped by using scanning or other monitoring devices. Instead of asking respondents about a president or policy position, there will be, at some point in the perhaps not-too-distant future, a way of measuring the appropriate section of the brain to see just how excited individuals really are when the name of the president or a policy alternative is put in front of them. Some college departments of psychology have even expanded their names and purviews to explicitly include these types of physiological measures—for example, at Dartmouth College in New Hampshire, it's the Department of Psychological and Brain Sciences.

But for all of their virtues, these questionless approaches have significant liabilities. One person's poison is another's cup of tea. Social scientists who study humans without asking questions certainly avoid the subjective mushiness that is the focus of this chapter, but they also miss out on the possibilities offered by taking advantage of the very special characteristic that put humans in a category uniquely distinct from all other animals: the ability to express thoughts, make judgments, recall past behavior, and project future behavior. It is the use of this very special characteristic that is at the heart of humanness, and on a much more limited scale gives polling such value.

Asking people questions is efficient and saves money. The researcher does not have to follow respondents around at their home or business for days on end recording what they do, or use other elaborate means to infer what's going on inside their heads. You just ask them. It saves time. It allows access to observations and information that would be difficult if not impossible for the scientist to obtain in any other way.

So it's not a great surprise that most polling today—correctly so—ends up asking respondents questions.

Here's how I like to look at it: polling as a partnership. The pollster asks respondents in a survey to be collaborators, to make observations and measurements of their own behavior and cognitive states under the direction of the researcher. (The pollster in some instances coaches the individual with such instructions as "Thinking back, can you recall any situations in which you have . . ." or [most famously] "If you had to vote today . . .") To use human beings as collaborators and/or deputized quasi-anthropologists in this way opens up the potential for extraordinary added value to the research process, taking advantage of people's capabilities of providing all sorts of information about themselves:

- Humans can report on their own current feelings and emotions.
- Humans can go back into history and recall and recollect what happened to them in the past.
- Humans can predict their future behavior.
- Humans can look around and report on what's happening in their environment, in essence acting like a thousand deputized anthropologists or reporters.

This latter situation provides information that is particularly valuable. A random sample of 1,000 people acting as collaborators is the same as having 1,000 spies out there in the culture—observing, watching, talking to people, and in general picking up on trends and patterns in ways that are almost impossible to duplicate.

Our overall goal as pollsters is to represent the thoughts and opinions and wise insights of the entire group of people who live in a society. We ask those people to examine themselves and tell us what they find. Our assumption is that this has great value.

## THE HUMAN FACTOR IN ATTITUDE MEASUREMENT

Taking advantage of the ability of humans to introspect and report back to us what they find may have inestimable potential, but it is sometimes (for lack of a better word) a messy process. It's this occasional untidiness that I want to focus on in this chapter.

There has been an enormous amount of study over the years of exactly what it is that we measure when we ask humans questions. It is not an easy objective. Even defining the simple term "attitude" is a very involved and complex process, as evidenced by the shelf of books written by social psychologists on the topic. And if we read all of those books, we come back again and again to the simple fact that the subject matter of polling—"attitudes," opinions, and projections of future behavior—is a little mushy. There is no direct way to access thoughts in people's brains. The person has to express them. Survey responses are thus obtained as written or verbal statements from a sampled respondent in reaction to a pollster's question. While it might seem that asking a question in a survey about an issue is a simple matter, it most assuredly is not. In fact, it turns out that this issue of how we attempt to elicit responses from those we survey can be one of the more complex and sometimes daunting challenges we face as pollsters.

Some people assume that a survey question simply taps into a hard-coded attitude resting in a human's cognitive filing cabinet, waiting to be quickly and efficiently measured. But that's far from accurate. What a survey question obtains about a given topic is better viewed as a more generalized *range of reaction* to the concept asked about in the question. That expressed range is often surprisingly narrow and quite stable over time, no matter how we ask about a given topic. But at other times, the responses to a question about a topic do vary, based on a number of factors, including in particular the exact words used in the question, the way in which alternatives are posed to the respondent, and occasionally the context of the question in the sense of what has come before it.

This variability is exacerbated by the fact that survey research relies not purely on measures obtained by an observing scientist but also on randomly selected laypeople to do their own observations and reporting. A survey scientist asks a respondent to observe a phenomenon—most often the respondent's own interior attitudes, past behavior, or projected future behavior—and then to report what is "found." The pollster's reliance on the amateur respondents to do their duty and answer the questions increases the chances of measurement variation.

## THE IMPACT OF QUESTION WORDING

Perhaps the most studied issue relating to this attitude measurement in polls has been the relationship between the way questions on a given topic are worded and the responses that are obtained.

- We know that a question asking about "preserving a woman's right to choose" will elicit a more positive response than one asking if one favors "legal abortion in all circumstances."
- We know that a question asking about going to war in the Persian Gulf in 1990 and 1991 obtained different responses when it included a reference to a United

Nations–backed coalition of nations than when it implied that the United States would be acting alone.

- We know that the public gave significantly different ratings when asked to rate President Clinton "as a person" than when asked just about his job performance.
- We know that support for tax cuts goes down when specific alternative uses for surplus federal money are given.
- We know that support for the death penalty drops when an alternative specifying that the criminal be sent to prison with no possibility of parole is offered.
- We know that perceptions of how well the education system works "in the United States" is more negative than when Americans are asked about the education system in their local community.
- We know that support for one's son going into politics is higher if one's daughter going into politics is asked about first, than if the questions are asked the other way around.

## The Meaning of This Variation

What do we do about variability—the fact that we sometimes get differences in the pattern of responses to survey questions on a specific topic because the questions are asked differently? Critics sometimes argue that such variability invalidates the entire survey process. If answers to questions on a given topic can vary based on such things as question wording or response order, then can we or should we pay attention to *any* survey findings? As critic Eric Burns noted in his article "Is Democracy Just a Numbers Game?" published in the October 1999 *Reader's Digest*, "Poll questions can be phrased to make the answers pointless, irrelevant or deceptive."[3] Another critic of polls, Matthew Robinson, wrote in his tendentious *Mobocracy*,

A poll's methodology is often the least understood part of a poll, and, for the media, too often the untold story. How a question is phrased can greatly change the response. A poll may be methodologically sound, yet with the addition of only a few words, a single lead-in question, or even just politically charged "code words," the results may be skewed and citizens' responses drastically changed.[4]

Despite the impression on the part of these and other critics that this is a newly discovered, secret flaw in the polling process, it is not. Pollsters and scholars have been focused on the impact of the way in which questions are asked for many years. As Dr. Norman Schwarz, an investigator of these issues, says, "Psychologists and social scientists have long been aware that collecting data by asking questions is an exercise that may yield many surprises."[5] George Gallup used to routinely conduct split sample experiments designed to measure the way in which different wordings of questions could affect the responses to his polls. Two sociologists, Howard Schuman and Stanley Presser, picked up on Gallup and others' work and rejuvenated interest in the impact of how questions were asked in their 1981 book, *Questions and Answers in Attitude Surveys: Experiments on Question Form, Wording, and Context.*[6] The book, as one might guess from its title, reviewed a substantial body of data focusing on survey response variation in relation to how questions are asked.

There has continued to be a great deal of research on this area in recent years, some of it quite involved and theoretical. Scholarly journals are full of articles addressing the issues involved in measuring what's in people's heads. Researchers spawn new theories about the fundamental processes that are involved when people are asked to answer questions about their interior states. The research on how respondents answer questions in a poll is fascinating and important. It's an exciting subdiscipline of the psychological and social sciences.

But as I've noted, a number of critics and users of poll results have a more negative view of the underlying cause of all this investigation. They argue that the variability of responses to questions on a given topic reflects the fact that there is "no there there"—or in other words, that there is nothing substantial being measured in the first place. I'm often confronted by questions from talk show callers or audience members after I give a speech who suggest that the fact that different wordings of questions produce different responses somehow invalidates the entire survey process. We also know that high-level policy makers and officeholders sometimes balk at using the results of polls because they cannot interpret conflicting (and therefore confusing) results on the same topic from poll to poll.

But I fundamentally disagree with this negative perspective. What we measure in polls is extremely important and extremely "real." Just because there is no one unvarying "attitude" on every topic, residing in hard-coded fashion in humans' heads and waiting to be tapped into by a pollster's query, doesn't mean that what we measure is worthless. Indeed, there's a lot of great value up there in people's minds, and if we play our cards right, we can do a good job of figuring out what it is. As I noted above, attitudes can be defined as the *tendencies* to behave in certain ways toward specific stimuli, and even though these tendencies can vary within certain ranges based on the circumstances in which they are measured, they are definable, stable, and valuable.

In fact, I contend that variations based on environmental and situational factors do not undermine the value of survey results as important scientific data, but actually enhance it. *Most scientific advances are based on the study of this type of variation, not despite it.* The fact that humans sometimes give different verbal or written responses to questions based on various types of conditions is of great value in helping us understand humans' approach to the subject matter under scrutiny. It is not dismaying. And it shouldn't raise doubts about the whole enterprise of understanding and measuring the public's opinion. This type of variation instead serves as the basis for a more thorough and compelling understanding of humans' views on important matters. The inherent variability of expressed attitudinal responses presents no more difficult a problem than much of what scientists encounter in dealing with very squishy subject matter in other branches of science. The science of polling is based on the assumption that this variability is either controlled (by virtue of standardized methodological procedures) or rigorously studied and used in the analysis of the survey results. And when used in this way, the variability provides important scientific information.

Our objective as pollsters becomes one of figuring out *why* responses sometimes vary according to question wording and other conditions. The issue becomes: what do the variations reveal about the attitudes and potential behavioral patterns and judgments of the humans who are doing the responding? Most variation is not meaningless, nor does it occur in a vacuum. Humans' varied responses do not indicate a flaw in the survey process, but are revealing and insightful. Science uses variability as keys to understanding. The goal is to investigate thoroughly enough to understand the variables that change in tandem with one another, and then to determine what the variation signifies. This, in turn, leads to understanding.

So pollsters certainly don't need to despair and throw up their hands at the nature of what they are trying to measure. Instead, they need to focus on careful, in-depth analysis and interpretation of their subject matter.

## EXAMPLES OF RESPONSE VARIABILITY

It is important to remember that a good deal of what we measure in polls is quite stable from poll to poll, regardless of how questions are phrased or the context in which the question is asked. As I've noted, responses to the same trend questions over months and years are more often than not remarkably constant. I'm often greatly surprised at the degree to which poll results are within one or two percentage points of what they were the year before and the year before that. The degree of stability has to do with what's being measured. Some variables are by their very nature intended to move up and down with rapid frequency—namely, those that measure mood or ratings of such labile phenomena as presidential job approval or how well the economy is doing. Others, particularly those dealing with more fundamental policy issues, don't change so much over time and display a great deal of stability from survey to survey and from year to year.

Still, as the examples above suggest, there are times when we do find differences in responses caused by variability in ways of asking about the same topic. And these examples provide special insights into the nature of public opinion on the topics with which they deal. They provide substantial grist for the scientists' mill. Indeed, differences based on question wording and other factors are so important to social scientists that pollsters have continued George Gallup's pioneering efforts to conduct experiments in which certain antecedent variables are controlled systematically in order to measure the impact of these variations on outcome or dependent variables. The results of those experiments, along with comparisons of different questions asked about the same topic, provide significant insights into the nature of public opinion.

Let's look at some of these specific examples in more detail.

## DEATH PENALTY

Here are two different questions asking the American public about the death penalty:

| Are you in favor of the death penalty for a person convicted of murder? | | |
|---|---|---|
| Favor | Oppose | Don't Know |
| 74% | 24% | 2% |
| If you could choose between the following two approaches, which do you think is the better penalty for murder—[ROTATED: the death penalty (or) life imprisonment with absolutely no possibility of parole]? | | |
| Death Penalty | Life Imprisonment | Don't Know |
| 53% | 44% | 3% |

Gallup poll data, 2003.

What are we to make of this? Is it only a bare majority of Americans—53 percent—who favor the death penalty, or is it a much more robust three-quarters?

The correct answer is both. One does not have to choose between these two as *the* attitude toward the death penalty. Instead, a careful analysis of both questions underscores the fact that there's a range of public opinion on the issue. The data give us excellent insights into the public's feeling and suggest that the overall public reaction to the use of the death penalty varies depending on circumstances. A sizable percentage of the population reacts in the affirmative when the basic concept of the death penalty in cases of murder is brought up. The public's "gut instinct," in other words, is to support the death penalty. At the same time, the data suggest that some Americans are not adamant about it. The drop to just 53 percent support when the life imprisonment alternative is given suggests that the case for another way of dealing with murders might have some sway with the public. Even so, the fact that support only drops to 53 percent tells us that even when the public is reminded that the alternative would be to put the murderer in prison for life, the death penalty would remain law if put to a vote of the public in a referendum. (Other questions asking about the use of the death penalty in the case of Oklahoma City bomber Timothy McVeigh in 2001 showed support levels above 75 percent, suggesting that in the instance of particularly heinous crimes, support for the use of the ultimate penalty is even higher.)

Public opinion on this important social issue, in short, is more complex than might seem at first glance, but careful analysis of poll results shows that support for use of the death penalty is above 50 percent regardless of the circumstances, but that precise levels of support vary depending on what Americans know about the situation involved.

## GAY RIGHTS

How do Americans feel about gay and lesbian rights? Here again we get substantially different answers depending on which aspect of this complex situation we ask about. Here are three questions out of a number that Gallup has tracked over the years on this topic:

| In general, do you think homosexuals should or should not have equal rights in terms of job opportunities? | | | |
| --- | --- | --- | --- |
| Yes, Should | No, Should Not | Depends (volunteered response) | No Opinion |
| 88% | 9% | 2% | 1% |

Gallup poll, May 5–7, 2003.

| Do you think homosexual relations between consenting adults should or should not be legal? | | |
|---|---|---|
| | Should Be Legal | Should Not Be Legal | No Opinion |
| July 25–27, 2003 | 48% | 46% | 6% |
| July 18–20, 2003 | 50% | 44% | 6% |
| May 19–21, 2003 | 59% | 37% | 4% |
| May 5–7, 2003 | 60% | 35% | 5% |

Gallup poll data.

| Do you think marriages between homosexuals should or should not be recognized by the law as valid, with the same rights as traditional marriages? | | |
|---|---|---|
| Should Be Valid | Should Not Be Recognized | No Opinion |
| 35% | 61% | 4% |

Gallup poll, October 24–26, 2003.

Once again, the evidence points to a complex set of attitudes. It is impossible to do an adequate job of describing and categorizing public opinion toward homosexuality by using just one question. The American public feels that discrimination in the workplace against gays and lesbians should be outlawed, while at the same time the majority is not in favor of the "legality" of such relations more generally. And the standing of the public on the contentious and emotional issue of gay marriage is clear: the significant majority opposes it.

I included the trend data on the legality of gay relations to underscore the importance of analyzing *change* in summarizing public opinion on this issue. It is obvious that something—most likely the U.S. Supreme Court decision overthrowing a Texas antisodomy law—caused a significant change in attitudes between May and July of 2003.

An analyst who focused only on the homosexual marriage question could conclude that Americans were homophobic, or at the least discriminatory in their attitudes. At the other end of the spectrum, an analyst who looked only at the job question might be struck by the degree to which Americans are nondiscriminatory and sympathetic toward gays. One's overall assessment needs to be contingent on all of the above. And when all of the data are taken into account, the same basic conclusion holds: different results to different questions on a topic illuminate and help us understand public opinion.

## THE 2003 IRAQ WAR

Pollsters asked a wide variety of questions in fall 2003 about the implications of the U.S. presence in Iraq. Consider this question:

| Again thinking about the goals versus the costs of the war, so far in your opinion has there been an acceptable or unacceptable number of U.S. military casualties in Iraq? | | |
|---|---|---|
| Acceptable | Unacceptable | No Opinion |
| 33% | 64% | 3% |

ABC/*Washington Post* poll, November 12–16, 2003.

This question, viewed in isolation, might lead one to a negative view of the situation in Iraq. But other questions don't paint as bleak a picture. Consider this Gallup poll question asking whether or not going to war with Iraq had been "worth it":

| All in all, do you think the situation in Iraq was worth going to war over, or not? | | |
| --- | --- | --- |
| Worth Going to War | Not Worth Going to War | No Opinion |
| 56% | 42% | 2% |

Gallup poll, November 14–16, 2003.

Here we find a majority of Americans saying the situation in Iraq was worth it, which most observers would interpret as a sign of majority support for the basic U.S. decision to intervene in that country.

So we learn a good deal from a comparison of the results of these two questions. We first and foremost learn that Americans don't like military casualties and—at the point in time at which this survey was in the field—found the casualties in Iraq to be unacceptable. But despite this negative view of the ongoing consequences of the conflict, there was apparently support for the general idea of the intervention. In other words, the negative reaction to the casualties had not yet caused a majority of Americans to doubt the basic premise of the war.

It perhaps comes as no great surprise to find that the public was holding complex views on the Iraqi situation in the fall of 2003, at a time when a variety of highly visible critics of the war were making their voices heard in the public debate. The analysis of poll questions on Iraq helps understand the underlying nature of those complex views.

## THE 1991 GULF WAR

Another example of the value of analyzing the effect of differences in question wording came about when Gallup asked Americans questions about the situation in Iraq and Kuwait in January 1991. The willingness of the American public to sanction going to war against the Iraqis—a very important public opinion issue at the time—varied, albeit not substantially, based on the inclusion or exclusion of several words or phrases in the questions. Here are two questions asked on a January 3–6, 1991, survey:

| *Version 1: Recently, the United Nations Security Council passed a resolution that allows Iraq one final opportunity to pull out of Kuwait by January 15 or else face possible military action. If Iraq lets this deadline pass, would you favor the United States and its allies going to war with Iraq in order to drive the Iraqis out of Kuwait, or not?* | | |
| --- | --- | --- |
| Favor Going to War | Do Not Favor Going to War | No Opinion |
| 62% | 32% | 6% |
| *Version 2: If the current situation in the Middle East involving Iraq and Kuwait does not change by January 15, would you favor or oppose the United States going to war with Iraq in order to drive the Iraqis out of Kuwait?* | | |
| Favor Going to War | Oppose Going to War | No Opinion |
| 52% | 39% | 9% |

Gallup poll data.

It is clear that something about the wording of the questions produced variations in response. The wording of version 1 invoked three key points that were not included in version 2: (a) "the United Nations Security Council,"

(b) the fact that the Iraqis were being given "one final opportunity," and (c) the statement that the war, if it did come, would be waged by "the United States and its allies."

What did we learn here? The analyst studying these results concludes that American public opinion on going to war operates within a range. It is not totally fixed, but rather contingent, to some degree, on the circumstances under which that war might be initiated. In other words—not surprisingly—the public apparently felt that there were some situational factors that would make war more acceptable.

Acceptance for the initiation of hostilities is higher to the degree to which it is stressed that the war would be a multilateral rather than a unilateral undertaking. The increase in positive responses that resulted from the inclusion of references to the United Nations in questions asking about going to war against Iraq suggests that the participation of a multinational body could be a factor that would encourage Americans to give their support for overseas incursions. The patterns of responses also suggested that Americans apparently favored the idea of giving the Iraqis an additional opportunity to avoid conflict. The difference in responses to the two questions, in short, helps to understand the thinking pattern of Americans as they contemplate a going-to-war decision.

## TAX CUTS

Here's a fascinating example of the impact of differences in how a question is asked based on two questions asked in March 1999 about federal tax cuts. Respondents in the survey were split into two equal groups. Each was asked a slightly different version of a question. For both versions, respondents were given the same "root" question about the best use of surplus federal government money. And in both versions, respondents were given two alternatives, one of which was always "to cut taxes." In one version, the second alternative was "to fund new retirement savings accounts, as well as increase spending on education, defense, Medicare, and other programs." In the second version, the alternative was "to increase spending on other government programs." In other words, the only difference between the two versions of the question was the way in which the alternative to tax cuts was phrased. Both questions began, "As you may know, the federal government is currently running a budget surplus, meaning it is taking in more money than it spends. President Clinton and the Republicans in Congress agree that *most* of the surplus money should be used for Social Security, but they disagree over what to do with the rest. How would you prefer to see the rest of the budget surplus used?" Besides "to cut taxes," version 1 gave this alternative: "To fund new retirement savings accounts, as well as increase spending on education, defense, Medicare, and other programs." This alternative was chosen by 59 percent; 36 percent chose cutting taxes, and 5 percent had no opinion.

When the alternative to tax cutting was changed in the second version to "to increase spending on other government programs," only 21 percent chose this alternative, and 74 percent chose the tax cut alternative (1 percent had no opinion).

The key here is the enormous difference in the responses based on the way in which the alternative to raising taxes is phrased. Obviously, simply offering an increase in generic "government spending" as an alternative to tax cuts sounds terrible to respondents, who immediately opt for the tax cuts given these two choices. On the other hand, spending government money rather than refunding it in tax cuts sounds much better to respondents when it is made clear that the spending would be on specific government programs such as Medicare and education.

These findings were in fact of great value in the spring and summer of 1999 when just these types of issues were being debated by Congress and President Clinton. This type of analysis of poll results helped analysts understand why there was not the public outpouring of support for congressionally approved tax cuts that the congressional leaders might have imagined. Pollsters concluded that there was a baseline level of support for tax cuts in the abstract (as evidenced by the high level of support when tax cuts are juxtaposed against "government spending") but that the public's support was not strongly held, as evidenced by the quick drop in support once the public was reminded that the money could be spent for important government programs.

Again, the bigger picture: the analysis of results of *variations* in question wording provided the researcher with a better and more in-depth understanding of public opinion.

## CLINTON "AS A PERSON"

Sometimes very small, seemingly innocuous changes in the way a question is worded can make a big difference in the responses obtained. An example of this occurred in the highly charged political environment of August 1998 when Bill Clinton made a speech to the nation regarding his previously denied relationship with White House intern Monica Lewinsky. An August 17, 1998, Gallup poll, conducted after this speech, asked respondents to rate Bill Clinton but used a slightly different wording than the usual Gallup polls.

The wording in the August 17 poll asked the respondent, "Now thinking about Bill Clinton as a person, do you have a favorable or unfavorable opinion of him?"

Previous polls had asked this question in a slightly different way: "Now I'd like to get your opinion about some
people in the news. As I read the name, please say if you
have a favorable or unfavorable opinion of this person."
(Gallup made the change for practical reasons. Since Clinton's favorability ratings were usually asked in the context
of a list of other people, the wording had to be changed to
ask the respondents to rate just one person.) To test the
implications of the wording change, both wordings were
included in an August 18 poll. The results:

| ASKING ABOUT BILL CLINTON IN SLIGHTLY DIFFERENT WAYS | | | |
|---|---|---|---|
| Poll Question | August 10–12 | August 17 | August 18 |
| Usual wording: "this person" | Favorable 60% Unfavorable 38% Don't Know 2% | | Favorable 55% Unfavorable 42% Don't Know 3% |
| "As a person" | | Favorable 40% Unfavorable 48% Don't Know 12% | Favorable 44% Unfavorable 48% Don't Know 8% |

Gallup poll data.

As can be seen, the wording "as a person" produced a
lower overall favorability rating of 44 percent in the August 18 polling, compared to the traditional wording that
produced a favorability rating of 55 percent. In a trend
context, importantly, the drop from the 60 percent favorable rating obtained earlier in August to the 40 percent on
the August 17 poll was apparently based, at least in part,
on the change in the wording, rather than an underlying
change in the public's responses to Bill Clinton. Apparently, even the slightest emphasis on Bill Clinton "the person" in the wording of a question depressed the public's
opinion of him, as contrasted to the public response to a
question that was more general.

It is worth noting that the effect of the wording differences is less pronounced in terms of the "unfavorables," which are only four points different between the two techniques. Apparently, adding the words "as a person" to the question creates a situation in which more respondents say they "don't know" rather than give a favorable opinion of Bill Clinton. Also, in sharp contrast, this type of slight wording change made little difference in relation to other famous figures. In fact, in the August 18 poll, there was no difference in the percent of those with a favorable opinion of Hillary Clinton produced by this same type of question-wording difference.

This analysis of the impact of wording variability gave us a richer understanding of the way in which Americans were reacting to Clinton than would have been possible if our questioning had been more limited. The data reinforced the conclusion that Americans had differentiated images of the two sides of Bill Clinton—his personal behavior on the one hand and his professional accomplishments on the other. This understanding of how the public evaluated Clinton in turn helped us understand why Americans were unwilling to endorse Clinton's impeachment, even while they were well aware of his affair with a White House intern and his subsequent attempts to cover it up.

## SON OR DAUGHTER INTO POLITICS

A classic Gallup question asking whether or not one's child should go into politics as a life's work provides a fascinating example of the impact of asking one question before another. Gallup has traditionally asked the question "If you had a son, would you like to see him go into politics as a life's work?" In a 1993 poll, Gallup asked the question about a daughter: "If you had a daughter, would

you like to see her go into politics as a life's work?" The
research split the sample such that half were asked about
the son first, and half about the daughter first. The results
were as follows:

| ALTERNATIVELY ASKING ABOUT SON/DAUGHTER FIRST _(Percent saying yes)_ | | |
| --- | --- | --- |
| | Son Question Asked First | Daughter Question Asked First |
| Son into politics | 22% | 42% |
| Daughter into politics | 24% | 41% |

Gallup poll, June 1993.

When the question about the son is asked first, a low
number of respondents (22 percent) said yes to allowing a
son to go into politics. And roughly the same percentage
(24 percent) then said that their daughter should go into
politics. When asked in this order (son first, daughter second), Americans don't seem to respect politics as a worthy
vocation for their children, regardless of gender.

But look what happens when the question about the
daughter is asked first. Almost twice as many respondents
say yes (41 percent). And when the son question is asked
after the daughter question, the positive responses jump to
42 percent. Interest in having one's child go into politics,
in other words, increases from the 20 percent range to the
40 percent range based on which gender is asked about
first in the question.

These responses are very revealing. The fact that the
"son as a politician" scores so low when the son question
is asked first might mean that the respondent is thinking
generically about politics as a vocation, not about the gender of the child. When the daughter into politics option is

asked first, on the other hand, might it be that some respondents were thinking about the question as one probing the issue of equality between men and women? The higher positive response in this daughter-first condition suggests that the respondent is saying, "Of course, my daughter should do whatever she wants to." This is born out by the results of the sequence in which the daughter question is asked second. Here, since the son question was asked first, respondents infer that the question is not about gender issues, but rather politics, and give much fewer "yes" responses to the daughter issue.

Now, we don't know that this is exactly what is going on here. I have extended one possible explanation for the findings, but further investigation is needed to determine if this or some other explanation can be verified using empirical data. But the comparison of the two ways of asking the question has shown us, above all else, that there is still gender sensitivity in the country. Furthermore, if this pattern were to change when the same set of questions is asked in the future, the researcher would be able to make additional assumptions about changes in gender norms over time.

## EDUCATION IN THIS COUNTRY VERSUS "MY" SCHOOLS

Much research has shown that Americans evaluate components of American life much differently based on whether the respondent is being asked to rate things on a national or on a local level. Americans tend to be much more positive the more local the focus. Nowhere is this phenomenon more apparent than when Americans are asked to rate schools. In the annual Gallup poll conducted for Phi Delta Kappa, respondents are asked to rate the nation's public schools, their local public schools, and, for public school parents, the public schools your child goes to. The results:

| RATING THE PUBLIC SCHOOLS<br>(Percent giving the public schools an A or a B grade) | | | |
|---|---|---|---|
| | Nation's Public Schools | Local Public Schools | Public Schools Attended by Your Oldest Child |
| Nationwide sample | 26% | 48% | — |
| Nationwide sample of public school parents | 26% | 55% | 68% |

Gallup poll for Phi Delta Kappa, June 2003.

This is a classic example of the difference in perceptions between what is happening "out there," as opposed to what is happening in a person's own backyard. Positive ratings of the nation's schools vary from 26 percent to 68 percent depending on which schools are being rated. Americans perceive that schools are in trouble in the nation as a whole, but most are quite positive about schools in their local area.

The same phenomenon shows up when respondents are asked to rate "Congress" and then their own personal congressperson, or when they are asked to rate "the health care system" and then their own personal doctors and health care availability. Americans generally have more negative views about these types of institutions when they are asked to evaluate them on a national scale than when the question asks them to focus locally on what they have experienced themselves. The latter is usually much more positive.

We can learn a great deal from this pattern, in particular the assumption that judgments about conditions "out there" across the country apparently reflect inferences based on media reports. These reports—at least as perceived by average citizens—apparently reflect more negative conditions than Americans find at home.

## THE MEANING OF RESPONSE VARIATION

I should point out again that the examples of the impact of question variations I've highlighted above are extreme ones. Many questions Gallup asks are remarkably robust, meaning that variations in wording or other variables associated with the interview situation don't make much difference in the responses. But the differences, when they do occur, though disturbing to some observers, are not cause for despair. They don't mean that polling is worthless or that the results from polls shouldn't be trusted. Instead, they should be viewed in just the opposite light. The study of this variation opens new windows into understanding public opinion and gives us a more detailed picture of how the public feels about and reacts to the major concerns of the day. Indeed—and this is my key point in this chapter— these types of differences provide a remarkable opportunity for us to learn more and understand better how the public reacts to various issues and the types of policies the public would like to see followed.

This type of analysis of the variation in the results of survey questions by experimental or observational condition is a basic part of science. Darwin's famous *On the Origin of Species* was based on his observation of the relationship between species and their environment. Most medical breakthroughs result when scientists examine the relationship between variable A (say, disease incidence) and variable B (doses of a drug, environmental conditions, and so forth). Analyzing polling results is, as I've emphasized, part of the same scientific method. Patterns of differences in responses obtained by researchers when humans are asked about a subject—based on variations in question wording and so forth—are meaningful and provide a valuable basis for understanding the phenomenon under consideration.

My approach to polling deemphasizes an orientation that argues there is such a thing as one fixed "attitude" inside respondents' heads and that the task of the pollster or survey researcher is to pinpoint it. I'm emphasizing instead that humans have tendencies to respond in certain ways to specific stimuli, and these reactions are, quite rightly, tempered by conditions and suppositions. The exact pattern of responses will vary depending on elements in the environment (most important, the exact form of the question) at the time of the survey. The task of the researcher is to describe and then understand the implications of these differential patterns of response and to use them as the basis for deriving the best possible depictions of where the public stands on the issues under consideration.

All in all, we're dealing here with a good news, bad news situation. The good news is that the intricacies of the ways in which people respond to poll questions provide us with a rich source of insight into public opinion and allow us to access the knowledge and wisdom of the people in ways not possible if we relied on one or two questions in isolation. The bad news is that this makes the whole polling process more complicated, and in particular puts pressure on those who are analyzing polls to capture this full complexity when the results are transmitted to the public, to decision makers, and to leaders.

## The Virtue of Analysis

In the previous sections of this chapter, I reviewed evidence showing that differences in question wording and the survey environment can make a difference in question responses. This variation in responses based on the structure of the survey tells us a great deal about the public's attitudes and approaches to the issues and policies being tested. We learn more, rather than less, when we have the opportunity to study these types of variations.

Most of the examples were based on asking questions in two different ways at the same point in time. This follows the experimental design model that is at the heart of science, assigning people randomly to two groups, applying different treatments to the groups, and then measuring the outcomes. If there are outcome differences, it is reasonable to attribute them to the differences in treatments. This type of experiment is the gold standard in science and provides us with an excellent basis for studying the complexities of public opinion on key issues.

But it's often not possible to do the kind of split sampling and random assignment to conditions necessary for this type of experimental analysis. Pollsters most often deal with situations in which there is no opportunity to incorporate experiments in surveys. Thus, it becomes extremely important for pollsters to do what they can with existing survey questions, reviewing and contrasting different ways in which poll questions are asked in different surveys at roughly the same times. The general idea is to collate, compare, and contrast results obtained from a wide variety of studies dealing with the same topic, something that needs to be done as frequently, and in as much depth, as possible (as I will emphasize in the final chapters of this book). There is great value, in other words, in comparing and contrasting the results of different ways of asking about the same topics.

This is a very familiar procedure in other forms of science. Physicists, chemists, and biologists take advantage of multiple studies to generate and test broad theories. Doctors review a wide variety of studies done on a topic (for example, the efficacy of mammograms in preventing deaths from breast cancer). Medical decisions are made on the basis of what the preponderance of the literature suggests, and rarely on the basis of one isolated study. It is my argument that pollsters benefit from following these same norms of science.

At Gallup, we routinely summarize data taken from a variety of studies that tell us how the American public feels about such things as the death penalty, abortion, smoking, defense spending, homosexuality, and gun control. There is no single question that allows us to understand the complexities of public opinion about any of these areas; we need the analysis of different questions from different studies to fully understand what is going on.

The public's judgment on many of the key issues about which societal direction is needed is often conditional and based on specification of circumstances. Americans support the death penalty in cases of murder but are more willing to back off this preference if it is made clear that the alternative is life imprisonment with no possibility of parole. Americans do not favor a constitutional amendment that would make all abortion illegal but *are* supportive of measures that would ban abortions in specific circumstances. Americans are hesitant to advocate U.S. involvement in foreign military actions but are more willing to sanction such involvement if there is clear evidence that other foreign nations are involved. Americans favor full extension of antidiscrimination laws to cover gays and lesbians but do not favor legalizing homosexual marriage. In all of these situations, the clearest understanding of the public's judgment on a given topic is discerned through a process of reviewing a wide variety of ways in which the people have been asked about the issue.

So, in many ways, pollsters needn't be faced with the (daunting) challenge of selecting exactly one or two precise questions to measure the phenomenon under consideration. It's more complicated than that. We need a variety of questions that come at the subject matter in different ways. Pollsters need to focus a major part of their effort on *analyzing the responses* to questions asked about a topic, rather than pursuing the elusive (and impossible) goal of deriving *the single question* that completely encapsulates where the public stands on the issue of concern. In many ways, the types of questions don't matter as long as there are enough of them. I'm not as concerned with question wording as I am with the study of the impact of wording differences after a study is completed. The problem, of course, is that this type of post hoc study requires a great deal of time and space—the important issue I'll tackle in the next two chapters.

But despite my emphasis on the importance of examining multiple questions on a topic of interest, I think it is important to emphasize that there is still value in the results of several specific types of questions even if used without this process of comparison and integration. This is particularly true in terms of: (a) the analysis of over-time trends, (b) questions that can be shown to predict other behaviors of interest, and (c) questions designed to measure reactions to specific situations or hypotheses.

## TRENDS

A single poll question can contribute to our understanding of public opinion when it has been asked in exactly the same way across time. This is particularly true in situations in which we are interested in knowing how attitudes have changed over months or years. Is the president's job approval higher or lower now than three months ago? Have attitudes toward the death penalty changed? Have the deaths of soldiers in Iraq decreased support for U.S. military involvement there? Is a candidate for president further behind or further ahead than he was a month ago?

It doesn't do us a lot of good to look at how responses to questions dealing with these issues have varied over time if the wording of the question or the survey environment has changed. These variations make it impossible to determine if any differences in the outcome are due to real, underlying changes in attitude in the population.

For that reason, most pollsters attempt to hold the survey environment rigidly constant when they are interested in measuring change in attitude over time. In other words, pollsters use exactly the same questions from survey to survey. This allows them to assess across-time change accurately, under the assumption that if everything—question wording and context—is held constant, then changes in the responses of the population must reflect real-world change.

These *trend questions* are in many ways the lifeblood of polling. We probably spend more time analyzing differences in response to trend questions than we do anything else when we face the task of summarizing public opinion on specific issues.

Let's look at attitudes toward the death penalty for a moment. In the 1930s, Gallup started asking Americans, "Do you favor or oppose the use of the death penalty in cases of murder?" The question is brief and avoids the complexities surrounding the issue, such as alternatives to the death penalty, the specifics of why the death penalty is imposed, etc. So, in and of itself, this question doesn't provide a complete understanding of this important area of American public opinion. But this exact question has been asked of Americans for more than fifty years and as a result provides us significant value of a different sort. If responses to this question have changed, something real is going on out there in the thinking of Americans on this key issue. In fact, that's what has happened over the years. Support for the death penalty as measured in this question fell in the 1960s, rose again after that, reaching an all-time high in 1994, and has been roughly stable ever since.

Our classic Gallup measure on presidential job approval provides another example of the power of trends. The question is seemingly simple and straightforward: "Do you approve or disapprove of the way [name of president] is performing his job as president?" We use this as a very basic way of assessing the public's overall feeling about a president. The question certainly doesn't begin to delve into the nuances of Americans' complex attitudes and feelings about a president. The results of many additional questions are needed in order to understand the public's views of a complex president like Bill Clinton. But our presidential job approval rating provides a useful summary measure, much as the vote for a president forces a respondent to summarize all of his or her feelings into one decision to vote for or against the candidate. And since this question is asked exactly the same way, survey after survey, month after month, and year after year, it does a good job of measuring real changes in the public's opinion of the president.

When we find that President George W. Bush has a job approval rating of 58 percent (as he did in the early months of 2003), for example, we can compare that to the 90 percent rating that he received just after September 11, 2001, the 89 percent his father had after the Persian Gulf War in 1991, the 29 percent his father received in the summer of 1992, the 48 percent Bill Clinton was receiving in 1995, a year and a half before his attempt to get reelected, and the average of 55 percent we have measured across all presidents since Harry S. Truman. The fact that the wording of the job approval question has been exactly the same over the years, in other words, provides us with a tremendous ability for understanding historic trends.

There are many other examples of trend questions Gallup has pioneered and tracked over the years. Trends don't solve the problem of the need for multiple indicators of public opinion on specific topics. They certainly don't provide us with all we need to understand the complexities of where the public stands on key issues. But they control for the impact of question wording and other survey factors and therefore allow us to do a better job of measuring real-world change.

## EXTERNAL VALIDITY

Another situation in which a single question has considerable value for the pollster is one in which that question has high external validity, or, in other words, a high degree of correlation with other, real-world indicators.

If responses to a particular question are related to a behavior or activity in which the researcher is interested, then the pollster has a good question—regardless of any considerations of how the question might have been phrased or worded, or how it relates to other questions. In some situations, we're not as interested in a full understanding of the background or origins of public opinion on a topic as much as we are in predicting a real-world outcome. The guiding criterion for researchers in that situation becomes one of determining how well a question predicts a specific result.

These situations occur frequently in marketing research, when the survey researcher is interested in finding measures that predict such things as market share or customer attrition. In the polling context, they probably occur most famously in certain preelection questions, which have a long history of documented external validity. There are a variety of ways in which pollsters can ask a respondent about his or her potential vote on election day. As we have discussed, it makes sense in some situations to ask all of these questions and then compare, contrast, and develop a full understanding of just what it is that is going through the voters' minds in the preelection environment. But the goal is often more straightforward than that: not to understand the various ways in which the respondent reacts to the candidates, but rather—more simply—to predict the vote. And with that in mind, pollsters have discovered that the simple question "If the election were held today, and you had to make a choice, would you vote for candidate A or candidate B?" is quite predictive. If the researcher wants to understand the nuances of a voter's preferences and feelings about candidates, then additional questions are needed. The response to one question asking for a simple vote choice would not be enough. If the researcher, on the other hand, is interested in predicting the vote, then this one vote question makes it all that is needed. And that's why the simple "if the election were held today" question has become one of the mainstays of the pollster's arsenal.

Another interesting example of the usefulness of simple questions comes from recent Gallup work in the area of employee attitudes. Gallup researchers have determined that a series of twelve questions, asked in surveys of employees, are very predictive of employee loyalty to a company and to actual profitability of specific business units. The higher the scores of the employees on the twelve questions, generally speaking, the higher are these outcome variables. One of the questions is "Do you have a best friend at work?" The implications of this question are puzzling. This isn't a question a researcher might choose to ask if he or she were initially developing a survey of employees. What the question means to respondents is not necessarily clear. However, these considerations are moot for the researcher who is interested in predicting loyalty and profitability. In this situation, all that needs to be known is that the responses to the "best friend" question help predict bottom-line outcomes, thus giving the question external validity and its value.

## THE VALUE OF SELF-PERCEPTIONS

As an interesting side note, I like to emphasize that certain questions that ask individuals to report on their own behavior, to describe the behavior of others, or to describe elements in their environment can have great value because they are so straightforward and do such a good job of predicting real-world outcomes. These include such questions as: How often do you go to church? What is your income? How often do you read a newspaper? How many children in your family? How many cars do you own? Do you own or rent your house? Do you live on a farm? How much time do you spend on the Internet? Although the ability to answer these questions may vary from person to person (some people are more forgetful than others, and some may have reasons to want to present themselves to the interviewer in certain ways), they all focus on a factual, "hard" reality.

In the broadest sense, these types of questions have less "mushiness" to them. These questions are closest to what would be obtained by outside observers if they were asked to measure physical or tangible elements in an individual's environment. Humans can be relied on to do a pretty good job in most situations of duplicating the accuracy with which a team of outside observers can measure purely external variables. (And it's obviously a lot cheaper to have respondents report on what they are doing, or have done in the past, than to have a scientist follow them around with a clipboard recording every action.) For example, we at Gallup like to use a measure of religiosity that asks respondents if they have been to church or synagogue over the past seven days. This is (we presume) a more accurate measure than asking more broadly if the respondent "usually" attends church.

The idea of asking people to review and report on their behavior just as an outside observer would has at least a theoretical virtue of being more specific and less subject to reporting error than a question that asks individuals to review what's in their brains. In fact, some researchers (myself included) think it's quite valuable to ask respondents to put themselves in the role of an observer. Asking "What specific comments have you made to colleagues about George W. Bush in the last week?" or "Would people who know you well say you are anti-Semitic" can be more illuminating than questions that ask people their attitudes about Bush and anti-Semitism in more abstract ways. As some researchers have pointed out, the best way to find out if one is in love is simply to observe one's reactions when the other person comes into the room, rather than to plumb the depths on one's inner self.

There are also situations in which the pollster wants to ask a specific question in a specific way because a phrase or a concept has been used publicly. A particular phrase or supposition sometimes takes on meaning in and of itself, and it can be important to measure the reaction of the population to that wording. For example, if a national leader says that "this country has a health care crisis" as part of a major speech, it can be useful to ask the public a question using just that phrase. If a presidential candidate asks in a debate, "Are you better off now than you were four years ago?" then it makes sense to put just that question in a poll. The responses don't necessarily help us understand the complexities of public opinion on the issue, nor are they valuable predictors of other behavior—but they allow us to obtain a quick sense of how well specific assertions play in the general population.

My central point is to emphasize that social scientists gain insights into public opinion by studying the responses to a wide variety of questions on a given topic. It's not so much how the public is asked about a given topic in a poll as it is how the public's responses to the poll questions are analyzed. Additionally, there's significant value in trend questions that give us solid indications of changes across time, questions that are highly correlated to specific behaviors of interest, and questions that ask respondents to report on their own behavior.

Nothing about the analysis of responses to survey questions is easy or necessarily straightforward. But the fact that response patterns to questions about a topic vary according to wording differences does not present insurmountable difficulties. It's all part of the challenge of maximizing the value of survey research.

1. Edward O. Wilson, *Consilience: The Unity of Knowledge* (New York: Alfred A. Knopf, 1998), 183.

2. Edward O. Laumann and James S. House, "Living Room Styles and Social Attributes: The Patterning of Material Artifacts in a Modern Urban Community," *Sociology and Social Research* 54 (1970): 321–42.

3. Eric Burns, "Is Democracy Just a Numbers Game?" *Reader's Digest*, October 1999, 31–36.

4. Matthew Robinson, *Mobocracy: How the Media's Obsession with Polling Twists the News, Alters Elections, and Undermines Democracy* (Roseville, CA: Prima Lifestyles, 2002), 147.

5. Norman Schwarz, *American Psychologist*, vol. 54, number 2, February 1999, 103.

6. Howard Schuman and Stanley Presser, *Questions and Answers in Attitude Surveys: Experiments on Question Form, Wording, and Context* (New York: Academic Press, 1981).

# CHAPTER 10

# The Media and Polls

Much of today's polling is designed to be reported back to the public directly and quickly in the news media. Quite often, however, there is not the time, space, or inclination to do the type of reporting of poll results that is warranted. Most media outlets have certainly learned enough to report a given poll's "margin of error" statistics, dates, and sample sizes. But these facts and figures, while important, are only a small part of what is required in evaluating much of contemporary survey research and polling in a way that captures its complexity and value.

Several years ago, Gallup released to the media its "Gallup Poll Social Audit on Black/White Relations in the United States." The data were presented at a press conference held in Washington where full documentation, including an in-depth report, was made available to the press. The poll itself was complex, consisting of more than fifty questions—some updates on trends dating back to the 1950s—and the sample size (more than 3,000 respondents, including 1,269 blacks) allowed for in-depth reporting.

But the way our results were reported in the media was, to say the least, confusing. Two headlines appearing on the same day emphasized two seemingly different conclusions:

- *USA Today*:          Poll: Whites Increasingly Accept Blacks[1]
- *New York Times*:   New Survey Shows Americans Pessimistic on Race Relations[2]

Other coverage similarly followed disparate paths:

- An editorial in the *Detroit News* took an optimistic approach: "Findings of a Gallup poll last week also showed racial tolerance and acceptance among whites to be at an all-time high: about 93 percent of whites polled noted that they were willing to vote for a black president. And 61 percent approve of interracial marriages now, versus 25 percent in 1972."[3]
- On the other hand, a *Detroit Free Press* editorial was quite negative: "As President Bill Clinton prepares to give the nation his personal vision for reaching accord between the races, one need look no further than the results of a recent Gallup poll to see just how difficult bridging the racial gap will be. On the most fundamental questions of whether different racial groups receive equal treatment, on the need for government leadership in promoting equality, and even on the question of how we're getting along as a nation, the disparities in perceptions between the races could not be more profound."[4]
- Perhaps the definitive word on the study was an Associated Press story with the headline, "Poll: Blacks Still See Racial Divide," followed by the lead sentence: "Blacks are far more pessimistic about how the races get along and how they are treated than are whites, according to a comprehensive survey released yesterday."[5] This was the story and spin picked up nationwide by newspapers using the AP as their basic national news source.

Although most news stories about the poll, including the ones in the newspapers referred to above, were accurate, they featured and emphasized significantly disparate aspects of the study. Thus, various segments of the public were exposed to sharply different conclusions about contemporary race relations, depending on which news outlet they happened to stumble across. As a result, the public was—if not confused—left with a less-than-complete understanding of this important area of American life.

This example underscores a critically important aspect of the polling process today: how information collected from the public is reported back to that same public through news and information channels.

We obviously want the public to obtain the most accurate, complete, and meaningful interpretation of polling results possible. But this has become increasingly hard to do. Many news media outlets today have less time and space to devote to an issue than they used to. There are also strong imperatives that push news media toward quicker, more simplistic reporting and away from complicated, more nuanced reporting. But, as readers of this book know well by this point, polling results are often complex and resist simplistic interpretation. Therein lies the problem.

These concerns about the news media's ability to report on complex subjects are not unique to survey research, of course. A number of situations involving journalistic reporting of stories about medicine and health have brought into focus the deficiency in this same "science to the public" link. Scientific research is often disseminated to the public too quickly and too superficially to do adequate justice to the complexities that lie behind it. As a *Philadelphia Inquirer* headline once put it, "Sound Bite Journalism Eating Away at Knowledge."[6]

The issue in all of these situations is the link between science, with its focus on systematically accumulating knowledge, and what the public ends up learning about these findings—a link that does not always work well. As a result, the public is sometimes exposed to scientific information that falls short on comprehensiveness and accuracy. Public opinion polling, which involves both a scientific underpinning and a strong emphasis on feedback to the public, is particularly susceptible to problematic linkages.

Compounding the situation is the increasing media demand for polling results. It's a good news, bad news state of affairs. News media are increasingly interested in reporting poll results, yet they are more challenged when it comes to reporting polls accurately and/or meaningfully.

## MEDIA IMPERATIVES

It has become clearer and clearer to me over the years that efficiently and accurately providing polling data and interpretation to the public faces substantial hurdles.

First, pollsters, unlike the researchers involved with other sciences, often don't have the luxury of spending days and weeks analyzing data and making decisions on what they mean. A lot of polling is, by its very nature, extremely time-sensitive. Polls often deal with public attitudes about an issue (or candidates in an election) at a particular point, and the data, once collected, need to be turned around and fed back to the public as quickly as possible. It doesn't make a lot of sense to conduct a poll on the status of a hotly contested presidential election and then wait a month to analyze the data before reporting them. By then it's of academic interest only.

The same is true for polls measuring reaction to fast-breaking news events, polls measuring the public's preferences on a key policy issue about to come to a vote in Congress, and so forth. It's not at all unusual to have a situation in which neither pollsters nor journalists have extended periods in which to carefully analyze poll data and to figure out how best to present them and their nuances to the public. It's often slam, bam, and out the door—particularly at election time.

Second, there is the issue of the special needs of journalists. News reporting is governed by a significant imperative that it be dramatic enough to arouse interest, yet simple enough to be understood quickly. These demands were evident in the "good old days" of yellow journalism and are even stronger today in the era of a fast-paced broadcast news environment with an increasing emphasis on the need to grab and hold viewers' attention. Even newspapers, despite their capacity to report news in more depth than is possible on television, face pressures to "dumb down" their news product and to make it flashy enough to attract coveted younger readers.

I've spent years dealing with the news media in terms of reporting polls. I've written thousands of polling articles, been interviewed by hundreds of print and broadcast journalists, anchored regular television reports, and have watched from an insider's perspective how our Gallup poll data have been treated in newspaper, radio, television, and online reporting.

Through this, it's important to note, I've learned that there are wide variations in media reporting of polls. Some media outlets, including in particular CNN and *USA Today*, with whom Gallup enjoys a strong working relationship, have the inclination to devote more time and space to analysis and interpretation. Some journalists are much better informed and better motivated than others to report the rich complexity of poll results. And, at the same time, some polls lend themselves to easier interpretation than others. So there are certainly many instances in which the public is well served by poll reports that do full justice to the underlying data.

Indeed, at Gallup, we worked with CNN to devise a new Gallup Studio approach—one that allows us to use big-screen graphics and extended periods of time to report poll results in greater depth. These reports are still often limited to only one and a half or two minutes (which is a long time by television standards), but this has been a significant improvement over a more normal television news pattern in which anchors only have time to simply read poll numbers and then go on to the next story. More generally, of course, CNN and other cable news networks have the capacity to allow analysts (and occasionally reporters) more extended periods of time in which to review polling results.

But these examples of expanded time for poll reporting are exceptions. The news media are simply too challenged by a variety of constraints to provide, on a regular basis, the kind of in-depth interpretation of polling that is needed.

And this isn't necessarily a new phenomenon. More than thirty years ago, Dr. George Gallup noted in his book *The Sophisticated Poll Watcher's Guide*, "The abbreviated format [in newspaper reports] does limit the writer of poll reports to a few outstanding facts that emerge from the findings. Ideally, there should be a way to provide a fuller description of the subtleties and the nuances of public attitudes."[7]

Let's come back to the main point. Poll findings are often complex, equivocal, and not necessarily straightforward or easy to explain. This complicated nature of public opinion has to be juxtaposed against the mandates of journalism and media coverage. Just as good science does not necessarily translate into good headline news, so scholarly, scientific assessment of public opinion on key issues does not always translate well into pithy sound bites and summary headlines. In short, media imperatives (and the nature of polling) are often at odds with the careful and deliberate assessment that polling deserves. Polling thus occupies a particularly sensitive position between the scientific motivation of understanding human behavior on the one hand and the need to inform the public on the other.

Producers, editors, and reporters faced with the prospect of presenting poll data in their particular medium, I believe, end up—at least subconsciously—following several "rules for media reporting of polls." To the extent that it is not possible to follow these rules, polling results have a much lower probability of being used.

1. A finding that public opinion is dominantly positive or dominantly negative is more likely to be reported than a finding that public opinion is mixed or split.
2. A simple or single conclusion about the results of a poll is better than a complex, equivocal, or conditional analysis.
3. A conclusion that contradicts conventional wisdom or generates conflict is better than a confirmatory ("boring") conclusion.
4. A conclusion that can be boldly stated up front is better than a conclusion that is inductively arrived at near the end of a story or broadcast package.

Basically, these media imperatives derive from the fact that news gatekeepers are under substantial pressure to produce news that is dramatic, eye-catching, and easily assimilated. All of us are familiar with the reality that some of the highest-rated news programming today on television features strongly opinionated hosts and guests, controversial topics, focuses on differences rather than agreement, and dramatically presents simplistic conclusions rather than conditional reviews of equivocal positions. While newspapers don't have this same structural pressure to titillate and hold viewer attention on a second-by-second basis, they do have pressures to grab reader attention with headlines and to compress the text of articles to fit into shorter and shorter news holes.

Regrettably, poll results often don't conform to the imperatives I've outlined here. In these cases, either polling is not reported at all, or reporters, editors, and producers are forced to dumb the results down or hype them up to make them more compatible with their medium's requirements.

## PUBLIC OPINION RESEARCH'S UNIQUE OPERATING PROCEDURE

The need for careful and accurate reporting is unusually acute in the case of polling. While some public opinion polling is conducted in a scientific context, for peer review and publication, a good deal is conducted *primarily* for immediate release—often within days or even hours of its completion—to a lay audience through print and electronic media, without moving through the more traditional scientific process. Thus, journalists are not given the usual safety blanket provided by scientifically refereed research results. There *is* no scientific analysis in the traditional sense. Journalists obviously have a higher probability of inaccurate or incomplete reporting when they summarize polling that is conducted without its having gone through a scientific or scholarly screening process.

This *direct-to-the-public* type of polling includes both survey research that is funded and conducted by media organizations themselves (such as the CNN/*USA Today*/Gallup poll, with which I'm associated, the *New York Times*/CBS Poll, etc.) and polling that is conducted by others with the primary intention of gaining release through the media (rather than via scholarly publication).

Some people might argue that direct-to-the-public polls actually simplify matters—because the needs of the media are specifically taken into account when the polling is done. In other words, when the encumbrances of the need for scientific reporting are not an issue, the execution and reporting of polls in "media-ready" form can be done much more quickly and in a fashion that is more targeted to reporters' needs. That's true, as far as it goes. Science has great benefits, but it's usually a slow, methodical process. Polls conducted for direct publication or broadcast, on the other hand, can be on top of the news and as fresh as the morning headlines.

But this simplification can come at a cost. In the drive to meet media requirements and to gain access to media channels, there's a risk of creating research and reporting that are more superficial or incomplete than might have been otherwise, particularly in terms of providing context and analysis.

Of course, direct-to-the-public polling does not always avoid or ignore scientific procedures. A good deal of this type of polling is built on a foundation of science and the scholarly approach to the accumulation of data. Many of the researchers who work for the media and report polling data directly back to the public are highly trained and experienced polling professionals themselves. But there are no universal requirements or standards in these situations, and thus, the quality of what is reported can suffer.

## IMPLICATIONS OF THE WAY IN WHICH THE MEDIA WORKS

Perhaps the most common way in which polls are reported today is as an *adjunct* to another news story. A newspaper article or television news story focuses on a topic, and then, almost as an afterthought, the article or anchor mentions a poll result that relates to the same topic.

In some situations, this type of reporting is appropriate and makes sense. For example, if the story is about a highly publicized execution, such as that of Oklahoma City bomber Timothy McVeigh in June 2001, then a quick reference to the fact that polls show that the American public favors the death penalty for murder might be sufficient. If the news story covers President George W. Bush signing a new bill that bans so-called partial-birth abortions, then a quick reference to polls showing that the public favors just such a bill may be appropriate. In many instances, however, this use of polls as an adjunct creates problems. The quick-shot reference to polling results in the context of a larger news story almost by definition requires a very selective and limited use of the poll information—most often the results of just one or two questions. These questions need to have a truly straightforward, unencumbered interpretation or to have implications that are immediately obvious or require little in the way of explanation or elaboration. Otherwise, the reader or viewer can be shortchanged.

On the other hand, polling data are sometimes used as the centerpiece of a *stand-alone* story. This is good. The stand-alone polling story gets more time or space, provides the opportunity for the writer to give a more complete picture of how survey respondents feel about an issue, and allows the author or the presenter to use graphs, charts, and diagrams. The stand-alone piece also lets the author or presenter make a more concerted effort to incorporate the fundamentals of scientific exposition, including context, hypothesis, and careful explanations. In other words, a stand-alone story can provide a fuller and more illuminating review of what the poll has to say. In a sense, the use of the polling data as a story in and of itself elevates the content to the level of other news stories of the day, rather than assuming that it should be an afterthought, filler, or line at the opening or the end of some other story coverage.

Unfortunately, poll results are not used as the primary basis for news stories very often, because polling results don't usually fit the bill of being the kind of fascinating, quickly involving news that producers and editors covet.

Television, in particular, is dependent on "good video," and a talking-head pollster doesn't always meet that requirement. Focusing a story only on poll results, in short, is often hard for media gatekeepers to justify.

Let me return to the implications of the "rules for media reporting of polls" that I outlined above. The underlying theme in those rules was the difficulty in finding ways for journalists to report poll results that don't lend themselves to dramatic, easy-to-summarize conclusions. Here's an example. A special 1997 Gallup poll on race included two seemingly similar questions that asked about responsibility for improving race-related problems. The two questions produced somewhat different results among the black population, as follows:

| *Question 1: Some people feel that the government in Washington, D.C., should make every possible effort to improve the social and economic position of blacks and other minority groups. Others feel that the government should not make any special effort to help minorities, because they should help themselves. How do you feel about this? (Black respondents only.)* | | |
| --- | --- | --- |
| Government Should Help | Minorities Should Help Themselves | Don't Know |
| 59% | 30% | 11% |
| *Question 2: Just your opinion, should blacks in America focus more on improving themselves and trying to get ahead, or focus more on changing the system in order to end discrimination and racism? (Black respondents only.)* | | |
| Improve Selves | Change System | Don't Know |
| 54% | 31% | 15% |

Gallup poll

These two questions represent an example of what I call the *conflicting results dilemma*, which occurs when more than one question is asked on a topic and the resulting answers do not line up neatly. Poll data are often complicated, and differing responses to questions on a given topic can seemingly contradict themselves. That's not bad in and of itself; it leads to all sorts of interesting analysis, and—as I've stressed in this book—furthers our understanding rather than hinders it.

But a journalist operating under deadlines or media restraints, when confronted by the race data presented above, might either report just one of these results or give up on the story and not report it at all. The results don't immediately lend themselves to a simple, straightforward story line. The advisable approach, of course, would be to use the seemingly conflicting results as the basis for in-depth discoveries about Americans' complex attitudes on this topic. Such an analysis would show that the difference in the responses to the two questions most probably resulted from the use of the term "government." Blacks apparently agree that the government should be involved in ameliorating issues relating to race, but when it comes to changing the "system" (perhaps in a revolutionary sense), they express more reluctance. But few pollsters or journalists would have time to get into all of this if pressed to summarize it in a paragraph or in one or two minutes on the air.

Questions Gallup asked about Microsoft also illustrate this conflicting results dilemma. The responses showed that Microsoft is well liked as a company, as is Bill Gates, Microsoft's CEO; that Microsoft is seen as having been good rather than bad for the computer industry; and that the public feels that Microsoft does not engage in illegal practices in terms of the sale of its software. But poll data also showed that at one point, a plurality of Americans felt that the Justice Department investigation of Microsoft under way at that time was justified and should continue. The presentation of any of these results in isolation or without further elaboration would fail to provide a complete picture or understanding of American attitudes on this topic. Reporters in a hurry who conveyed just the data on attitudes toward the continuing Justice Department investigation could have misled readers into thinking that Americans didn't like or didn't trust Microsoft. In fact, a more detailed and analytic approach to these findings would need to focus on helping readers and viewers understand the positive reaction to the investigation's continuation even in the face of the favorable attitudes toward the company that was the object of the investigation.

A famous example of a conflicting results dilemma happened in 1998 and early 1999 when Bill Clinton faced an impeachment crisis in the Lewinsky matter. Clinton's job approval rating stayed high throughout the crisis, in the 60 percent range—and only about a third of Americans wanted Clinton impeached and removed from office. At the same time, other polling results showed that Americans were keenly aware of Clinton's sexual misconduct, that they felt he had not only had sexual relations with "that woman" but had also lied about it, and that they gave him low marks for his personal integrity and morality. To report any of these results in isolation was to fail to allow the readers or the viewers to understand the full nuances of the story. But to report them in depth required a commitment of time and space on the part of media gatekeepers that was not always forthcoming.

Another question from the Gallup race poll illustrates a slightly different problem, the *muddled results dilemma*, which often occurs when responses are split, with no strong majority tilt. Here's how black Americans answered a question about how well blacks are treated in their local communities as compared to whites:

- Same as whites:     49 percent
- Not very well:      38 percent
- Badly:              7 percent

One observer could interpret the 49 percent figure as high, arguing that it exceeds expectations. Another observer could interpret the 49 percent figure as low, emphasizing that almost half of all black Americans (45 percent) feel that they are treated less well ("not very well" or "badly") than whites in their local communities. There is no right or wrong interpretation in this case. The best treatment of this type of result is to put it in context by using trends over time, or in comparison to other questions, or by comparing the black responses to those for other relevant segments of the population. Thus, in this situation, a more careful, analytic approach—one that takes more time or space—would note how the percentage of blacks saying that they are treated the same as whites has changed over time (on a relative basis, 49 percent for the "same as whites" response is the highest reading for blacks among any of the Gallup polls in which this question has been asked) and how it is still significantly lower than the response to the same question among whites (76 percent). But again, that would take the time that many pollsters or journalists simply don't have.

In the most general sense, I'm making this point: the push within media today for quickly presented, easily digested, and (if possible) controversial news, along with the mandates of the formats in which the news is presented, moves science reporting toward selective presentations that can only skim the surface of what are often complex, layered, and even contradictory scientific research findings. Polling, a scientific approach to measuring human attitudes and opinions, shares these problems. Additionally, as I've noted, polling is in some ways susceptible to more general quality control problems than other forms of scientific investigation. That is, survey research is often not subject to the same type of scrutiny and peer review that helps maintain quality in other realms of science.

Science typically controls the quality of research through publication in scientific, refereed journals. No doubt a fair amount of bad science is conducted in this country, but the elaborate processes of the scientific publishing system are designed to make it harder for bad science to be disseminated to both fellow scientists and the public at large. And, once published, most scientific research results are subject to continuing review and replication attempts by other scientists. Results have to stand the test of scrutiny and review by the entire group of scientists in a given area before they become recognized as significant.

To its credit, the press often takes advantage of these scientific processes in terms of hard-science results, picking up and reporting on scientific research after it has been recognized or published using a system of scientific review. A review of articles reported in the science section of the Tuesday *New York Times*, for example, shows that the articles typically rely on scientific results that have first been published in such carefully controlled journals as *Nature*, *Science*, the *New England Journal of Medicine*, and the *Journal of the American Medical Association*. These journals serve as a filter before the findings reach the general public.

The way in which polls are conducted today, on the other hand, bypasses a great deal of the checks and balances developed as part of the normal scientific process. Many polls are sponsored by the media outlets that report them. The quality control and interpretation of these polls is therefore dependent on the level of training and sophistication of the people working at the media outlet.

Polls are also frequently sponsored by associations and entities with particular agendas, and the results sent by these groups to media outlets are often released without much scrutiny. (Much of this is possible because polls today can be conducted quickly, and at relatively low cost.) This procedure is akin to a drug company conducting a scientific investigation into the efficacy of a new drug and then sending the results directly to media outlets rather than publishing the results through normal scientific procedures. News editors and producers often feel that attributing the origin of a poll to its sponsor and giving the margin of error exonerate them from responsibility for the quality of the poll's content. But the reader or viewer still gets the bad results. Most journalists who deal with polls are also familiar with the fact that pollsters working for political candidates often "leak" poll results selectively in order to spin news coverage in a favorable way.

Again, it's not that a lot of this polling is conducted badly. In fact, much of it is done quite well. But there are no guarantees, and the fact that news media sometimes appear willing to report on almost any poll results that come in the door—without any type of quality control or peer review—results in a situation in which bad polling is frequently reported as if it were good polling.

## WHAT SHOULD BE DONE?

There's little question that a variety of factors make it difficult to get poll results back to the people (and leaders) in a way that is understandable, comprehensive, and accurate. So what should be done?

As a starting point, we would clearly be better off if there were fewer bad polls conducted in the first place. Bad polling, like bad science or bad journalism, doesn't help anyone (except perhaps the people who commission the polling if the results are favorable to their cause or position). But trying to eliminate bad polls is easier said than done. It is sadly true that we will almost certainly continue to see shoddy polls conducted by inexperienced pollsters or by those who have a vested interest in producing results that prove particular points about the American public.

Indeed, it may be easier to conduct bad polls than to conduct bad science in other areas because there are relatively few barriers to entrance for those who wish to become pollsters. Technological advances make it much simpler than it used to be for interested persons to conduct polls. Specialized companies can provide various poll components "off the shelf" cheaply and efficiently, allowing anyone who so desires to quite easily "do a poll" without much training or experience. Additionally, the Internet now provides a handy database of millions of potential poll respondents, and it is necessary to reach only a small fraction of them to conduct a poll. Robotic computers can call thousands of phone numbers and conduct interviews by having respondents punch in their answers, allowing those interested in conducting a poll to obviate the cost of live human interviewers.

All of this makes it nearly impossible to prevent bad polls from being conducted in the first place. This in turn puts a great burden on the shoulders of media gatekeepers whose job it is to decide which polls should be reported and which should not.

There have been many efforts to police polls over the years. A major review of survey research commissioned by the National Research Council in the 1980s recommended quite reasonably that those who use and publish polls should "discriminate among surveys according to the quality of their research procedures."[8] From time to time, there are suggestions to license pollsters or establish criteria for regulating survey research that would allow only qualified professionals to conduct polls. There are also professional groups to which pollsters belong that enforce standards in polling, much as is done by professional associations in the medical and legal fields. But these groups have had relatively little success in reducing the number of bad polls. Indeed, various state and national organizations make it mandatory that lawyers pass bar exams and that doctors pass medical licensing exams, yet these standards haven't weeded out all bad doctors and bad lawyers. It is hard to see that an official program that restricted pollsters to those who were somehow established as qualified could be much more effective (or, perhaps more important, possible).

But, looking at the situation from a more positive perspective, it is clear that another step in the process of improving media reporting of polls can involve better education of the journalists, editors, and producers who are the gatekeepers of media outlets. News organizations can be encouraged to do a better job of hiring experienced and well-trained polling professionals to help report on and analyze polls and to educate journalists who deal with polls once hired.

Everyone would be better off if there were savvy polling experts in positions of responsibility at media outlets. Many of the media constraints that plague the reporting of polls are essentially structural and have nothing directly to do with the people involved, but there's still a great deal of good that comes when editors, reporters, and producers know more about what they are covering.

There are indeed well-trained professionals in place at some media outlets, particularly the large cable and broadcast news networks and major newspapers. But for hundreds of other small newspapers and television stations (and unfortunately, even at some larger ones), the persons who report poll results know little more than the average American about the intricacies of survey research. And the resulting polling coverage reflects this.

There's actually been a considerable amount of effort on the part of pollsters over the years to help train reporters and editors. The National Council on Public Polls, of which I am a board member, has offered seminars and daylong teaching sessions for reporters and journalists, to explain and discuss how polling is done and how it should be reported (unfortunately, these have never generated a great deal of interest from journalists). There has also been talk from time to time about requiring more training in survey methodology and interpretation in journalism schools, but that's still far from the norm.

The National Research Council review I mentioned above went so far as to recommend that independent peer review should be made "a part of the design, analysis and reporting of surveys. If voluntary reviews are not available, then a portion of the resources of the survey should be allocated to obtain paid reviews."[9] This would certainly be a new twist if publicly released polls were put out for intensive voluntary review, and would no doubt enhance the quality of data received by the public. Unfortunately, not much has come about along these lines in the years since this recommendation was included in the Research Council's 1984 report. In part, as I've discussed, the need for speed in reporting many news-sensitive polls makes the laborious process of peer review impossible.

In the final analysis, even if there are good polls produced by dedicated professionals, media imperatives continue to hinder the process of reporting even high-quality polls in appropriate fashion. That brings us back to the question of what else managers of the major media outlets might do or change that would enhance the way polling results are presented to the public. Everyone, of course, would like the media to do the best possible job of reporting *all* the news of the day, not just polls. So in a way we're talking here about a subset of very big and complicated questions that journalism faces in terms of doing its job well regardless of the subject matter. These issues, of course, are a continuing focus of the journalism community and for the most part far beyond the scope of this book.

But it is important to keep in mind that one of the principal values of having up-to-date, well-done polls is to provide feedback to the public at large about what the collective body of the citizens of the country is thinking and feeling concerning the great issues of the day. The news media are a vital part of this process. Media gatekeepers recognize this. That's why we have media outlets sponsoring polls and devoting time and space to poll reporting on a frequent basis. But the structural demands of modern newspapers, television, and radio diminish the chances that the polling is reported in the depth and detail that is needed.

Dr. George Gallup in essence circumvented some of these constraints in the early years of the Gallup poll by preparing full-page inserts that newspapers paid for and published exactly as they received them. That allowed Gallup and his assistants to control the process of interpreting and presenting their poll results (Gallup even had his own typesetters put the inserts together) and also gave Gallup enough space to explain poll results in greater depth than might otherwise have been possible.

Those days are gone. But the advent of the Internet has provided somewhat of a throwback to the way polls used to be presented. The Gallup organization and other polling firms today use their Web sites to present data and analysis "directly to the people" in new and innovative ways. And, along these same lines, pollsters and media outlets may profitably find themselves using the essentially limitless space on their Web sites for expanded poll coverage in the years ahead. The quality of poll reporting can be improved by circumventing traditional media constraints in a process by which pollsters essentially publish poll analysis themselves on the Internet.

But this "direct to the customer" process is going to

take a while to become widespread. Internet use is still nowhere near universal. In the meanwhile, most Americans still hear and read about poll results through standard news media coverage. Thus, much of the challenge of improved reporting of polling will continue to rest with journalists using their traditional news media.

I think one way poll reporting can be improved is to encourage media gatekeepers to use the results from as many high-quality, scientific, independent polls as possible. This puts the onus on journalists to sift through a large quantity of poll information, but would provide needed checks and balances to prevent bad polls from having undue impact. As is true in much of science, more is better. Generally, the more polling there is, the more data there will be for us to analyze and compare. Having many well-done polls allows us to do a better job of providing context for poll results. This helps ensure that bad polls are exposed and/or more carefully questioned.

Another important way to improve media coverage of polls is to use reporting formats that allow for more detailed, complete analysis.

This is in many ways the major focus of my discussion in this chapter. Throwing poll results around in brief sound bites on television, or giving them a few sentences in a newspaper article, usually doesn't cut the mustard. We need to focus on developing ways to spend more time and to devote more space to presenting what polling scientists find.

Of course, when this recommendation is presented to news editors and producers, we get the usual objections: (a) there's not enough time or space to do justice to almost any news story—not just polling; (b) the pace of television newscasts in general has to be kept very fast or the viewer's attention is lost; (c) polling lacks the dramatic elements that increase ratings or readership. Still, I'm not willing to give up on my conclusion that Americans are greatly interested in what their fellow citizens are thinking and feeling about the issues of the day, and that polling results can be presented in ways other than compressing them into brief one- or two-sentence reports or having them included in shouting matches between dueling pundits.

I spent a number of years doing market research for media outlets around the country. In the process, I conducted tens of thousands of interviews with television news viewers and newspaper readers. Ultimately, I came away with a conviction that media-delivered news provides five basic benefits for Americans:

- News is of interest when it stimulates the emotions (hence the enduring emphasis on crime, police, fire, sex, and pathos in much local news coverage).
- News satisfies humans' deep desire to learn and acquire new information.
- News provides the benefit of satisfying humans' desire to be associated with other people (even if vicariously) and to learn about one's friends and neighbors.
- News fulfills a "surveillance" need to know what is happening in one's environment.
- News can help people acquire new skills for dealing with life.

These are general reasons why people like news. Do they apply to news about polling? I think so. Polling certainly doesn't fully provide *all* of these benefits. But if polling results are presented correctly, they satisfy humans' needs to learn and understand new information, they provide surveillance information by which individuals keep up on what is going on around them, and they provide a connection with the thoughts and feelings of other people. (Actually, when I make a speech about polling, I often find an emotional connection with some information that deals with deeply held beliefs on topics like God, abortion, death, and sex—but that's probably the exception rather than the rule.)

Most important, I think it is hard to overstate the importance polling has in helping to fulfill the fundamental human desire to learn and acquire new information and understanding, a desire that probably developed through evolution as a mechanism to ensure the species' survival. If polling can be presented in a way that allows readers and viewers to come to new understandings and insights about the way their fellow humans are thinking and feeling about issues, its appeal can be very significant indeed.

The subject matter of polling is inherently interesting because polling is about *us*. Humans love to compare and contrast their thinking on issues to the thinking of others. What more appealing topic can be presented in newspapers and on television than the in-depth discussion and analysis of humans themselves? Media gatekeepers must agree in principle. They obviously believe that polling is of interest to their readers and viewers in small doses; these gatekeepers need to be convinced that it is of interest in larger doses as well.

Along these lines, we need more meta-analyses, more summaries, and more big-picture reviews of what the polling data on particular topics tell us. Medical science has gravitated more and more in this direction. Doctors now have access to a wide variety of summaries when they need information on a particular condition, diagnosis, symptom, disease, or remedy. Medical Web sites intended for the general public have duplicated this process.

Polling needs to move in exactly this direction. The public's opinion about such complex topics as gay rights, abortion, school vouchers, welfare, and civil rights cannot be easily summed up in the responses to one or two questions. There has to be a commitment to greater review and analysis of polling data on a topic on television and in print—probing into the nuances of public sentiment in

POLLING MATTERS

order to achieve a reasonable and accurate portrait of how and where the public's judgment will allow society to progress. This involves a heightened emphasis on the comparing and contrasting of poll results. As I've emphasized throughout this book, we need reporting based on multiple indicators—varied questions on a given topic coming from different directions and in different ways. And we also need the context provided by across-time trending.

In the most general sense, all of this calls for a reevaluation of how poll results are dealt with by the news media. As I've pointed out in this chapter, polling results have several strikes against them even before they arrive on the desks of journalists. Polling data usually don't have the advantage of the strict peer review process that provides quality control for other science. Polls are easy and relatively inexpensive to produce, which increases the chances that bad polls are produced. Polls are also deceptively easy to analyze and report at a surface level, because it doesn't take much analytic genius to tell viewers or readers that X percent of the public responded in Y way to a question. Then, as noted, there are the constraints of today's news media environment that militate against complex and nuanced reporting of scientific results, constraints that push what poll reporting there is toward that which is brief, simplistic, controversial, or exciting.

But there is hope. Media executives obviously believe in the value of polls. Polls have become a staple of news coverage, albeit in brief doses. I believe that ultimately the interest of the audience in hearing and reading more in-depth reporting of what the people around them think and feel can win out, and that new ways of presenting polls can be achieved.

1. *USA Today*, June 11, 1997.

2. *New York Times*, June 11, 1997.

3. *Detroit News*, June 17, 1997.

4. *Detroit Free Press*, June 14, 1997.

5. *Daily News*, June 11, 1997.

6. *Philadelphia Inquirer*, May 10, 1998.

7. George Gallup, *The Sophisticated Poll Watcher's Guide* (Princeton, NJ: Princeton Opinion Press, 1972), 115.

8. Charles F. Turner and Elizabeth Martin, eds., *Surveying Subjective Phenomena*, vol. 1 (New York: Russell Sage Foundation, 1984), 310.

9. Ibid., 313.

# CHAPTER 11

# Making Polls Work in a Democracy

Polling doesn't do much good in a democracy if it's hidden from view. Better reporting of polling in the news media encourages the dissemination of the collective views of the public to everyone, which in turn helps all citizens in a democracy understand where their fellow citizens stand on the key issues of the day. The previous chapter reviewed a variety of ways in which this delivery of polling data to the public can be improved.

Polling also doesn't do a lot of good if it is ignored by the society's elected leaders, who in a representative democracy—like the United States—occupy the key roles as the day-to-day stewards of the power of the people. Indeed, my personal conviction on this point should be clear by now. Leaders should regularly avail themselves of the tremendous wisdom bound up in the collective experiences and insights of the people they represent. And this is best done by virtue of polls.

Some elected representatives may not feel this is necessary. Many politicians believe they are well aware of the views and dynamics of their constituencies. Representatives pay attention to mail, telephone calls, e-mail, district or state newspapers, communications from lobbying groups and contributors, and what they hear when they return to the area they represent. They claim to have a good feel for the basic sentiment "back home" and are certainly aware of major eruptions of dissatisfaction on an issue, organized campaigns for or against specific legislation, and the sentiment of powerful elites and party officials.

But there is evidence that leaders often do not have as good a feel for the views of their constituents as they may think they do and that they often don't make decisions that conform to what the public wants (as examined in detail in Jacobs and Shapiro's insightful *Politicians Don't Pander*[1]). More important, it is clear that the people themselves perceive that the politicians they send off to represent them are out of touch. I believe in large part that this out-of-touchness has helped set off the modest voter revolt we're seeing in this country, exemplified by the initiative and referendum movement, the extraordinary California recall election of 2003, and feelings of disdain that Americans have for their representatives and politicians.

It is not a resounding vote of confidence when senators and congresspeople have honesty and ethics ratings of only 20 percent and 19 percent respectively, which is near the bottom of the list of a variety of professions we test in this fashion. Moreover, it's revealing that only 29 percent of Americans have a great deal or quite a lot of confidence in Congress as an institution. The Congress, of course, is the branch of government set up to represent the interests of the people. Something is certainly out of kilter when the people appear to have such a lack of respect for it.

There is no greater witness to this voter dissatisfaction than former governor Gray Davis of California, who initially fought hard against the recall effort that removed him from office in October 2003, but who finally came to the realization that he had ignored the people to his peril. "I didn't stay in touch with the people," said Davis.

"That's clearly my biggest regret. Voters are the source of all wisdom."

This valedictory message in many ways sums up the key thesis of this book. Still, the question remains: why don't officeholders and decision makers use polls more often?

It is not that politicians are unfamiliar with polls or how they work. That's often a problem for average citizens, many of whom aren't comfortable with polls and don't understand the sampling process, but it isn't a problem for most elected representatives. Indeed, I would estimate that the vast majority of politicians have a great deal of respect for polling for the simple reason that they use polls to get elected. Many politicians and elected officials make major monetary and career decisions on the basis of polls. Most wouldn't consider running for office without the advice of a trusted and experienced pollster at their side. The pollster has become an integral and indispensable part of the election campaign team for most politicians today, and many of the polling industry's best and brightest minds provide complex and involved polling for politicians.

So why don't politicians use polls more often *between* elections? Many politicians apparently believe, in all sincerity, that they are already in touch with their constituents and know how the people they represent think and feel about the issues. These politicians argue that the additional input provided by polls would be superfluous. Besides, they argue, if the voters don't feel they are being well represented, they can simply vote the elected officials out of office.

But politicians aren't nearly as in touch with their constituents as they might believe. Furthermore, the idea of letting voters eventually get rid of politicians who don't pay attention to the people's views may work in the long run, but is inefficient. A lot of people are so turned off by this type of system that they don't care anymore, and they tend to grow apathetic. That may be one reason why we have the seemingly contradictory situation in which the people have low esteem for Congress and the representative system on the one hand, but they don't vote in great numbers and when they do vote they return incumbents back to office on the other. Many citizens may well believe that the system isn't going to work well regardless of who's in office. It apparently takes a galvanizing situation like the one that occurred in California to convince voters that they can do something about it. But we need to be able to use the input from all of the people all of the time, not just the votes of smaller percentages when elections roll around.

I'm arguing that elected officials should be availing themselves of the people's opinion on a regular basis because it's the right and philosophically correct thing to do. Society needs guidance, the wisdom of the people is a fundamentally sound source of that guidance, and those charged with making the decisions for society need to take it into account.

## TOO DIFFICULT?

Some politicians, although they use polls in their personal election campaigns, may feel it is too difficult to use polling on a regular basis because they don't control the way in which poll results are obtained. Most politicians don't themselves commission and conduct polls between elections.

Left to use "other people's" polls, politicians sometimes throw up their hands in bewilderment. Some of this reaction derives from real-world experiences. Politicians are besieged by lobbying and other pressure groups touting polls that often appear to have conflicting results, in much the way I described it in the previous chapter. Politicians may despair—even if motivated to use polls at some basic level—of their ability to use polls to ascertain what the people think on a routine basis.

Scholars Steven Kull and I. M. Destler, in the course of their research for *Misreading the Public,* interviewed members of Congress and their staffs, executive branch officials, and professionals in the media and nongovernmental organizations in Washington in an attempt to figure out why there was such a gap between what policy makers felt was the opinion of the public on key foreign policy issues and what was actually the case. One persistent finding was just what I've outlined—the distrust felt by these officials for polls because of the often confusing results:

> A number of policy practitioners emphasized that they discounted polls because of their seemingly contradictory results. In some cases this was presented as an inadequacy of the polls, but in as many cases respondents expressed frustration and bewilderment with their own efforts to make sense out of the welter of numbers. For example, a high-level congressional staff member said that there are "just so many polls out there." On reading one "you think you might have a good idea of what people might be thinking," but shortly "there's another one that comes out that could point out a different trend."[2]

There is no question that these types of complaints have a grain of truth to them. In some cases (but by no means all), there are indeed seemingly conflicting results from poll to poll on the same topic. As I have discussed, subtle changes in how questions are worded or presented to respondents can make a difference in the responses obtained.

But my overarching intent in this book is to emphasize that this fact of life is not a "deal stopper," but rather an opportunity and challenge. There is much to be learned from a set of questions asked about a given topic, even if they appear to produce conflicting results—as long as those involved are willing to take the time and trouble to work at it. With effort, these seemingly conflicting and off-putting poll differences can be woven into an exciting and revealing pattern that goes a long way toward providing a firm grip on what it is that the public would like to see done.

Again, politicians have already figured out how to measure—quite carefully—the views of the people when it comes to elections. Candidates for office hire professional pollsters, some very smart, who make it their business to figure out the views of the people, and who in turn brief the candidates so that poll data can be used effectively and efficiently. To be sure, elections present a somewhat more limited challenge than figuring out citizen preferences across a wide variety of policies and issues. But the principles involved are the same. With the right amount of effort, the wisdom of the public can be just as effectively ascertained between elections as campaign strategy can be developed during them.

The bottom line is that representatives can and should spend a great deal more time and effort in the attempt to understand their constituencies. This is not an easy challenge. It involves a sharp change from the current setup for many elected representatives, whose office staffs are often employed to sit back and wait to monitor sporadic input from the people back home. Elected representatives need to adopt a much more proactive stance, and above all else use available scientific tools to assess the views of their constituents in significantly greater detail. Politicians upgrade their computer and phone systems to take advantage of the latest technological developments; why not upgrade the systems they use to understand the people they represent?

In short, politicians need to hire more pollsters. This is

a seemingly alarming recommendation to those who have a basic fear of the influence of the people, and to those who revere the image of the sage politician wisely pondering the great issues of the day in relative isolation. But I believe the most important members of a representative's staff, in many ways, could turn out to be public opinion scientists whose duties would be focused on studying and summarizing the views and insights of the people. This scientific measurement of public opinion in the home district or state would be much more than the simple monitoring of incoming calls and letters. It would represent the application of available technology and science to the most important challenge an elected representative has—making decisions that affect the course of society.

With all of this, I'm sure there's still the lurking suspicion in the minds of some that the voices of the people simply aren't worth paying attention to—at least between elections. There is probably no better exemplification of this sentiment than the statements of two Texans, former senator Phil Gramm, who said, "The people of Texas, wise people, fair people, didn't elect me to read those polls," and George W. Bush, who said, "If elected president I will not use my office to reflect public opinion."

My response to these misguided sentiments has occupied a good deal of this book. I believe that it is not only perfectly acceptable for politicians to distill and use the wisdom of the people through polling but that it is exceedingly important.

I'm not talking here about direct democracy as it is usually defined—a system in which citizens vote directly on all major issues put before them in classic referendum style. Having citizens vote on issues—in addition to obviating the role of the representative—has other problems, among them the fact that only a portion of the people vote, and that voters are limited to a yes or no input on most specific issues. No, we're talking here about a change in the philosophy or orientation in the way elected representatives approach their jobs as delegates of the people. The constitutional framework says nothing about the input representatives take into account as they go about their jobs. I say the most valuable input comes from the people themselves. The long and short of it is that officeholders need to focus more on the wisdom of the people and less on almost everything else.

Keep in mind that elected representatives already embrace the general idea of obtaining help when they make decisions. Senators and representatives hold extensive committee meetings, listen to expert testimony, hear from important and influential constituents, pay attention to powerful lobbyists, and seek advice and consent from party leaders. It is the systematic consultation with the people that is often left out of the process. This is not good. Our elected representatives need to move to the point where they give as much or more credence to the accurately measured views of the people as they do to their own attitudes, the views of experts, or the views of special interests. I'm really talking about doing nothing more than getting elected representatives to make more use of the wisdom that is available direct from the people.

In response to this, politicians might rather defensively admit that they *are* willing to use polling to help figure out the best way to *communicate* their positions to constituents, but not to determine the basic positions in the first place. In fact, this is an oft-cited position of politicians who seem to shy away from admitting that they might take assessments of the public's opinion into account in formulating policy. This is misguided. There is no reason why the views of the people, as measured through polls, shouldn't be used directly as a primary basis for establishing or modifying laws or policies. This is nothing to be ashamed of and is no affront to the men and women who are elected to office. It is how things should be. And it is what the people themselves want to be done.

## THE POLLSTER CANDIDATE

I like to imagine a scenario in which a candidate runs for office and proclaims that he or she has essentially no personal issue positions, but is proposing to serve only as a *conduit* for the wishes of the public. This candidate would pledge to do nothing but attempt to mirror constituent wishes. Let's call this person the Pollster Candidate. Although this is an extreme, hypothetical situation that probably wouldn't work for a number of reasons, it illuminates some of the positive implications of taking the people seriously.

The Pollster Candidate would be a blank slate, a true neutral who pledged to do no deep thinking, no massive inner searches of his or her conscience to decide how to vote, but rather to be a delegate pledged to reflect the wishes of the voters. The Pollster Candidate would spend most of an election campaign demonstrating to the voters that he or she was able to accurately reflect their wishes. When asked about positions on such issues as abortion, foreign aid, defense spending, gays in the military, education, and health care, the Pollster Candidate would do his or her best to discern and reflect the opinions of the people of the district or state represented. In order to predict how the Pollster Candidate would vote when sent to Washington, the voters would need to understand how they themselves feel on the same issues.

The Pollster Candidate would have little personally to do with lobbying, campaign finance, and influence from special interests. Because the Pollster Candidate would rely on the collective opinions of constituents in deciding how to vote, those who would attempt to influence his or her vote would essentially be wasting time by attempting to curry favor or buy influence. Instead, those who wanted to obtain the Pollster Candidate's vote would need to go out and influence the people themselves. The Pollster Candidate's vote would be changed to the degree that the people's sentiments were changed. The people of the district would be the jury, and lobbyists and special interest groups would play to them, not to their representatives.

Positive benefits to society would accrue. It is likely that the people of the country would prefer that lobbying money would be spent on taking messages and arguments to them (the voters) rather than going into the campaign coffers of the candidates and parties (who in turn spend it on attempting to get elected). The public might well come to appreciate its role as being more in charge and the fact that its opinions were being regularly taken into account by its representatives in Washington. The clearer it became that the public's views were going to be called on to influence votes directly, the more the public might spend time studying and following the events of the day. And this would probably decrease the short-term impact of attempts to sway public opinion through misleading or misguided ad campaigns. Perhaps ratings of Congress would go up. People would get more involved. And the chances of making the best decisions for the future of the society would be significantly greater.

## POLLING MATTERS

Even with skilled pollsters and survey scientists, how reasonable is it that public opinion can be increasingly taken into account in governing a country? Even if one accepts the idea that the people of the society should have their opinions used by government and elected representatives on a regular basis, it is of course impossible to enlist the public's help in making each of the thousands of decisions that come up in any given year. Moreover, some of these decisions involve technical issues that are beyond the understanding of the majority of the population. A government large enough to run a major state or a country has a huge range of activity. As a result, it assembles legions of bureaucrats, experts, commissions, and task forces to help in making daily decisions and moving forward. There is no doubt that the citizens—no matter how powerfully one believes in democracy—cannot be involved in all of what goes on. The issue becomes one of how frequently and in how much detail the people of the society can and should be asked for guidance. George Gallup addressed this concern more than sixty years ago:

> There is something tempting about the view that an aristocracy of specialists should lead the people . . . We must agree that most people do not and in the nature of things, cannot have the necessary knowledge to judge the intimate details of policy . . . There are things that cannot be done by public opinion, just as there are things that can only be done by public opinion . . . The ultimate values of politics and economics, the judgments on which public policy is based, do not come from special knowledge or from intelligence alone. They are compounded from the day-to-day experience of the men and women who together make up the society we live in. That is why public opinion polls are important today. Instead of being attempts to sabotage representative government, kidnap the members of Congress, and substitute the taxi driver for the experts in politics, as some critics insist, public opinion research is a necessary and valuable aid to truly representative government. What is evident here is that representatives will be better able to represent if they have an accurate measure of the wishes, aspirations, and needs of different groups within the general public.[3]

Dr. Gallup's point is straightforward: the people of an entity of almost any size can be and should be trusted to provide input into its day-to-day running. The people of a societal entity *can* make decisions on the *overall direction* of the world in which they live. I'm not talking about specific decisions on daily minutiae or choices among involved and technical policy alternatives, but on the broad direction and general policies that their representatives adopt and that ultimately affect them. The people of a society can be trusted to operate as a board of directors, giving insight and input into the broader direction of what the people they elected should do.

If the fundamental idea behind a democracy is recognizing the wisdom in the aggregated experiences of its citizens, then *polling is actually a more efficient way to collect this wisdom than the vote.*

This is a particularly important insight. Our object as citizens is to move the society forward in the best possible fashion. For that purpose we cannot afford to miss out on the opinions of the lazy and those who choose not to participate in voting. Society needs the input of all its citizens. Indeed, some countries take this idea to the extreme and have made voting mandatory. The United States is not yet at that point, and the proportion of the population that votes is now down to 50 percent in some presidential elections, with the proportion lower still in other elections. A "wisdom at any cost" position argues that polls conducted more frequently among all of the people provide valuable input that is missing if the views of voters are all that is taken into account.

In the most general case, one reaction to the central theme of this book—that the views of the people must be continually assessed and used as the basis for decision making—is that it's hard to do. That's true. It is difficult; it takes a lot of commitment and hard work to collect and understand this wisdom. But it's worth it.

All in all, a society can't have it both ways. Either the people are the best source of decisions on how to run the society or they are not. The basic principle of democracy is that the people are ultimately a better source for making decisions on what the collectivity should do than is any other alternative. There are good reasons for the hybrid model we have today, wherein people vote for representatives or experts they put in place to facilitate the society's day-to-day functioning. But leaving the people's opinions out of the picture until the next vote is a way of saying that the people have only limited brainpower and can be trusted only so far. That's wrong. Representatives need to spend more time between elections maximizing the valuable insights derivable from the public they represent. To ignore the wisdom of the people is folly to the extreme.

If the people can be trusted to vote for representatives, they should certainly have their wisdom taken into account after elections as well. Our best path to progress is to commit to the idea that polls can and should be a positive, fundamentally important element of a well-functioning democratic society. The people's voice is wise, and almost always on target, forming what Dr. George Gallup proclaimed as the true pulse of democracy.

1. Lawrence R. Jacobs and Robert Y. Shapiro, *Politicians Don't Pander: Political Manipulation and the Loss of Democratic Responsiveness* (Chicago: University of Chicago Press, 2000).

2. Steven Kull and I. M. Destler, *Misreading the Public: The Myth of New Isolationism* (Washington, DC: Brookings Institute, 1999), 209.

3. George Gallup and Saul Forbes Rae, *The Pulse of Democracy* (New York: Simon & Schuster, 1940), 266.

# ACKNOWLEDGMENTS

As the reader of this book will have figured out by this time, I owe a great debt to a man I never met, Dr. George Gallup, who passed away in 1984, long before I arrived at Gallup. Through his written works and writings, I found a man who above all else believed passionately in the fundamental wisdom bound up in the opinions of the common people, an idea that he pursued with integrity and vigor all his life. To him I owe my greatest debt as the inspiration for this book.

I have been very lucky to work on a daily basis with Dr. Gallup's two sons, Alec and George, who have carried on their father's tradition throughout their entire working lives. Alec has been a constant companion and wonderful mentor in the years during which I've been at Gallup. George is an inspiration with his abiding belief in the value of survey research for shedding light on the personal, spiritual side of human life.

I was introduced to the value of a scientific approach to the study of human social life by a series of extraordinary professors, including Ted Hefner at Baylor University and Mike Flynn at the University of Michigan. Mike was an instrumental factor in making my tenure at Michigan the rewarding experience it was, and the type of mentoring he provided wasn't formally rewarded or even acknowledged by the academic system of which Mike was a part. So I'm using this belated opportunity to provide a personal thanks to Mike for what he did for me.

I have been very fortunate to work for a number of years now with the chairman and CEO of Gallup, Jim Clifton, who has his own personal belief in the value of scientific assessments of asking people questions, and a never-wavering commitment to the value of the Gallup poll. Jim is a personal friend from whom I have learned a great deal, and as head of Gallup he has created the environment that has allowed the Gallup poll to flourish.

At a different juncture in my life, Lance Tarrance was my boss and mentor, and Lance provided me with a superb example of what dedication to truth through empirical survey research can show. Although Lance operated in the political world, he was driven by data, and never once to my knowledge did he allow political judgments or desires of clients to affect his scientific interpretation of the survey results. I owe Lance a great deal.

I want to thank Marcus Buckingham, whose insights and faith in the importance and timeliness of the concept of this book were a great encouragement in helping it get written and published.

We have had an extraordinary team of survey research professionals here at Gallup, including David Moore, Lydia Saad, and Jeff Jones, and each has helped the points in this book come to life in the real world.

Judith Keneman at Gallup has been of great help in the preparation of this book, including her uncanny ability to decipher what is universally accepted to be my nearly illegible handwriting. I also received significant assistance from Joe Carroll, Leslie Terhune, and Maura Strausberg. Geoff Brewer worked tirelessly to help facilitate the practical details of getting this book published, and I also thank Mark Stiemann at Gallup and Andie Avila and a team of very competent copyeditors at Warner Books for their editorial and logistical expertise.

Tom Uhlman, Marcus Buckingham, Lydia Saad, Jon Krosnick, Keating Holland, Jack Ludwig, Cal Newport, and Kim Newport all read portions of this book and provided their comments and viewpoints. Each of these people vigorously expressed opinions and in some cases disagreements with what they read. As each will attest, I was not able to take into account all of their viewpoints, so I want to make it clear that any flaws, oversights, or illegitimate arguments that remain in the book are in no way things for which anyone other than myself should be held accountable.

Personally, as I'm sure is almost universally the case, writing a book turns out to be a much more challenging task than was initially anticipated. There is a vast gulf between having thoughts and ideas and the challenge of getting them organized, written on paper, and then relentlessly edited and shaped into a coherent whole. My wife, Kim, has been the driving force and encourager behind the scenes in helping push me forward with this project, and for that as well as the thousand other ways in which she has contributed to my life, I dedicate this book to her.

# INDEX